FREE Study Skills DVD Offer

Dear Customer,

Thank you for your purchase from Mometrix! We consider it an honor and privilege that you have purchased our product and want to ensure your satisfaction.

As a way of showing our appreciation and to help us better serve you, we have developed a Study Skills DVD that we would like to give you for <u>FREE</u>. **This DVD covers our "best practices" for studying for your exam, from using our study materials to preparing for the day of the test.**

All that we ask is that you email us your feedback that would describe your experience so far with our product. Good, bad or indifferent, we want to know what you think!

To get your **FREE Study Skills DVD**, email <u>freedvd@mometrix.com</u> with "FREE STUDY SKILLS DVD" in the subject line and the following information in the body of the email:

    a. The name of the product you purchased.

    b. Your product rating on a scale of 1-5, with 5 being the highest rating.

    c. Your feedback. It can be long, short, or anything in-between, just your impressions and experience so far with our product. Good feedback might include how our study material met your needs and will highlight features of the product that you found helpful.

    d. Your full name and shipping address where you would like us to send your free DVD.

If you have any questions or concerns, please don't hesitate to contact me directly.

Thanks again!

Sincerely,

Jay Willis
Vice President
<u>jay.willis@mometrix.com</u>
1-800-673-8175

GACE English

SECRETS

Study Guide
Your Key to Exam Success

**GACE Test Review for the
Georgia Assessments for the
Certification of Educators**

Dear Future Exam Success Story:

First of all, **THANK YOU** for purchasing Mometrix study materials!

Second, congratulations! You are one of the few determined test-takers who are committed to doing whatever it takes to excel on your exam. **You have come to the right place.** We developed these study materials with one goal in mind: to deliver you the information you need in a format that's concise and easy to use.

In addition to optimizing your guide for the content of the test, we've outlined our recommended steps for breaking down the preparation process into small, attainable goals so you can make sure you stay on track.

We've also analyzed the entire test-taking process, identifying the most common pitfalls and showing how you can overcome them and be ready for any curveball the test throws you.

Standardized testing is one of the biggest obstacles on your road to success, which only increases the importance of doing well in the high-pressure, high-stakes environment of test day. Your results on this test could have a significant impact on your future, and this guide provides the information and practical advice to help you achieve your full potential on test day.

Your success is our success

We would love to hear from you! If you would like to share the story of your exam success or if you have any questions or comments in regard to our products, please contact us at **800-673-8175** or **support@mometrix.com**.

Thanks again for your business and we wish you continued success!

Sincerely,
The Mometrix Test Preparation Team

Need more help? Check out our flashcards at: http://MometrixFlashcards.com/GACE

TABLE OF CONTENTS

Introduction

Thank you for purchasing this resource! You have made the choice to prepare yourself for a test that could have a huge impact on your future, and this guide is designed to help you be fully ready for test day. Obviously, it's important to have a solid understanding of the test material, but you also need to be prepared for the unique environment and stressors of the test, so that you can perform to the best of your abilities.

For this purpose, the first section that appears in this guide is the **Secret Keys**. We've devoted countless hours to meticulously researching what works and what doesn't, and we've boiled down our findings to the five most impactful steps you can take to improve your performance on the test. We start at the beginning with study planning and move through the preparation process, all the way to the testing strategies that will help you get the most out of what you know when you're finally sitting in front of the test.

We recommend that you start preparing for your test as far in advance as possible. However, if you've bought this guide as a last-minute study resource and only have a few days before your test, we recommend that you skip over the first two Secret Keys since they address a long-term study plan.

If you struggle with **test anxiety**, we strongly encourage you to check out our recommendations for how you can overcome it. Test anxiety is a formidable foe, but it can be beaten, and we want to make sure you have the tools you need to defeat it.

Secret Key #1 – Plan Big, Study Small

There's a lot riding on your performance. If you want to ace this test, you're going to need to keep your skills sharp and the material fresh in your mind. You need a plan that lets you review everything you need to know while still fitting in your schedule. We'll break this strategy down into three categories.

Information Organization

Start with the information you already have: the official test outline. From this, you can make a complete list of all the concepts you need to cover before the test. Organize these concepts into groups that can be studied together, and create a list of any related vocabulary you need to learn so you can brush up on any difficult terms. You'll want to keep this vocabulary list handy once you actually start studying since you may need to add to it along the way.

Time Management

Once you have your set of study concepts, decide how to spread them out over the time you have left before the test. Break your study plan into small, clear goals so you have a manageable task for each day and know exactly what you're doing. Then just focus on one small step at a time. When you manage your time this way, you don't need to spend hours at a time studying. Studying a small block of content for a short period each day helps you retain information better and avoid stressing over how much you have left to do. You can relax knowing that you have a plan to cover everything in time. In order for this strategy to be effective though, you have to start studying early and stick to your schedule. Avoid the exhaustion and futility that comes from last-minute cramming!

Study Environment

The environment you study in has a big impact on your learning. Studying in a coffee shop, while probably more enjoyable, is not likely to be as fruitful as studying in a quiet room. It's important to keep distractions to a minimum. You're only planning to study for a short block of time, so make the most of it. Don't pause to check your phone or get up to find a snack. It's also important to **avoid multitasking**. Research has consistently shown that multitasking will make your studying dramatically less effective. Your study area should also be comfortable and well-lit so you don't have the distraction of straining your eyes or sitting on an uncomfortable chair.

The time of day you study is also important. You want to be rested and alert. Don't wait until just before bedtime. Study when you'll be most likely to comprehend and remember. Even better, if you know what time of day your test will be, set that time aside for study. That way your brain will be used to working on that subject at that specific time and you'll have a better chance of recalling information.

Finally, it can be helpful to team up with others who are studying for the same test. Your actual studying should be done in as isolated an environment as possible, but the work of organizing the information and setting up the study plan can be divided up. In between study sessions, you can discuss with your teammates the concepts that you're all studying and quiz each other on the details. Just be sure that your teammates are as serious about the test as you are. If you find that your study time is being replaced with social time, you might need to find a new team.

Secret Key #2 – Make Your Studying Count

You're devoting a lot of time and effort to preparing for this test, so you want to be absolutely certain it will pay off. This means doing more than just reading the content and hoping you can remember it on test day. It's important to make every minute of study count. There are two main areas you can focus on to make your studying count:

Retention

It doesn't matter how much time you study if you can't remember the material. You need to make sure you are retaining the concepts. To check your retention of the information you're learning, try recalling it at later times with minimal prompting. Try carrying around flashcards and glance at one or two from time to time or ask a friend who's also studying for the test to quiz you.

To enhance your retention, look for ways to put the information into practice so that you can apply it rather than simply recalling it. If you're using the information in practical ways, it will be much easier to remember. Similarly, it helps to solidify a concept in your mind if you're not only reading it to yourself but also explaining it to someone else. Ask a friend to let you teach them about a concept you're a little shaky on (or speak aloud to an imaginary audience if necessary). As you try to summarize, define, give examples, and answer your friend's questions, you'll understand the concepts better and they will stay with you longer. Finally, step back for a big picture view and ask yourself how each piece of information fits with the whole subject. When you link the different concepts together and see them working together as a whole, it's easier to remember the individual components.

Finally, practice showing your work on any multi-step problems, even if you're just studying. Writing out each step you take to solve a problem will help solidify the process in your mind, and you'll be more likely to remember it during the test.

Modality

Modality simply refers to the means or method by which you study. Choosing a study modality that fits your own individual learning style is crucial. No two people learn best in exactly the same way, so it's important to know your strengths and use them to your advantage.

For example, if you learn best by visualization, focus on visualizing a concept in your mind and draw an image or a diagram. Try color-coding your notes, illustrating them, or creating symbols that will trigger your mind to recall a learned concept. If you learn best by hearing or discussing information, find a study partner who learns the same way or read aloud to yourself. Think about how to put the information in your own words. Imagine that you are giving a lecture on the topic and record yourself so you can listen to it later.

For any learning style, flashcards can be helpful. Organize the information so you can take advantage of spare moments to review. Underline key words or phrases. Use different colors for different categories. Mnemonic devices (such as creating a short list in which every item starts with the same letter) can also help with retention. Find what works best for you and use it to store the information in your mind most effectively and easily.

Secret Key #3 – Practice the Right Way

Your success on test day depends not only on how many hours you put into preparing, but also on whether you prepared the right way. It's good to check along the way to see if your studying is paying off. One of the most effective ways to do this is by taking practice tests to evaluate your progress. Practice tests are useful because they show exactly where you need to improve. Every time you take a practice test, pay special attention to these three groups of questions:

- The questions you got wrong
- The questions you had to guess on, even if you guessed right
- The questions you found difficult or slow to work through

This will show you exactly what your weak areas are, and where you need to devote more study time. Ask yourself why each of these questions gave you trouble. Was it because you didn't understand the material? Was it because you didn't remember the vocabulary? Do you need more repetitions on this type of question to build speed and confidence? Dig into those questions and figure out how you can strengthen your weak areas as you go back to review the material.

Additionally, many practice tests have a section explaining the answer choices. It can be tempting to read the explanation and think that you now have a good understanding of the concept. However, an explanation likely only covers part of the question's broader context. Even if the explanation makes sense, **go back and investigate** every concept related to the question until you're positive you have a thorough understanding.

As you go along, keep in mind that the practice test is just that: practice. Memorizing these questions and answers will not be very helpful on the actual test because it is unlikely to have any of the same exact questions. If you only know the right answers to the sample questions, you won't be prepared for the real thing. **Study the concepts** until you understand them fully, and then you'll be able to answer any question that shows up on the test.

It's important to wait on the practice tests until you're ready. If you take a test on your first day of study, you may be overwhelmed by the amount of material covered and how much you need to learn. Work up to it gradually.

On test day, you'll need to be prepared for answering questions, managing your time, and using the test-taking strategies you've learned. It's a lot to balance, like a mental marathon that will have a big impact on your future. Like training for a marathon, you'll need to start slowly and work your way up. When test day arrives, you'll be ready.

Start with the strategies you've read in the first two Secret Keys—plan your course and study in the way that works best for you. If you have time, consider using multiple study resources to get different approaches to the same concepts. It can be helpful to see difficult concepts from more than one angle. Then find a good source for practice tests. Many times, the test website will suggest potential study resources or provide sample tests.

Practice Test Strategy

When you're ready to start taking practice tests, follow this strategy:

Untimed and Open-Book Practice

Take the first test with no time constraints and with your notes and study guide handy. Take your time and focus on applying the strategies you've learned.

Timed and Open-Book Practice

Take the second practice test open-book as well, but set a timer and practice pacing yourself to finish in time.

Timed and Closed-Book Practice

Take any other practice tests as if it were test day. Set a timer and put away your study materials. Sit at a table or desk in a quiet room, imagine yourself at the testing center, and answer questions as quickly and accurately as possible.

Keep repeating timed and closed-book tests on a regular basis until you run out of practice tests or it's time for the actual test. Your mind will be ready for the schedule and stress of test day, and you'll be able to focus on recalling the material you've learned.

Secret Key #4 – Pace Yourself

Once you're fully prepared for the material on the test, your biggest challenge on test day will be managing your time. Just knowing that the clock is ticking can make you panic even if you have plenty of time left. Work on pacing yourself so you can build confidence against the time constraints of the exam. Pacing is a difficult skill to master, especially in a high-pressure environment, so **practice is vital**.

Set time expectations for your pace based on how much time is available. For example, if a section has 60 questions and the time limit is 30 minutes, you know you have to average 30 seconds or less per question in order to answer them all. Although 30 seconds is the hard limit, set 25 seconds per question as your goal, so you reserve extra time to spend on harder questions. When you budget extra time for the harder questions, you no longer have any reason to stress when those questions take longer to answer.

Don't let this time expectation distract you from working through the test at a calm, steady pace, but keep it in mind so you don't spend too much time on any one question. Recognize that taking extra time on one question you don't understand may keep you from answering two that you do understand later in the test. If your time limit for a question is up and you're still not sure of the answer, mark it and move on, and come back to it later if the time and the test format allow. If the testing format doesn't allow you to return to earlier questions, just make an educated guess; then put it out of your mind and move on.

On the easier questions, be careful not to rush. It may seem wise to hurry through them so you have more time for the challenging ones, but it's not worth missing one if you know the concept and just didn't take the time to read the question fully. Work efficiently but make sure you understand the question and have looked at all of the answer choices, since more than one may seem right at first.

Even if you're paying attention to the time, you may find yourself a little behind at some point. You should speed up to get back on track, but do so wisely. Don't panic; just take a few seconds less on each question until you're caught up. Don't guess without thinking, but do look through the answer choices and eliminate any you know are wrong. If you can get down to two choices, it is often worthwhile to guess from those. Once you've chosen an answer, move on and don't dwell on any that you skipped or had to hurry through. If a question was taking too long, chances are it was one of the harder ones, so you weren't as likely to get it right anyway.

On the other hand, if you find yourself getting ahead of schedule, it may be beneficial to slow down a little. The more quickly you work, the more likely you are to make a careless mistake that will affect your score. You've budgeted time for each question, so don't be afraid to spend that time. Practice an efficient but careful pace to get the most out of the time you have.

Secret Key #5 – Have a Plan for Guessing

When you're taking the test, you may find yourself stuck on a question. Some of the answer choices seem better than others, but you don't see the one answer choice that is obviously correct. What do you do?

The scenario described above is very common, yet most test takers have not effectively prepared for it. Developing and practicing a plan for guessing may be one of the single most effective uses of your time as you get ready for the exam.

In developing your plan for guessing, there are three questions to address:

- When should you start the guessing process?
- How should you narrow down the choices?
- Which answer should you choose?

When to Start the Guessing Process

Unless your plan for guessing is to select C every time (which, despite its merits, is not what we recommend), you need to leave yourself enough time to apply your answer elimination strategies. Since you have a limited amount of time for each question, that means that if you're going to give yourself the best shot at guessing correctly, you have to decide quickly whether or not you will guess.

Of course, the best-case scenario is that you don't have to guess at all, so first, see if you can answer the question based on your knowledge of the subject and basic reasoning skills. Focus on the key words in the question and try to jog your memory of related topics. Give yourself a chance to bring the knowledge to mind, but once you realize that you don't have (or you can't access) the knowledge you need to answer the question, it's time to start the guessing process.

It's almost always better to start the guessing process too early than too late. It only takes a few seconds to remember something and answer the question from knowledge. Carefully eliminating wrong answer choices takes longer. Plus, going through the process of eliminating answer choices can actually help jog your memory.

Summary: Start the guessing process as soon as you decide that you can't answer the question based on your knowledge.

How to Narrow Down the Choices

The next chapter in this book (**Test-Taking Strategies**) includes a wide range of strategies for how to approach questions and how to look for answer choices to eliminate. You will definitely want to read those carefully, practice them, and figure out which ones work best for you. Here though, we're going to address a mindset rather than a particular strategy.

Your chances of guessing an answer correctly depend on how many options you are choosing from.

How many choices you have	How likely you are to guess correctly
5	20%
4	25%
3	33%
2	50%
1	100%

You can see from this chart just how valuable it is to be able to eliminate incorrect answers and make an educated guess, but there are two things that many test takers do that cause them to miss out on the benefits of guessing:

- Accidentally eliminating the correct answer
- Selecting an answer based on an impression

We'll look at the first one here, and the second one in the next section.

To avoid accidentally eliminating the correct answer, we recommend a thought exercise called **the $5 challenge**. In this challenge, you only eliminate an answer choice from contention if you are willing to bet $5 on it being wrong. Why $5? Five dollars is a small but not insignificant amount of money. It's an amount you could afford to lose but wouldn't want to throw away. And while losing $5 once might not hurt too much, doing it twenty times will set you back $100. In the same way, each small decision you make—eliminating a choice here, guessing on a question there—won't by itself impact your score very much, but when you put them all together, they can make a big difference. By holding each answer choice elimination decision to a higher standard, you can reduce the risk of accidentally eliminating the correct answer.

The $5 challenge can also be applied in a positive sense: If you are willing to bet $5 that an answer choice *is* correct, go ahead and mark it as correct.

Summary: Only eliminate an answer choice if you are willing to bet $5 that it is wrong.

Which Answer to Choose

You're taking the test. You've run into a hard question and decided you'll have to guess. You've eliminated all the answer choices you're willing to bet $5 on. Now you have to pick an answer. Why do we even need to talk about this? Why can't you just pick whichever one you feel like when the time comes?

The answer to these questions is that if you don't come into the test with a plan, you'll rely on your impression to select an answer choice, and if you do that, you risk falling into a trap. The test writers know that everyone who takes their test will be guessing on some of the questions, so they intentionally write wrong answer choices to seem plausible. You still have to pick an answer though, and if the wrong answer choices are designed to look right, how can you ever be sure that you're not falling for their trap? The best solution we've found to this dilemma is to take the decision out of your hands entirely. Here is the process we recommend:

Once you've eliminated any choices that you are confident (willing to bet $5) are wrong, select the first remaining choice as your answer.

Whether you choose to select the first remaining choice, the second, or the last, the important thing is that you use some preselected standard. Using this approach guarantees that you will not be enticed into selecting an answer choice that looks right, because you are not basing your decision on how the answer choices look.

This is not meant to make you question your knowledge. Instead, it is to help you recognize the difference between your knowledge and your impressions. There's a huge difference between thinking an answer is right because of what you know, and thinking an answer is right because it looks or sounds like it should be right.

Summary: To ensure that your selection is appropriately random, make a predetermined selection from among all answer choices you have not eliminated.

Test-Taking Strategies

This section contains a list of test-taking strategies that you may find helpful as you work through the test. By taking what you know and applying logical thought, you can maximize your chances of answering any question correctly!

It is very important to realize that every question is different and every person is different: no single strategy will work on every question, and no single strategy will work for every person. That's why we've included all of them here, so you can try them out and determine which ones work best for different types of questions and which ones work best for you.

Question Strategies

Read Carefully

Read the question and answer choices carefully. Don't miss the question because you misread the terms. You have plenty of time to read each question thoroughly and make sure you understand what is being asked. Yet a happy medium must be attained, so don't waste too much time. You must read carefully, but efficiently.

Contextual Clues

Look for contextual clues. If the question includes a word you are not familiar with, look at the immediate context for some indication of what the word might mean. Contextual clues can often give you all the information you need to decipher the meaning of an unfamiliar word. Even if you can't determine the meaning, you may be able to narrow down the possibilities enough to make a solid guess at the answer to the question.

Prefixes

If you're having trouble with a word in the question or answer choices, try dissecting it. Take advantage of every clue that the word might include. Prefixes and suffixes can be a huge help. Usually they allow you to determine a basic meaning. Pre- means before, post- means after, pro - is positive, de- is negative. From prefixes and suffixes, you can get an idea of the general meaning of the word and try to put it into context.

Hedge Words

Watch out for critical hedge words, such as *likely, may, can, sometimes, often, almost, mostly, usually, generally, rarely*, and *sometimes*. Question writers insert these hedge phrases to cover every possibility. Often an answer choice will be wrong simply because it leaves no room for exception. Be on guard for answer choices that have definitive words such as *exactly* and *always*.

Switchback Words

Stay alert for *switchbacks*. These are the words and phrases frequently used to alert you to shifts in thought. The most common switchback words are *but, although*, and *however*. Others include *nevertheless, on the other hand, even though, while, in spite of, despite, regardless of*. Switchback words are important to catch because they can change the direction of the question or an answer choice.

Face Value

When in doubt, use common sense. Accept the situation in the problem at face value. Don't read too much into it. These problems will not require you to make wild assumptions. If you have to go beyond creativity and warp time or space in order to have an answer choice fit the question, then you should move on and consider the other answer choices. These are normal problems rooted in reality. The applicable relationship or explanation may not be readily apparent, but it is there for you to figure out. Use your common sense to interpret anything that isn't clear.

Answer Choice Strategies

Answer Selection

The most thorough way to pick an answer choice is to identify and eliminate wrong answers until only one is left, then confirm it is the correct answer. Sometimes an answer choice may immediately seem right, but be careful. The test writers will usually put more than one reasonable answer choice on each question, so take a second to read all of them and make sure that the other choices are not equally obvious. As long as you have time left, it is better to read every answer choice than to pick the first one that looks right without checking the others.

Answer Choice Families

An answer choice family consists of two (in rare cases, three) answer choices that are very similar in construction and cannot all be true at the same time. If you see two answer choices that are direct opposites or parallels, one of them is usually the correct answer. For instance, if one answer choice says that quantity x increases and another either says that quantity x decreases (opposite) or says that quantity y increases (parallel), then those answer choices would fall into the same family. An answer choice that doesn't match the construction of the answer choice family is more likely to be incorrect. Most questions will not have answer choice families, but when they do appear, you should be prepared to recognize them.

Eliminate Answers

Eliminate answer choices as soon as you realize they are wrong, but make sure you consider all possibilities. If you are eliminating answer choices and realize that the last one you are left with is also wrong, don't panic. Start over and consider each choice again. There may be something you missed the first time that you will realize on the second pass.

Avoid Fact Traps

Don't be distracted by an answer choice that is factually true but doesn't answer the question. You are looking for the choice that answers the question. Stay focused on what the question is asking for so you don't accidentally pick an answer that is true but incorrect. Always go back to the question and make sure the answer choice you've selected actually answers the question and is not merely a true statement.

Extreme Statements

In general, you should avoid answers that put forth extreme actions as standard practice or proclaim controversial ideas as established fact. An answer choice that states the "process should be used in certain situations, if…" is much more likely to be correct than one that states the "process should be discontinued completely." The first is a calm rational statement and doesn't even make a definitive, uncompromising stance, using a hedge word *if* to provide wiggle room, whereas the second choice is a radical idea and far more extreme.

Benchmark

As you read through the answer choices and you come across one that seems to answer the question well, mentally select that answer choice. This is not your final answer, but it's the one that will help you evaluate the other answer choices. The one that you selected is your benchmark or standard for judging each of the other answer choices. Every other answer choice must be compared to your benchmark. That choice is correct until proven otherwise by another answer choice beating it. If you find a better answer, then that one becomes your new benchmark. Once you've decided that no other choice answers the question as well as your benchmark, you have your final answer.

Predict the Answer

Before you even start looking at the answer choices, it is often best to try to predict the answer. When you come up with the answer on your own, it is easier to avoid distractions and traps because you will know exactly what to look for. The right answer choice is unlikely to be word-for-word what you came up with, but it should be a close match. Even if you are confident that you have the right answer, you should still take the time to read each option before moving on.

General Strategies

Tough Questions

If you are stumped on a problem or it appears too hard or too difficult, don't waste time. Move on! Remember though, if you can quickly check for obviously incorrect answer choices, your chances of guessing correctly are greatly improved. Before you completely give up, at least try to knock out a couple of possible answers. Eliminate what you can and then guess at the remaining answer choices before moving on.

Check Your Work

Since you will probably not know every term listed and the answer to every question, it is important that you get credit for the ones that you do know. Don't miss any questions through careless mistakes. If at all possible, try to take a second to look back over your answer selection and make sure you've selected the correct answer choice and haven't made a costly careless mistake (such as marking an answer choice that you didn't mean to mark). This quick double check should more than pay for itself in caught mistakes for the time it costs.

Pace Yourself

It's easy to be overwhelmed when you're looking at a page full of questions; your mind is confused and full of random thoughts, and the clock is ticking down faster than you would like. Calm down and maintain the pace that you have set for yourself. Especially as you get down to the last few minutes of the test, don't let the small numbers on the clock make you panic. As long as you are on track by monitoring your pace, you are guaranteed to have time for each question.

Don't Rush

It is very easy to make errors when you are in a hurry. Maintaining a fast pace in answering questions is pointless if it makes you miss questions that you would have gotten right otherwise. Test writers like to include distracting information and wrong answers that seem right. Taking a little extra time to avoid careless mistakes can make all the difference in your test score. Find a pace that allows you to be confident in the answers that you select.

Keep Moving

Panicking will not help you pass the test, so do your best to stay calm and keep moving. Taking deep breaths and going through the answer elimination steps you practiced can help to break through a stress barrier and keep your pace.

Final Notes

The combination of a solid foundation of content knowledge and the confidence that comes from practicing your plan for applying that knowledge is the key to maximizing your performance on test day. As your foundation of content knowledge is built up and strengthened, you'll find that the strategies included in this chapter become more and more effective in helping you quickly sift through the distractions and traps of the test to isolate the correct answer.

Now it's time to move on to the test content chapters of this book, but be sure to keep your goal in mind. As you read, think about how you will be able to apply this information on the test. If you've already seen sample questions for the test and you have an idea of the question format and style, try to come up with questions of your own that you can answer based on what you're reading. This will give you valuable practice applying your knowledge in the same ways you can expect to on test day.

Good luck and good studying!

Language

Vocabulary and Syntax

Dialect

Dialect is the form of a language spoken by people according to their geographical region, social class, cultural group, or any other distinctive group. It includes pronunciation, grammar, and spelling. Literary authors often use dialect when writing dialogue to illustrate the social and geographical backgrounds of specific characters, which supports character development. For example, in *The Adventures of Huckleberry Finn* (1885), Mark Twain's novel is written in the dialect of the young and uneducated white Southern character, opening with this sentence: "You don't know about me without you have read a book by the name of The Adventures of Tom Sawyer, but that ain't no matter." Twain uses a different and exaggerated dialect to represent the speech of the African-American slave Jim: "We's safe, Huck, we's safe! Jump up and crack yo' heels. Dat's de good ole Cairo at las', I jis knows it."

In *To Kill a Mockingbird,* author Harper Lee used dialect in the characters' dialogue to portray an uneducated boy in the American South: "Reckon I have. Almost died the first year I come to school and et them pecans—folks say he pizened 'em." Lee also uses many Southern regional expressions, such as "right stove up," "What in the sam holy hill?", "sit a spell," "fess" (meaning "confess"), "jim-dandy," and "hush your fussing." These contribute to Lee's characterization of the people she describes, who live in a small town in Alabama circa the 1930s. In *Wuthering Heights* (1847), Emily Bronte reproduces Britain's 18th-19th-century Yorkshire dialect in the speech of servant Joseph: "Running after t'lads, as usuald!... If I war yah, maister, I'd just slam t'boards i' their faces all on 'em, gentle and simple! Never a day ut yah're off, but yon cat o' Linton comes sneaking hither; and Miss Nelly, shoo's a fine lass!"

In addition to using dialects to support character development in novels, plays, poems, and other literary works, authors also manipulate dialects to accomplish various purposes with their intended reading audiences. For example, in an English Language Arts lesson plan for eighth graders (Groome and Gibbs, 2008), teachers point out author Frances O'Roark Dowell set her novel *Dovey Coe* (2000) in the Western North Carolina mountains of 1928. Dowell writes protagonist Dovey's narration in the regional Appalachian Mountain dialect to remind readers of the significance of the novel's setting. This lesson plan further includes two poems by African-American author Paul Laurence Dunbar: "When Malindy Sings" and "We Wear the Mask." Students are asked why Dunbar wrote the former poem in Southern slave dialect and the latter in Standard English. Exercises include identifying dialect/Standard English features, rewriting dialect in Standard English, identifying audiences, and identifying how author choices of dialects or Standard English affect readers and accomplish author purposes.

Dialect vs. Diction

When written as characters' dialogue in literary works, dialect represents the particular pronunciation, grammar, and figurative expressions used by certain groups of people based on their geographic region, social class, and cultural background. For example, when a character says, "There's gold up in them thar hills," the author is using dialect to add to the characterization of that individual. Diction is more related to individual characters than to groups of people. The way in which a specific character speaks, including his or her choice of words, manner of expressing himself or herself, and use of grammar all represent individual types of diction. For example, two

- 15 -

characters in the same novel might describe the same action or event using different diction: One says "I'm heading uptown for the evening," and the other says "I'm going out for a night on the town." These convey the same literal meaning, but due to their variations in diction they are expressed in different ways.

Review Video: Dialogue, Paradox, and Dialect
Visit mometrix.com/academy and enter code: 684341

Simple Survey Research into Linguistic Dialects

To learn about different dialects spoken in different geographic regions, social classes, and cultural groups, students can undertake simple surveys of small groups of informants. Students should first make a list of words they have heard used in certain dialects. Then they can ask their respondents to identify the words they know. Students can also ask respondents to identify words they have heard of but cannot define. Using their lists of dialect words, students can ask informants to identify which words they use in their day-to-day conversations. For a more multidimensional survey, a student can ask the sampled informants all three questions—words that they know, those that they have heard of but do not know the meanings, and those that they use in their speech.

Influences on Regional Dialect

Linguistic researchers have identified regional variations in vocabulary choices, which have evolved because of differences in local climates and how they influence human behaviors. For example, in the Southern United States, the Linguistic Atlas of the Gulf States (LAGS) Project by Dr. Lee Pederson of Emory University discovered and documented that people living in the northern or Upland section of the Piedmont plateau region call the fungal infection commonly known as athlete's foot "toe itch," but people living in the southern or Lowland section call it "ground itch." The explanation for this difference is that in the north, temperatures are cooler and people accordingly wear shoes, so they associate the itching with the feet in their description, but in the south, temperatures are hotter and people traditionally went barefoot, so they associated the itching with the ground that presumably transmitted the infection.

Affixes

Affixes in the English language are morphemes that are added to words to create related but different words. Derivational affixes form new words based on and related to the original words. For example, the affix –ness added to the end of the adjective *happy* forms the noun *happiness.* Inflectional affixes form different grammatical versions of words. For example, the plural affix –s changes the singular noun *book* to the plural noun *books*, and the past tense affix –ed changes the present tense verb *look* to the past tense *looked.* Prefixes are affixes placed in front of words. For example, *heat* means to make hot; *preheat* means to heat in advance. Suffixes are affixes placed at the ends of words. The *happiness* example above contains the suffix –ness. Circumfixes add parts both before and after words, such as how *light* becomes *enlighten* with the prefix *en-* and the suffix –en. Interfixes create compound words via central affixes: *speed* and *meter* become *speedometer* via the interfix –o–.

Word Roots, Prefixes, and Suffixes to Help Determine Meanings of Words

Many English words were formed from combining multiple sources. For example, the Latin *habēre* means "to have," and the prefixes *in-* and *im-* mean a lack or prevention of something, as in *insufficient* and *imperfect*. Latin combined *in-* with *habēre* to form *inhibēre,* whose past participle was *inhibitus*. This is the origin of the English word *inhibit,* meaning to prevent from having. Hence by knowing the meanings of both the prefix and the root, one can decipher the word meaning. In Greek, the root *enkephalo-* refers to the brain. Many medical terms are based on this root, such as encephalitis and hydrocephalus. Understanding the prefix and suffix meanings (*-itis* means inflammation; *hydro-* means water) allows a person to deduce that encephalitis refers to brain inflammation and hydrocephalus refers to water (or other fluid) on the brain

> **Review Video: Determining Word Meanings**
> Visit mometrix.com/academy and enter code: 894894

Prefixes

While knowing prefix meanings helps ESL and beginning readers learn new words, other readers take for granted the meanings of known words. However, prefix knowledge will also benefit them for determining meanings or definitions of unfamiliar words. For example, native English speakers and readers familiar with recipes know what *preheat* means. Knowing that *pre-* means in advance can also inform them that *presume* means to assume in advance, that *prejudice* means advance judgment, and that this understanding can be applied to many other words beginning with *pre-*. Knowing that the prefix *dis-* indicates opposition informs the meanings of words like *disbar, disagree, disestablish,* and many more. Knowing *dys-* means bad, impaired, abnormal, or difficult informs *dyslogistic, dysfunctional, dysphagia,* and *dysplasia.*

> **Review Video: Prefixes**
> Visit mometrix.com/academy and enter code: 361382

Suffixes

In English, certain suffixes generally indicate both that a word is a noun, and that the noun represents a state of being or quality. For example, *-ness* is commonly used to change an adjective into its noun form, as with *happy* and *happiness, nice* and *niceness,* and so on. The suffix *–tion* is commonly used to transform a verb into its noun form, as with *converse* and *conversation or move* and *motion.* Thus, if readers are unfamiliar with the second form of a word, knowing the meaning of the transforming suffix can help them determine meaning.

> **Review Video: Suffixes**
> Visit mometrix.com/academy and enter code: 106442

Context Clues to Help Determine Meanings of Words

If readers simply bypass unknown words, they can reach unclear conclusions about what they read. However, if they look for the definition of every unfamiliar word in the dictionary, it can slow their reading progress. Moreover, the dictionary may list multiple definitions for a word, so readers must search the word's context for meaning. Hence context is important to new vocabulary regardless of reader methods. Four types of context clues are examples, definitions, descriptive words, and opposites. Authors may use a certain word, and then follow it with several different examples of what it describes. Sometimes authors actually supply a definition of a word they use, which is especially true in informational and technical texts. Authors may use descriptive words that elaborate upon a vocabulary word they just used. Authors may also use opposites with negation that help define meaning.

Examples and Definitions

An author may use a word and then give examples that illustrate its meaning. Consider this text: "For students who are deaf or hard of hearing, teachers who do not know how to use sign language can help them understand certain instructions by using gestures instead, like pointing their fingers to indicate which direction to look or go; holding up a hand, palm outward, to indicate stopping; holding the hand(s) flat, palm(s) up, curling a finger toward oneself in a beckoning motion to indicate 'come here'; or curling all fingers toward oneself repeatedly to indicate 'come on', 'more', or 'continue.'" The author of this text has used the word "gestures" and then followed it with examples, so a reader unfamiliar with the word could deduce from the examples that "gestures" means "hand motions." Readers can find examples by looking for signal words "for example," "for instance," "like" "such as," and "e.g."

While readers sometimes have to look for definitions of unfamiliar words in a dictionary and/or do some work to determine a word's meaning from its surrounding context, at other times an author may make it easier for readers by defining certain words. For example, an author may write, "The company did not have sufficient capital, that is, available money, to continue operations." The author defined "capital" as "available money," and heralded the definition with the phrase "that is." Another way that authors supply word definitions is with appositives. Rather than being introduced by a signal phrase like "that is," "namely," or "meaning," an appositive comes after the vocabulary word it defines and is enclosed within two commas. For example, an author may write, "The Indians introduced the Pilgrims to pemmican, cakes they made of lean meat dried and mixed with fat, which proved greatly beneficial to keep settlers from starving while trapping." In this example, the appositive phrase following "pemmican" and preceding "which" defines the word "pemmican."

Descriptions

When readers encounter a word they do not recognize in a text, the author may expand on that word to illustrate it better. While the author may do this to make the prose more picturesque and vivid, the reader can also take advantage of this description to provide context clues to the meaning of the unfamiliar word. For example, an author may write, "The man sitting next to me on the airplane was obese. His shirt stretched across his vast expanse of flesh, strained almost to bursting." The descriptive second sentence elaborates on and helps to define the previous sentence's word "obese" to mean extremely fat. One author described someone who was obese simply, yet very descriptively, as "an epic in bloat." A reader unfamiliar with the word "repugnant" can decipher its meaning through an author's accompanying description: "The way the child grimaced and shuddered as he swallowed the medicine showed that its taste was particularly repugnant."

Opposites

Text authors sometimes introduce a contrasting or opposing idea before or after a concept they present. They may do this to emphasize or heighten the idea they present by contrasting it with something that is the reverse. However, readers can also use these context clues to understand familiar words. For example, an author may write, "Our conversation was not cheery. We sat and talked very solemnly about his experience, and a number of similar events." The reader who is not familiar with the word "solemnly" can deduce by the author's preceding use of "not cheery" that "solemn" means the opposite of cheery or happy, so it must mean serious or sad. Or if someone writes, "Don't condemn his entire project because you couldn't find anything good to say about it," readers unfamiliar with "condemn" can understand from the sentence structure that it means the opposite of saying anything good, so it must mean reject, dismiss, or disapprove. "Entire" adds another context clue, meaning total or complete rejection.

Syntax to Determine Part of Speech and Meanings of Words

Syntax refers to sentence structure and word order. Suppose that a reader encounters an unfamiliar word when reading a text. To illustrate, consider an invented word like "splunch." If this word is used in a sentence like "Please splunch that ball to me," the reader can assume from syntactic context that "splunch" is a verb. We would not use a noun, adjective, adverb, or preposition with the object "that ball," and the prepositional phrase "to me" further indicates "splunch" represents an action. However, in the sentence, "Please hand that splunch to me," the reader can assume that "splunch" is a noun. Demonstrative adjectives like "that" modify nouns. Also, we hand someone some*thing*—a thing being a noun; we do not hand someone a verb, adjective, or adverb. Some sentences contain further clues. For example, from the sentence, "The princess wore the glittering splunch on her head," the reader can deduce that it is a crown, tiara, or something similar from the syntactic context, without knowing the word.

Syntax to Indicate Different Meanings of Similar Sentences

The syntax, or structure, of a sentence affords grammatical cues that aid readers in comprehending the meanings of words, phrases, and sentences in the texts that they read. Seemingly minor differences in how the words or phrases in a sentence are ordered can make major differences in meaning. For example, two sentences can use exactly the same words but have different meanings based on the word order: (1) "The man with a broken arm sat in a chair." (2) "The man sat in a chair with a broken arm." While both sentences indicate that a man sat in a chair, differing syntax indicates whether the man's or chair's arm was broken.

Nuances of Word Meaning Relative to Connotation, Denotation, Diction, and Usage

A word's denotation is simply its objective dictionary definition. However, its connotation refers to the subjective associations, often emotional, that specific words evoke in listeners and readers. Two or more words can have the same dictionary meaning, but very different connotations. Writers use diction (a style element) to convey various nuances of thought and emotion by selecting synonyms for other words that best communicate the associations they want to trigger for readers. For example, a car engine is naturally greasy; in this sense, "greasy" is a neutral term. But when a person's smile, appearance, or clothing is described as "greasy," it has a negative connotation. Because of usages that have occurred in recent times, many words have gained additional and/or different meanings. The word "gay" originally meant happy or festive, as in the Christmas carol "Deck the Halls" lyrics, "Don we now our gay apparel," but in the 20th century, it also came to indicate a sexual preference.

> **Review Video: Denotation and Connotation**
> Visit mometrix.com/academy and enter code: 310092
>
> **Review Video: Word Usage**
> Visit mometrix.com/academy and enter code: 197863

Figures of Speech

A figure of speech is a verbal expression whose meaning is figurative rather than literal. For example, the phrase "butterflies in the stomach" does not refer to actual butterflies in a person's stomach. It is a metaphor representing the fluttery feelings experienced when a person is nervous or excited—or when one "falls in love," which does not mean physically falling. "Hitting a sales target" does not mean physically hitting a target with arrows as in archery; it is a metaphor for meeting a sales quota. "Climbing the ladder of success" metaphorically likens advancing in one's career to ascending ladder rungs. Similes, such as "light as a feather" (meaning very light, not a feather's actual weight), and hyperbole, like "I'm starving/freezing/roasting," are also figures of speech.

Review Video: Figure of Speech
Visit mometrix.com/academy and enter code: 111295

Parts of Speech

Nouns are words for persons, places, or things. The words *girl, town*, and *house* are all nouns. Nouns are frequently the sentence subjects. Proper nouns are names. Pronouns replace nouns, including personal pronouns specifying person, number, gender, or case. Some common pronouns are *I, you, he, she, it, none*, and *which*. Personal pronouns may be subjective, such as sentence/clause subjects, or objective, like the objects of verbs or prepositions. Verbs are words for actions or states of being. Verbs are often sentence predicates. Adjectives are descriptive words modifying nouns, for example, *big* girl, *red* house, or other adjectives, such as *great* big house. Adverbs are descriptive words modifying verbs, adjectives, or other adverbs (including clauses), often ending in *–ly*. Examples include running *quickly* and *patiently* waiting. Conjunctive adverbs connect two clauses. The words *also, finally, however, furthermore, consequently, instead, meanwhile, next, still, then, therefore, indeed, incidentally,* and *likewise* are all conjunctive adverbs. Prepositions connect nouns/pronouns/phrases to other words in sentences, such as *on, in, behind, under, beside, against, beneath, over,* and *during*. Prepositional phrases include prepositions, their objects, and associated adjectives/adverbs. Conjunctions connect words/phrases/clauses. Common conjunctions include *and, when, but, or/nor, for, so,* and *yet*.

Review Video: Nouns and Pronouns
Visit mometrix.com/academy and enter code: 312073

Fragments and Run-On Sentences

A sentence fragment is missing some essential component: a subject, predicate, or independent clause. An example of the latter is: "Although I knew that." This is incomplete because "although" makes it a dependent clause with no independent clause to complete the thought. By adding an independent clause, the sentence becomes complete: "Although I knew that, I forgot it." The statement "Going to dinner" has a subject (the gerund "going," a verbal functioning as a noun) and a prepositional phrase ("to dinner") but it does not have a proper subject. Again, adding a subject solves the problem: "We are going to dinner." To repair the statement "The friendly woman Mary," simply add a verb: "The friendly woman is Mary."

Run-on sentences lack necessary punctuation and/or connecting words: "We went to their party we had a very good time we plan to go again." This can be corrected several ways: "We went to their party. We had a very good time. We plan to go again." Or, less choppily: "We went to their party; we had a very good time, and we plan to go again."

Review Video: Fragments and Run-On Sentences
Visit mometrix.com/academy and enter code: 541989

Colons vs. Semicolons, Its vs. It's, and Saw vs. Seen

Semicolons separate independent clauses, such as "She likes music; she likes to dance." Colons separate clauses when the second explains or illustrates the first: "She likes music: she likes to dance to it." People often misuse semicolons. For example, business letter salutations should use colons. "Dear Mr. Johnson:" is correct, while "Dear Mr. Johnson;" is not. Another common error is inserting an apostrophe into "its" to indicate possession. For example, the sentence, "The house is old; *its* paint is peeling" is correct. People often incorrectly spell this possessive personal pronoun as "it's." Their error is because some possessive nouns/pronouns use apostrophes, such as "Barbara's idea" or "the man's hat." But "its," along with "yours," "hers," and "theirs" (without noun objects) do not. The only correct usage of "it's" is as a contraction of "it" and "is," as in "It's raining outside." "Saw" is the past tense of "to see." "Seen" is the perfect tense, used with auxiliary verbs to form present perfect "have seen," or past perfect, "had seen." This is why "I seen you" and "I have saw" are both incorrect.

> **Review Video: Colons**
> Visit mometrix.com/academy and enter code: 868673
>
> **Review Video: Semicolon Usage**
> Visit mometrix.com/academy and enter code: 370605
>
> **Review Video: Apostrophes**
> Visit mometrix.com/academy and enter code: 213068

Phrases, Clauses, and Independent and Dependent Clauses

A clause has a subject and a predicate and the other elements of a sentence. An independent clause can stand on its own as a sentence. A dependent clause has a subject and a predicate, but it also has a subordinating conjunction, a relative pronoun, or some other connecting word or phrase that makes it unable to stand alone without an accompanying independent clause. For example, "I knew she was not at home" is an independent clause that can be a sentence on its own. But "because I saw her leave" is a dependent clause due to the subordinating conjunction "because," which makes it depend on the independent clause. The two clauses, joined together, form the complex sentence, "I knew she was not at home because I saw her leave." A phrase is neither a complete sentence nor a clause. It lacks a subject, or a predicate, or both. For example, "late at night" is an adverb phrase; "into the house" is a prepositional phrase. Phrases modify other sentence parts.

> **Review Video: Clauses**
> Visit mometrix.com/academy and enter code: 940170

Inconsistent Verb Tenses and Non-Parallel Structure

While changing verb tenses in writing can indicate temporal relationships, switching tenses in a sentence if both or all verbs represent the same time frame is incorrect. For example, "The professor explained the theory to students who ask questions" uses inconsistent verb tenses. The verbs should be either "explained" and "asked" or "explains" and "asks." It is also incorrect to maintain the same verb tense when the time frame shifts among actions. The sentence, "Before they even saw the evidence, they decided" should actually read, "Before they even saw the evidence, they *had* decided" because "decided" occurred prior to "saw." "Susie loves the puppy she adopted" is correct: present-tense "loves" is true currently, while past-tense "adopted" is something Susie did previously and is not doing currently. An example of non-parallel structure is: "She enjoys skating, skiing, swimming, and to sail a boat." Because the first three objects are all gerunds ("-ing"

- 21 -

participles used as nouns), the fourth should be "sailing" to be consistent, not the inconsistent infinitive "to sail."

Review Video: Verb Tenses
Visit mometrix.com/academy and enter code: 809578

Simple, Compound, and Complex Sentences

A simple sentence is an independent clause. It states a complete thought and includes a subject and predicate/verb. An example is, "Some students cram before tests." "Students" is the subject; "some" is a modifying adjective. "Cram" is the verb; "before tests" is a modifying prepositional phrase. A compound sentence includes two independent clauses connected by a coordinator (*for, and, nor, but, or, yet, so*). For example, "Andrew likes history, but Cynthia prefers math" is a compound sentence. Independent clauses can also be joined by a semicolon instead of a coordinator: "Andrew likes history; Cynthia prefers math." A complex sentence has an independent clause and dependent clause, joined by a subordinator: "While Andrew likes history, Cynthia prefers math." The subordinating conjunction "while" makes the first clause dependent on the second. In the complex sentence, "Students are tired on exam day when they have crammed all night," the second clause, made subordinate by "when," depends on the independent clause that came first.

Compound, Complex, and Compound-Complex Sentences

Compound sentences consist of two independent clauses, joined by a coordinating conjunction or punctuation like a semicolon, a colon, or sometimes a comma (for example, "He likes coffee, she likes tea"). Complex sentences consist of an independent clause and a dependent clause, connected by a subordinating word, making one clause subordinate to/dependent on the other. A compound-complex sentence includes two independent clauses, plus one or more dependent clauses. "Susan likes art, and Emily prefers science" is a compound sentence. "Although Susan likes art, Emily prefers science" is a complex sentence. An example of a compound-complex sentence is, "Susan, who draws well, likes art, but Emily, who is very methodical, prefers science." "Susan likes art" is an independent clause. "Who draws well" is a dependent clause with subordinator "who" modifying subject "Susan." "Emily prefers science" is another independent clause. "Who is very methodical" is another dependent clause with subordinator "who" modifying subject "Emily." "But" is the coordinating conjunction joining the two independent clauses.

Review Video: Variation of Sentence Types
Visit mometrix.com/academy and enter code: 845700

Lie vs. Lay

"To lie" is the infinitive form of the verb, as in "It is restful to lie down on a bed." Many people incorrectly use "lay down" instead. "To lay" is always a transitive verb, which means that it requires an object, and it means to make something lie down or to set something down, as in, "Lay that book on the table." The non-infinitive "lay" is the past tense of "to lie," e.g., "Yesterday I lay down." But the past tense of the transitive verb "to lay" is "laid," as in, "Yesterday I laid the book on the table." The present perfect and past perfect tenses of the intransitive verb "to lie" are both "lain," as in "I have lain here a long time" or "I had lain there all day before they came." However, the present and past perfect tenses of the transitive verb "to lay" are both "laid," as in "I have laid this book down for now" and "I had laid this book down last week."

- 22 -

Compound Words

Compound words are words that consist of two single words that are used together to give a more specific meaning so commonly or often that they have been combined to form one word. These may be any part of speech, but are often nouns or adjectives. Some examples of nouns are *footsteps*, *heartbeat*, *countertop*, *gunshot*, *housewife*, *household*, *bookshelf*, *songbook*, *storybook*, *timetable*, *halfway*, *aftermath*, and *upkeep*. Some examples among adjectives include *paint-chipped*, *two-person*, *beat-up*, *pock-marked*, *war-torn*, *world-weary*, and *evidence-based*. Compound adjectives are often hyphenated, but not always, as in *bloodstained*. Also, authors may create compound adjectives when writing descriptively, as in *acne-scarred*, *hail-pitted*, and *flower-adorned*, to name a few.

Dangling Participles and Squinting Modifiers

Dangling participles are common writing errors. They occur when someone writes a participial ("-ing") phrase followed by a clause, but the syntax makes the participle seemingly modify that clause when it really modifies something else that is unstated. Consider the following sentence, "Always getting into trouble, her life changes." The participle "getting" should modify an absent "she," but it incorrectly modifies "her life" instead. Her life is not always getting into trouble, she is. Or another example, "After eating his lunch, we left the restaurant." The dangling participle makes it sound as if we both ate his lunch. If the writer meant to indicate he ate, it should read, "After he ate his lunch, we left the restaurant." "Joanne's mother left when she was young" has a squinting modifier, making unclear who was young when the mother left—Joanne, her mother, or both. Possible corrections include: "When Joanne was young, her mother left," "Joanne's mother left as a young woman," or "Her young mother left when Joanne was a young child."

Misplaced Modifiers

Misplaced modifiers are in the wrong part of a sentence, appearing to modify the wrong thing. For example, "This author creates a drama revolving around one character's journey in his new publication." This sounds like the new publication is a part of the character's journey. Correction involves moving the prepositional phrase: "In his new publication, this author creates a drama revolving around one character's journey."

Some other simple examples of how modifier placement affects meaning include: "She ate only fruit" versus "She only ate fruit." The first sentence means she ate nothing except fruit; the second means she did not plant, pick, wash, or cook fruit, but only ate it. Or, "He failed nearly every class he took" versus "He nearly failed every class he took." The former means he actually failed most of the classes he took, while the latter means he passed every class he took, but just barely. "Covered with flowers, she admired the field" means she was covered with flowers; "She admired the field covered with flowers" is correct.

> ### Review Video: Misplaced Modifiers
> Visit mometrix.com/academy and enter code: 312681

Inconsistent Verb Tense

A narrative includes the following: "Anticipating the explosion, the insurgent watched the Humvees drive out of range. He frowned. Impatiently he jerks at the wire connected to the grenade's pin. But the handle was caught on something and had not detonated the grenade." This narrative switches tenses. To correct this, the verbs should be consistent in tense: "watched... frowned... jerked... was (caught)... had not detonated." Conversely, they could also be "watches... frowns... jerks... is (caught)... has not detonated." When the main narrative is in the past tense, the reference to something occurring earlier should be in the past perfect tense; when narrative is in the present tense, the reference should be in the present perfect tense.

Phrases vs. Clauses and Transitive vs. Intransitive Verbs

A clause makes a complete sentence, which can be just a subject and verb. However, the verb must be intransitive—one that does not require an object—for the sentence to be complete. For example, "I am," "I live," and "I love" are all complete sentences, but "I like" (or "I hate") is not because "like" needs an object—I like what? "I like it," "I like food," "I like to eat," and "I like eating" are all examples of complete sentences and independent clauses. A phrase lacks either a subject or a verb. For example, while "I like to go swimming" is a clause/sentence, "to go swimming" is a phrase: it has a verb but no subject. The imperative "Go now" is a complete sentence wherein the subject "you" is understood; the meaning is "[You] go now."

Punctuation Errors in Possessive Pronouns

Many people make the error of misspelling the possessive pronoun "its" as "it's" when the apostrophe is only ever used in the contraction of "it is," and never in the possessive. Another common error is misspelling other possessive pronouns by using apostrophes, such as "your's" and "her's." These are always incorrect. A possessive pronoun taking a noun as its object, such as "his hat," "your hat," or "her hat" is not complicated by any –s ending. However, when the possessive pronoun does not have any noun object, the –s ending is added: "It is hers," "That hat is yours," or "She is a friend of theirs." Just like other possessive pronouns without –s endings (such as "mine"), the possessive pronouns ending with –s never include an apostrophe.

Drawbacks to Wordprocessing Spell Checkers

Microsoft Word is one of the most popular word processing programs. It has many excellent features facilitating composition. However, students and other writers must realize that its spell checkers, and those of similar programs, are far from perfect. One cannot rely on them without paying attention to what they do. For example, a college student writing a paper on Sophocles' *Oedipus Rex* correctly typed the name of key character Laius, king of Thebes and father of Oedipus, throughout his paper. However, his spell checker, not recognizing the name, "corrected" it to Louis. The student only realized this at the last minute while on his way to class, paper in hand, without a computer or printer nearby, and he had to rewrite every instance of the name by hand. Spell checkers commonly fail to recognize proper names and foreign language words. To eliminate the red zigzag underline that Word uses to indicate a misspelling, simply right-click and select "Add to dictionary" from the drop-down menu. Students and writers must consciously proofread everything they write, rather than assume spell checkers are always correct.

Microsoft Word's grammar check identifies many common errors, but is often incorrect. It does not recognize reflexive verbs, such as "assess themselves" or "do it for themselves," and suggests changing "themselves" to "them." Many writers and students get perplexed when writing a complete sentence to find Word underlining it with a green zigzag, labeling it a "fragment." Sometimes this reflects a true error, like leaving the verb out of a clause. But other times, it makes no sense by current writing standards. Right-clicking, selecting "Grammar" from the drop-down menu, and selecting "Ignore rule" eliminates such wrong "corrections." (Another option is to simply ignore the markups.) If they have questions, writers and students can consult reputable grammar experts' websites about suspect "corrections."

The grammar checkers in popular word processing software programs like Microsoft Word can catch many inadvertent errors often caused by hurried typing and/or careless writing. However, these programs are not always correct, and in fact are often incorrect. Not only will Word's grammar checker incorrectly label some constructions incorrect when they are not, but it will also fail to identify other errors. For example, Noam Chomsky's famous sample sentence, "Colorless green ideas sleep furiously" is grammatically, morphologically, and syntactically correct in its construction, but makes no sense semantically—which was Chomsky's point. Grammar checkers are not people who can think, reason, and understand; they are simply programmed to identify certain things categorized as errors. So the grammar checker has no problem with Chomsky's sentence and does not flag anything in it as wrong. This is an example of how grammar checkers not only over-correct by identifying correct usages as incorrect, but also under-correct by not identifying incorrect usages. Writers and students must use their own judgment and knowledge and consult grammatical experts and/or their websites when needed.

Persuasive Techniques

To appeal using reason, writers present logical arguments, such as using "If... then... because" statements. To appeal to emotions, authors ask readers how they would feel about something or to put themselves in another's place, present their point as making them feel best, and tell readers how they should feel. To appeal to character, morality, or ethics, authors present their points to readers as the right or most moral choices. Authors cite expert opinions to show readers that someone very knowledgeable about the subject or viewpoint agrees. Testimonials, via anecdotes about or quotations, add support. Bandwagon appeals persuade readers that everybody else agrees with the author's views. Authors appeal to greed by presenting their choice as cheaper, free, and/or more valuable for less cost. They appeal to laziness by presenting their views as more convenient, easy, or relaxing. Authors also anticipate potential objections and argue against them before audiences think of them, thereby depicting those objections as weak.

Authors can use comparisons like analogies, similes, and metaphors to persuade audiences. For example, a writer might represent excessive expenses as "hemorrhaging" money, which the author's recommended solution will stop. Authors can use negative word connotations to make some choices unappealing to readers, and positive word connotations to make others more appealing. Using humor can relax readers and garner their agreement. However, writers must take care: ridiculing opponents works with readers who already agree, but otherwise can backfire by angering other readers. Rhetorical questions need no answer, but create effect that can force agreement, such as asking the question, "Wouldn't you rather be paid more than less?" Generalizations persuade readers by being impossible to disagree with; writers can make these appear to support their viewpoints, like saying, "We all want peace, not war" regarding more specific political arguments. Transfer and association persuade by example: if advertisements show attractive actors enjoying their products, audiences imagine they will experience the same. Repetition, can also sometimes effectively persuade audiences.

> **Review Video: Rhetorical Strategy of Persuasion**
> Visit mometrix.com/academy and enter code: 302658

Critical Evaluation of Effectiveness of Persuasive Methods

First, readers should identify the author's thesis—what s/he argues for or against. They should consider the argument's content and why the author saw a need to present it. Does the author offer solutions to problems raised? If so, are they realistic? Note all central ideas and evidence supporting the author's thesis. Research any unfamiliar subjects or vocabulary. Readers should then outline or summarize the work in their own words. Identify which type(s) of appeal(s) the author uses. Readers should evaluate how well the author communicated meaning from the reader's perspective: Did they respond to emotional appeals with anger, concern, happiness, etc.? If so, why? Decide if the author's reasoning sufficed for changing the reader's mind. Determine whether the content and presentation were accurate, cohesive, and clear. Readers should also ask themselves whether they found the author believable or not, and why or why not.

Classical Author Appeals

In his *On Rhetoric,* ancient Greek philosopher Aristotle defined three basic types of appeal used in writing, which he called pathos, ethos, and logos. *Pathos* means suffering or experience and refers to appeals to the emotions (the English word "pathetic" comes from this root). Writing that is meant to entertain audiences, by making them either happy, as with comedy, or sad, as with tragedy, uses pathos. Aristotle's *Poetics* states that evoking the emotions of terror and pity is one of the criteria for writing tragedy. *Ethos* means character and connotes ideology (the English word "ethics" comes from this root). Writing that appeals to credibility, based on academic, professional, or personal merit uses ethos. *Logos* means "I say" and refers to a plea, opinion, expectation, word or speech, account, opinion, or reason. (The English word "logic" comes from this root.) Aristotle used it to mean persuasion that appeals to the audience through reasoning and logic to influence their opinions.

Author's Argument in Argumentative Writing

When an author writes in argumentative mode, the argument is a belief, position, or opinion that the author wants to convince readers to believe as well. For the first step, readers should identify the issue. Some issues are controversial, meaning people disagree about them. Gun control, foreign policy, and the death penalty are all controversial issues. The next step is to determine the author's position on the issue. That position or viewpoint constitutes the author's argument. Readers should then identify the author's assumptions: things s/he accepts, believes, or takes for granted without needing proof. Inaccurate or illogical assumptions produce flawed arguments and can mislead readers. Readers should identify what kinds of supporting evidence the author offers—research results, personal observations or experiences, case studies, facts, examples, expert testimony and opinions, and comparisons. Readers should decide how relevant this support is to the argument.

The first three reader steps to evaluate an author's argument are to identify the author's assumptions, identify the supporting evidence, and decide whether the evidence is relevant. For example, if an author is not an expert on a particular topic, then that author's personal experience or opinion might not be relevant. The fourth step is to assess the author's objectivity. For example, consider whether the author introduces clear, understandable supporting evidence and facts to support the argument. The fifth step is evaluating whether the author's argument is complete. When authors give sufficient support for their arguments and also anticipate and respond effectively to opposing arguments or objections to their points, their arguments are complete. However, some authors omit information that could detract from their arguments. If instead they stated this information and refuted it, it would strengthen their arguments. The sixth step in evaluating an author's argumentative writing is to assess whether the argument is valid. Providing clear, logical reasoning makes an author's argument valid. Readers should ask themselves whether the author's points follow a sequence that makes sense, and whether each point leads to the next. The seventh step is to determine whether the author's argument is credible, meaning that it is convincing and believable. Arguments that are not valid are not credible, so step seven depends on step six. Readers should be mindful of their own biases as they evaluate and should not expect authors to conclusively prove their arguments, but rather to provide effective support and reason.

Logical Fallacies

Post hoc ergo propter hoc is Latin for "After this, therefore because of this." This equates to reasoning that because X happened before Y, X must have caused Y. But just as correlation does not imply causation, neither does chronological sequence. For example, one cannot assume that because most rapists read pornography as teenagers that pornography causes rape. A red herring is irrelevant information introduced to distract others from the pertinent issue. For example, one author claims that welfare dependence raises crime rates, while another argues plausibly that some increase in crime is justified in addressing poverty. However, if the second author argued instead, "But how can the poor survive without help?" that would be a red herring. Slippery slopes, when fallacious, are arguments that one event will cause others without demonstrating any cause-and-effect relationship—hence non-sequiturs. For example, arguing that legalizing one drug will cause all drugs to be legalized is obviously false. Straw man is refuting an exaggeration or caricature of someone's argument, not the real argument.

Rationales for Knowing Logical Fallacies

For persuasive and argumentative writing, logic is necessary, but so are supporting facts, insights, and the plausibility of an argument. Although logic by itself may show that the answer to a question discussed is unknown, the most plausible argument can still convince audiences. One reason for knowing the names and processes of logical fallacies is enabling writers to identify flawed reasoning by those presenting opposing viewpoints—and identify them precisely by supplying a Latin name for each. Another reason is that by identifying logical fallacies, the author does not simply make an opponent's argument weaker or less convincing, but s/he actually eliminates it from the debate. Rather than counterarguments—allowing opponents' rhetoric proving their arguments' importance—this makes audiences question the validity, and even existence, of the opposing argument. If the other author cannot justify it strongly, that argument can be negated, and so the audience does not even consider it.

Steps or Strategies to Draw Attention to Logical Fallacies in Opposing Arguments

The writer should first restate the targeted opposing argument. Then s/he points out this argument is a logical fallacy and identifies it by name. The writer then explains the meaning of this logical fallacy and why it involves erroneous reasoning. Writers must not let their language become pompous or pedantic in tone during this explanation. Instead, they appeal more to audiences by stating the meaning of the fallacy as though their perceptive readers and listeners already know it. For example, if a writer identifies an opposing writer's use of an appeal to public opinion, s/he defines this by pointing out that majority agreement with a position does not make it right. Writers then give overt examples of a fallacy's incorrectness—such as historical beliefs that the world was flat or that slavery was acceptable. Finally, writers call for the erroneous argument to be ruled out, leaving their opponents with an untenable position.

Argumentum ad antiquitatem means an argument to tradition or antiquity. We have often read or heard this used when people write or say, "We have always done it this way." An example might be that the governments of all major societies have always supplied state funding for cultural pursuits and the arts. However, it is not logical that this intrinsically warrants continuing to do it. An inherent weakness of this argument is that others can refute it easily just by drawing attention to it. Therefore, it should not be a writer's first choice. If one feels the need to use this argument, one way to support it is to offer a reason for respecting the tradition cited. One might support arguing for a tradition with the evolutionary principle of natural selection—such as saying that the reason all known civilizations practice this tradition is because those that ignored it failed to survive.

Argumentum ad hominem is against the person, not the person's statements/ideas. The arguer attacks a person's motives or character, not what s/he wrote or said. This is less often by name-calling, such as "He is a communist/fascist/greedy capitalist," but more commonly by attacking the person as an information source. If one cites ending the Vietnam War, signing environmental laws, and opening China as positive accomplishments of Richard Nixon, and quotes him regarding free trade, then the *ad hominem* arguer might cite the Watergate scandal as evidence Nixon was a "crook" and liar, so nobody can believe anything he said. Arguments *ad hominem* also are used against people arguing for anything that would benefit them and against anything that would disadvantage them—like owners of corporate conglomerates arguing against anti-trust laws—shifting focus away from the argument's validity to focus on who makes it. Many *ad hominem* arguments may be restated about ideas versus people—such as not claiming someone is a fascist, but his/her position is.

Argumentum ad ignorantiam is an argument appealing to ignorance. In other words, the arguer presumes the truth of something based on its not being proven untrue. For example, one would do better by presenting actual data to prove climate change than by arguing it is true because nobody has proven it false. The burden of proof is a key factor for determining whether this argument is fallacious or not. As an analogy, in the United States legal system, a defendant is innocent until proven guilty—rather than guilty until proven innocent as in some other court systems. Thus defense attorneys can argue that their client is not guilty because the prosecution has not proven him/her guilty. However, prosecuting attorneys cannot argue that the defendant must be guilty of committing a crime because s/he has no alibi. Both arguments constitute *ad ignorantiam*, but in the American legal system, the burden of proof is on the prosecution rather than the defense. Similarly, in rhetoric, the proposer typically has the burden of proof.

The logical fallacy *argumentum ad logicam*, or argument/appeal to logic, presumes something is untrue based on an invalid argument or proof. This is fallacious because other, valid arguments could exist. The *argumentum ad logicam* frequently occurs within the context of the *straw man* fallacy, which argues against a distortion or exaggeration of a position, not the actual position. The *ad logicam* appeal is determined as fallacious or not through the burden of proof: If the proposer of the original position does not prove it, s/he loses the debate even though other arguments not presented could have proven it. Also, if one side disproves another's point as invalid, it will be judged invalid, regardless of whether the proposer could have proven it with a better argument because s/he did not do so; the burden of proof is on the proposer. This determination of fallacy or validity via burden of proof is comparable to that used with *argumentum ad ignorantiam*.

Argumentum ad misericordiam means argument/appeal to pity. This is often employed by those pleading to others for donations and other assistance to help starving children, abused animals, and poor people. Of course many pity such victims and want to help, but what makes this appeal illogical is that by itself, it cannot make expenses free, make true something untrue, or render something possible that is impossible. It is valid, however, to emphasize a problem's significance as a way of supporting one's proposing a particular solution to that problem. The proposer of the solution must then be able to address such objections as whether that solution is possible or feasible; what negative impacts it could have on others, even while providing positive impacts on those it would help; and its expenses and how to provide for those. Appealing to pity is acceptable to support arguments that a proposal's benefits justify its costs, but unacceptable as the sole response to objections without otherwise addressing them.

Argumentum ad nauseam translates literally as argument to the point of nausea. In other words, this tactic involves repeating one's point over and over until listeners are so disgusted that they cannot tolerate hearing it any longer. Reiterating a true statement over and over is not fallacious in

- 28 -

itself, but expecting such repetition to replace actual logic is. Despite the absence of reasoning, repetition has a powerful effect of convincing listeners. This makes *argumentum ad nauseam* very popular. When one side in a spoken or written debate or controversy has used this technique of constant repetition without supplying any evidence to support or document the assertion, the other side can refute it by pointing out that the repeated statement has not been substantiated with any proof.

Argumentum ad numerum, translated as argument or appeal to numbers, is a rhetorical device of citing mathematical figures as "proof" that something is true. For example, one might argue, "80 percent of the public supports this legislation." The fallacy here is that the agreement of the majority does not make something true. The 80 percent of the public that supports a law could be wrong in doing so—like in the antebellum Southern United States, where the majority of the public supported slavery. They had considerable incentive to take this position to preserve the entire foundation of their economy and way of life, but they were not morally justified in doing so. *Argumentum ad numerum* resembles *argumentum ad populum*—appeal to popularity or to the people. Their minor difference is that arguing to the people appeals directly to the nearby public, while appealing to numbers attempts to persuade others based on citing how many other people agree. These are similar enough to be often used interchangeably in rhetoric.

The meaning of *argumentum ad verecundiam* is arguing or appealing to authority. This is attempting to prove one's position by citing the opinion of someone who is not an expert in the specific subject at issue. For example, Enrico Fermi and Albert Einstein were both pacifists, and objected strenuously to having their science applied for building bombs. While some agree and some do not, the fact is that Fermi and Einstein were experts in nuclear physics, but not in politics or foreign policy. Citing or quoting authorities in the subject under discussion, though, is not fallacious. It is also acceptable to quote a non-expert who nevertheless made an eloquent statement appropriate to one's argument. Unacceptable uses of the appeal to authority include using unqualified sources to verify facts and/or implying that a given position has to be correct just because a certain person believes it is.

Circulus in demonstrando is Latin for a circular argument. This means that by trying to use the assertion or idea they want to prove is itself a part of their proof, people using circular argumentation are actually "talking in circles." As an example, someone argues, "X is illegal. Because it is illegal, one should not do it. Because one shouldn't do it, the government should prevent people from doing it. This is why it is illegal." In this example, the circular nature of the argument is obvious. However, some arguments are circular but less easily recognized. Some politicians and political commentators are notorious for using circular arguments. To refute the fallacy of *circulus in demonstrando,* one can summarize the arguer's statement as "You are saying that X is true because X is true," and then additionally point out that the arguer has not provided any actual proof.

"Complex question" refers to a rhetorical tactic that implicitly presumes something as true before it has been established. An obvious example is when reporters or lawyers ask someone, "Have you stopped embezzling?" when there is no proof that the person questioned ever embezzled. This tactic is employed to trick people into admitting things they would not admit in direct questioning. A less obvious example is asking someone, "Since most African-Americans are poor, do you believe the measures proposed would be effective?" The first clause is not true, but the person questioned could be so focused on the second clause and how to answer it as to overlook the falsehood. This is more effective in spoken than written language: in real-time spoken interactions, it can confuse someone; in a written piece, the reader has time to reconsider it and realize it is untrue. A major drawback is that if the person questioned notices the falsehood and confronts the questioner, it makes the questioner appear foolish.

Cum hoc ergo propter hoc means in Latin, "With this, therefore because of this." In other words, because these occur together, one causes the other. A parallel fallacy in scientific research is assuming that correlation indicates causation. Things can occur together out of coincidence: people may attribute economic improvement to a certain president's administration when it may be more due to technological advances. Things can occur together, but one is an effect of prior causes: an improved economy during one president's administration can be the result of an earlier president's actions. Things can occur together and be unrelated to each other, but both related to a common reason: as an economic remedy, one president enacts downsizing measures, which many voters dislike, so they consequently elect a different president, and benefits of the previous president's downsizing appear after the election of the subsequent president. Whereas correlation can never mean causation in scientific research, in rhetoric one may attribute causation to correlation if one can provide sufficiently convincing reasons for it.

The Latin *dicto simpliciter* literally means "spoken simply," a figuratively sweeping generalization. When people make sweeping proclamations they presume are always true, they are stereotyping—which is another term for this. An example is generalizing that as a group, women are not as strong physically as men and assuming that therefore, they cannot serve equally in the military. While the first statement is true in general, it is not always true of specific individuals: some women are stronger than some men. In rhetoric, it is typically sufficient simply to state why a sweeping generalization does not prove someone's point without using the official terminology or pointing out its logical fallacy. Sweeping generalizations are understood by the public without instruction in rhetorical devices. Hence, experts also advise that naming the fallacy in Latin in this case seems condescending. Non-fallacious generalizations are always true individually, such as "Normal human females have two X chromosomes; normal human males have an X and a Y chromosome."

The appeal to nature assumes that anything natural or part of nature is good, and/or that anything not natural is bad. For example, some people may argue that birth control or homosexuality is wrong because these are not natural. In addition to the problem of defining the meaning of "natural," it is also illogical to equate "unnatural" or non-natural with wrong. Human beings use fire, construct and use tools, wear clothing, and farm the soil; these can be deemed "unnatural," yet they are both common and beneficial. Because of these inherent weaknesses, this argument is not effective. For instance, defending environmentalism only on the basis of preserving natural resources or wildernesses does not provide strong enough reasons. However, this can be defended more strongly by appealing to humans on the basis of their own survival by arguing that humans live within a complex ecosystem that is easily damaged by certain human activities which could destroy both the ecosystem and thus humanity as a part of it.

In the naturalistic fallacy, one draws conclusions regarding values—in other words, right and wrong or good and bad—based only on factual statements. This is fallacious because any logical inferences based on facts alone will constitute simply more statements of fact, rather than statements of value. A statement of value must be used together with facts to make a conclusion about values For instance, the statement, "This medication will keep you from dying" might seem to connect to a conclusion, "You should take this medication." However, the former is a statement of fact, the latter one of value. For the conclusion to be logically valid, an additional premise is needed, "You should do what you need to do to stay alive."

Argumentum ad antiquitatem, or appeal to tradition (something is right because it has always been done) and the appeal to nature (something is right because it is natural), are forms of the naturalistic fallacy: they draw conclusions about values using statements of fact without any statement(s) of value to connect logically with conclusions. Facts represent what is; values represent what ought to be. Philosopher David Hume described these fallacies as attempts to bridge the "is-ought gap." Initial axioms of value are not necessarily justifiable via pure logic. However, rhetoric is not limited to pure logic. Three ways to rebut an axiom of value, such as "Anything natural is good," are: (1) Ask if anybody—yourself, the judge of a debate, or even your opponent who stated it—truly believes this; (2) present another value axiom that competes with it, like "Anything that improves people's lives is good," so the judge is forced to choose between the two; and (3) cite logical ramifications of the statement's contradiction of basic morality.

In Latin, *non sequitur* means "It does not follow." If someone says, for instance, "Racism is wrong; thus affirmative action is necessary," this conclusion does not logically follow the initial premise. If one says instead, "Racism is wrong; affirmative action would decrease racism; thus affirmative action is needed," the logical connection is supplied. Some rhetoricians include *non sequiturs* in their opening arguments strategically to avoid giving away to their opponents a counterargument they anticipate. Except in the cases of significant, obvious counterarguments that should be anticipated and answered early, it is more strategic to wait for an opponent to raise an argument to rebut, rather than waste time and energy answering unstated objections. It is inadvisable to claim *non sequitur* whenever an opponent does not anticipate each of one's counterarguments. The best application for pointing out this fallacy is when an opponent attempts to show a causal chain without proving each link. Identifying each unsubstantiated step ultimately reveals such attempted chains as weak and implausible.

Petitio principii means "begging the question": when attempting to prove something, one assumes the same thing one wants to prove. In terms of logical structure, this is the same as using a circular argument. Although the meaning of "begging the question" is quite specific, many people misuse this term in rhetorical arguments. A question is begged if it is asked during a conversation but never answered, and meanwhile the parties in the discussion come to a conclusion about a related issue. For example, someone might argue, "Some people campaign for legalizing pornography because it is a medium for freedom of expression. However, this 'begs the question' of what freedom of expression means." This uses the term incorrectly. Some issues and discussions motivate questions rather than begging them. A more correct example of "begging the question" would be if someone argued, "Because we believe that pornography should be legalized, it constitutes a valid medium of free expression. Being free expression, it therefore should not be banned."

Translated from Latin, *tu quoque* means "you too." The old saying "Two wrongs don't make a right" addresses this fallacy. In rhetoric, one commits an error in logic—for example, making unproven claims—and defends it by rejoining that the opposition did the same. That both sides made the same error does not excuse either one. Though *tu quoque* is an obvious fallacy, it is often used to significant advantage in rhetoric: Disregarding whether any proposition is true or false, debaters can show which side made the better performance in arguing. For example, if both sides have equally appealed to audience pity (*argumentum ad misericordiam*), or both have used equal *ad hominem* arguments (attacking the person, not what s/he says), then to be fair a judge must penalize both equally, not just one. Additionally, it is not fallacious to show that "non-unique" advantages or disadvantages that apply equally to both sides cannot warrant preferring either position. *Tu quoque* can ensure that judging is only according to differentiating factors between sides.

> **Review Video: Reading Logical Fallacies**
> Visit mometrix.com/academy and enter code: 644845

Research Writing

A research question or problem is what a researcher wants to answer or resolve. In a research paper, the problem statement clearly identifies the issue, tells why the researcher cares about this issue, defines the scope of the research by focusing on specific variables, and shows why those variables matter. The problem statement follows the title and abstract in the research paper, supplying context for the rest and getting the reader's attention. Whether professionals or students, when researchers conduct academic research projects, their literature reviews, which thoroughly examine the extant body of literature on their chosen research topic, form a necessary component of the project by showing what work has already been done toward answering the research question that they have chosen to investigate.

Addressing Research Questions

When asking a research question, the researcher may find through making a careful review of the existing literature that the question s/he has chosen have already been answered definitively. In this case, the researcher should modify the question or ask a different one. If the question has not been answered in the literature, researchers should consider the existing knowledge, the chronological sequence in which knowledge has been developed, whether there are any gaps in the knowledge, what needs and opportunities for additional research have been identified, and how one plans to fill in these gaps. Researchers should also consider whether consensus or controversy exists about pertinent matters and, with the latter, which positions exist. One should also consider research trajectories suggested by others' work and the most productive research direction indicated by the literature. Finally, researchers should realize there are no absolute answers: they must decide what is important in the context of their work.

Literature Review

One main part of a literature review is searching through existing literature. The other is actually writing the review. Researchers must take care not to get lost in the information without making any progress in their research goal. A good precaution is to write out the research question and keep it nearby. It is also wise to make a search plan and establish a time limit in advance. Finding a seemingly endless number of references indicates a need to revisit the research question because it is too broad. Finding too little material means that the research topic is too narrow. With cutting-edge research, one may find that nobody has investigated this particular question. This requires systematic searching, using abstracts in periodicals for an overview of available literature, research papers or other specific sources to explore its reference, and references in books and general sources.

When searching published literature on a research topic, one must take thorough notes. It is common to find a reference that could be useful later but is not needed now, so it is helpful to make a note of it so it will be easy to find later. These notes can be grouped in a word processing document, which also allows for easy compiling of links and quotes from Internet research. Researchers should connect to the Internet regularly, view resources for their research often, learn how to use resources correctly and efficiently, experiment with resources available within the discipline(s), open and examine databases, become familiar with reference desk materials, find

- 32 -

publications with abstracts of articles and books on one's topic, use papers' references to locate the most utile journals and important authors, identify keywords for refining and narrowing database searches, and peruse library catalogues online for available sources—all while taking notes.

As one searches the available literature, one will gradually develop an overview of the body of literature for his or her subject. This signals the time to prepare for writing the literature review. The researcher should assemble his or her notes along with copies of all the journal articles and all the books acquired. Then one should again write the research question at the top of a page and list below it all of the author names and keywords discovered while searching. It is also helpful to observe whether any groups or pairs of these stand out. These activities are parts of structuring one's literature review—the first step for writing a thesis, dissertation, or research paper. Writers should rewrite as necessary rather than expecting to make only one draft. However, stopping to edit along the way can distract from the momentum of the first draft. It may be better to skip to a later portion of the paper and revisit the problem section at another time.

Body and Conclusion in Literature Review

The first step of a literature review paper is to create a rough draft. The next step is to edit: rewrite for clarity, eliminate unnecessary verbiage, and change terminology that could confuse readers. After editing, a writer should ask others to read and give feedback. Additionally, the writer should read the paper aloud to hear how it sounds, editing as needed. Throughout a literature review, the writer should not only summarize and comment on each source reviewed, but should also relate these findings to the original research question. The writer should explicitly state in the conclusion how the research question and pertinent literature interaction is developed throughout the body, reflecting on insights gained through the process.

Primary and Secondary Sources

In literature review, one may examine both primary and secondary sources. Primary sources contain original information, like reports other researchers have made of their findings and other first-hand accounts written by experimenters or witnesses of discoveries or events. They may be found in academic books, journals and other periodicals, and authoritative databases. Secondary sources refer to information originally given by other people or found in other places. They may be cited, quoted, or described in books, magazines, newspapers, films, audio and video materials, databases, and websites. Accounts of research and its results are always informed and directed by reviews of the pertinent literature. These depict the present research as a cumulative process integral to the scientific method. Literature reviews also test the research question in relation to the existing knowledge about the topic.

Editing and Revising

After composing a rough draft of a research paper, the writer should edit it. The purpose of the paper is to communicate the answer to one's research question in an efficient and effective manner. This should be as concise and clear as possible, and the style should also be consistent. Editing is often easier to do after writing the first draft than during it, as distance allows writers to be more objective. If the paper includes an abstract and an introduction, the writer should compose these after writing the rest, when s/he will have a better grasp of the theme and arguments. Not all readers understand technical terminology or long words, so writers should use these sparingly. Finally, writers should keep a writing and style guide available to answer questions as they edit.

> **Review Video: Revising and Editing**
> Visit mometrix.com/academy and enter code: 674181

Citing Sources

Formal research writers must cite all sources used—books, articles, interviews, conversations, and anything else that contributed to the research. One reason is to avoid plagiarism and give others credit for their ideas. Another reason is to help readers find more information about the subject for further reading and research. Additionally, citing sources helps to make a paper academically authoritative. To prepare, research writers should keep a running list of sources consulted, in an electronic file or on file cards. For every source used, the writer needs specific information. For books, a writer needs to record the author and/or editor name, title, publication date, city, and publisher name. For articles, one needs the author name, title, journal (or magazine or newspaper) name, volume and issue number, publication date, and page numbers. For electronic resources, a writer will need the article information plus the URL, database name, name of the database's publisher, and the date of access.

Three common reference styles are MLA (Modern Language Association), APA (American Psychological Association), and Turabian (by expert author Kate Turabian). Each style formats citation information differently. Professors and instructors often specify that students use one of these. Generally, APA style is used in psychology and sociology papers, and MLA style is used in English literature papers and similar scholarly projects.

To refer to authoritative sources for citing more complicated or specialized resources, such as legislative publications, audiovisual resources, or manuscripts, see http://library.csudh.edu/cyberlib/research.htm, the section on Research and Writing Resources from the library website of California State University Dominguez Hills (CSUDH). The APA Manual is available in print: *Publication Manual of the American Psychological Association,* 6th ed., July 2009, and electronically in a Kindle edition. (The sixth is the latest edition as of February 2014.) APA has also adapted from this edition the *APA Style Guide to Electronic References,* and a pocket guide, *Concise Rules of APA Style.* Garner and Smith's *The Complete Guide to Citing Government Information Resources: A Manual for Writers and Librarians,* June 1993 (revised edition) is available in paperback on Amazon.com. *MLA Handbook for Writers of Research Papers* (7th edition, 2009) is available at MLA Bookstore's website. Turabian's *A Manual for Writers of Research Papers, Theses, and Dissertations* (8th edition, revised, 2013) is available from the University of Chicago Press website.

Integrating References and Quotations

In research papers, one can include studies whose conclusions agree with one's position (Reed 284; Becker and Fagen 93), as well as studies that disagree (Limbaugh 442, Beck 69) by including parenthetical citations as demonstrated in this sentence. Quotations should be selective: writers should compose an original sentence and incorporate only a few words from a research source. If students cannot use more original words than quotation, they are likely padding their compositions.

When quoting sources, writers should work quotations and references seamlessly into their sentences instead of interrupting the flow of their own argument to summarize a source. Summarizing others' content is often a ploy to bolster word counts. Writing that analyzes the content, evaluates it, and synthesizes material from various sources demonstrates critical thinking skills and is thus more valuable.

> **Review Video: Quotes**
> Visit mometrix.com/academy and enter code: 191037

Incorporating Outside Sources

Writers do better to include short quotations rather than long. For example, six to eight long passages quoted in a 10-page paper are excessive. It is also better to avoid wording like "This quotation shows," "As you can see from this quotation," or "It talks about." These are amateurish, feeble efforts to interact with other authors' ideas. Also, writing about sources and quotations wastes words that should be used to develop one's own ideas. Quotations should be used to stimulate discussion rather than taking its place. Ending a paragraph, section, or paper with a quotation is not incorrect per se, but using it to prove a point, without anything more in one's own words regarding the point or subject, is avoiding thinking critically about the topic and considering multiple alternatives. It can also be a tactic to dissuade readers from challenging one's propositions. Writers should include references and quotations that disagree as well as agree with their thesis statements. Presenting evidence on both sides of an issue makes it easier for reasonably skeptical readers to agree with a writer's viewpoint.

SSBI Classroom Teaching Approach

Language teaching and learning have evolved from a traditional focus on teaching and teachers to a more current focus on learning and learners. Educators have come to realize that regardless of teacher performance, if students are not learning and motivated, more emphasis on learners is needed. More learner-centered instruction is necessarily more interactive, self-directed, and independent. However, many students lack awareness of learning strategies. Language acquisition requires not only memory formation and retention, but also relevant and continuing practice. Classroom teachers can train students in purposeful, systematic learning methods to support and facilitate these components. Styles- and Strategies-based Instruction (SSBI) (cf. Oxford, 200a; Cohen and Dörnyei, 2002) combines training activities in learning strategies and styles with day-to-day language instruction. Its basis is a combination of classroom language learning opportunities with more efficient, effective use of language learned. Explicit and implicit instruction in language learning and strategy use are integrated in classrooms to promote strategy awareness, organization, systematic and effective application, and transfers to new learning and contexts of use.

Components

The first component of the SSBI approach is Strategy Preparation. This involves teachers discovering which learning strategies students already know, and how they are able to apply them. Most students have developed some strategies, but they often do not apply them systematically or effectively. The second component of SSBI is Strategy Awareness-Raising. Its aim is for teachers to make students aware of learning strategies they may never have considered, or had thought about but have never actually utilized. Five SSBI tasks of awareness raising are to determine: (1) what comprises the learning process; (2) students' individual approaches to learning generally and/or preferences in learning styles; (3) which types of strategies they already use, plus strategies the teachers and classmates suggest; (4) how much responsibility individual students assume for their own learning; and (5) methods for assessing students' use of learning strategies.

Following the first two phases of SSBI—Strategy Preparation and Strategy Awareness-Raising—the third component is the Strategy Training phase. This involves explicit instruction by classroom teachers to teach students why, when, and how specific learning strategies are used to support activities for learning and using language. Strategies may be used singly, in clusters, or in sequences. In a typical scenario of classroom training in learning strategies, a teacher would describe strategies that could prove useful to students, model the application of these strategies, and give the students several examples of each strategy to illustrate them. The teacher would also have students contribute more examples from their own learning experiences. The teacher leads whole-class and/or small-group discussions about three things: rationales for using various strategies, planning their approaches to specified activities, and assessing the efficacy of the strategies that they select. The teacher can also invite students to experiment with applying a wide array of strategies.

The fourth phase of SSBI is Strategy Practice. Teachers ask students to experiment with a wide range of learning strategies. Awareness of and training in a strategy are insufficient: students must additionally have plenty of opportunities to practice applying them to many different tasks in language learning and use. This phase incorporates activities that are "strategy-friendly," meaning they reinforce strategies that students have previously learned, and they afford ample time for students to combine their learning of subject course content with practice in using the various strategies. SSBI activities are prescribed to refer explicitly to strategies employed for task completion. Hence, either students plan which strategies to use for a certain activity, or teachers call their attention to which strategies they are using at the time. Teachers may also "debrief" students in their strategy applications and their comparative efficacy following an activity.

SSBI includes Strategy Preparation; Strategy Awareness-Raising; Strategy Training; Strategy Practice; and finally, Personalization of Strategies. During this final component, students personalize what they have learned about various systematic strategies for language learning. They self-assess their application of the strategies they have learned, and they examine how they can transfer these strategies to different contexts. Those who plan, write, and implement curriculum within the SSBI approach have the responsibility of ensuring that day-to-day classroom materials and activities have systematic learning strategies integrated into them, and that the linguistic tasks they assign to students embed these strategies, both implicitly and explicitly, for practice in different contexts. Teachers can begin with existing course matter and then decide which strategies to incorporate, begin with a set of selected strategies and then build activities around these, or they can spontaneously include indicated or suitable strategies during lessons. SSBI activities aim to give students strategy awareness; training; practice; personalization; and spontaneous, independent, and unprompted selection of strategies they prefer.

Research-Based Instruction for Vocabulary Development

The National Reading Technical Assistance Center (NRTAC, 2010) has reviewed current research on vocabulary instruction and synthesized salient findings. According to the National Reading Panel (NRP), children often must learn the meanings of specific words to understand specific subject matter and/or lessons. Therefore, teachers must give direct instruction in the vocabulary found in specific texts. Researchers also find that students need to be exposed to vocabulary words multiple times, and they additionally warn that word repetition not be simply drilling, but rather repeated encounters with the same words in varied contexts. Studies demonstrate that students should learn high-frequency vocabulary words and be able to apply them in multiple and varied contexts. Vocabulary learning is found to take a developmental course. Researchers also find that teachers should restructure vocabulary exercises as needed because once students understand expectations, they tend to learn faster.

Research Findings About Vocabulary Instruction

Among a number of conclusions that reviewers of the research literature on vocabulary instruction have made, they find that learners achieve more effective vocabulary acquisition when vocabulary learning is not limited to knowing word definitions but also involves active student engagement. Some researchers define a child's "knowing" a word as not simply knowing the dictionary definition of a word and how it is related logically to other words, but moreover by the way that the word works in various contexts. Also, research in 2000 by the National Institute of Child Health and Human Development (NICHD) found computer technology very useful in vocabulary instruction, but not many teaching applications revealed in literature. Additional research finds that students' long-term vocabulary development is significantly influenced by their reading volume, which promotes incidental learning of vocabulary. Researchers recommend independent reading at home and school, plus structured read-aloud sessions and discussions.

Areas Needing Further Study

According to the National Institute of Child Health and Human Development (NICHD), optimum vocabulary learning by students will not proceed from relying on only one instructional method. Multiple researchers and educators find that students must learn not only word definitions, but also how words fit into the world's context. Crucial aspects of vocabulary learning include receptive vocabulary understanding versus productive vocabulary expression, printed or written vocabulary versus spoken vocabulary, and vocabulary depth versus vocabulary breadth. These are all topics in which extant research indicates the need for additional study. Moreover, other researchers have found the means of measuring vocabulary knowledge, in which the words students are learning, their levels of vocabulary knowledge, and variability among students in their vocabulary sizes need to be taken into account to understand vocabulary learning. The National Reading Panel (NRP) reported (NICHD, 2000) that while vocabulary instruction increases comprehension, teaching methods must fit reader ability and age, and that research has not yet definitively identified the best instructional methods for vocabulary.

Consensus Conclusions Regarding What Is Most Effective

Researchers find that when young children are repeatedly exposed to targeted vocabulary words, as in repeated readings of the same storybooks, they are more likely to understand the words' meanings, remember them, and use them more often than children who hear a story only once. Rereading is also found effective for children at risk for reading problems. Researchers note that children gain semantic and lexical knowledge gradually through frequent exposure to targeted words. Other findings suggest that children with comprehension deficits in lexical learning may experience these due to variations in semantic learning instead of phonological learning. Studies have shown that explicit instruction of word meanings during read-aloud sessions in addition to rereading increases children's vocabulary comprehension more than rereading alone. Also, students are found to progress even more when asked to give their own definitions of target words than when they are told explanations for unknown words. Researchers find that contextual instructional approaches increase vocabulary more than lessons teaching word definitions.

Multimedia and Questions and Comments

Studies find that children learn definitions of new words more easily than they can recall pronunciations. Some researchers examined multimedia applications for enhancing read-aloud sessions and vocabulary instruction with preschoolers through second-graders, including both native English speakers and English language learners (ELLs). While findings for adding multimedia with native English-speaking students were not statistically significant, they were for ELL students. Gaps between ELLs and native English speakers were reduced, not just for vocabulary words targeted, but also for more generalized knowledge of English vocabulary. Researchers have also found that when teachers use questions and comments to call attention to target vocabulary words, children are more likely to learn the meanings of those words. Investigators have ruled out previous knowledge by using storybooks that included nonsense words; children still comprehended and remembered meanings assigned to the nonsense words better when teachers asked them questions and gave them comments about the word meanings.

Scaffolding, Question Demand, and Student Engagement

Some investigators have evaluated how using low-demand and high-demand questions and scaffolding (graduated support) influence young children's vocabulary learning during storybook read-alouds. The experimenters found that when teachers used scaffolding by asking children low-demand questions and gradually adding more complexity until their questions eventually reached high-demand status, preschool children showed more progress in learning new words. Others have examined engagement in linguistic student-teacher interactions and its effects on vocabulary acquisition. Some have found that amounts of time spent in early literacy activities vary widely among preschool classes; that learning environments cover a range, from language-centered to mainly non-literacy-based learning activities; and furthermore, that even children in the same classrooms have strikingly varied learning opportunities and experiences. This indicates a significant relationship between children's experience and background knowledge, and their learning results. Other studies show that preschoolers and kindergarteners learn and remember vocabulary better through interactive approaches than through embedded or incidental vocabulary exposure during read-aloud sessions.

Reading for Literature

Historical Background for English Literature

The ancient Greek Athenian elite were a highly educated society, developing philosophies and writing about principles for creating poetry and drama. During the Roman Empire, the Romans assimilated and adapted the culture of the Greeks they conquered into their own society. For example, the gods of Roman mythology were essentially the same as in Greek myth, only renamed in Latin. However, after the fall of the Roman Empire, the many European countries formerly united under Roman rule became fragmented. There followed a 1,000-year period of general public ignorance and illiteracy—called the Dark Ages as well as the Middle Ages. Only the Church remained a bastion of literacy: monks and priests laboriously copied manuscripts one at a time by hand. Johannes Gutenberg's 1450 invention of the movable-type printing press changed everything: multiple copies of books could be printed much faster. This enabled a public return to literacy, leading to the Renaissance, or "rebirth"—reviving access and interest for Greek and Roman classics, and generating a creative explosion in all arts.

Medieval Poetry

The medieval time period was heavily influenced by Greek and Latin Stoic philosophies. Medieval Christians appreciated Greek and Latin Stoic philosophies for their assigning more importance to spiritual virtues than material. Pagan stoic values were often adapted to Christian beliefs, and these were incorporated into early English literature.

Geoffrey Chaucer

The Canterbury Tales

Medieval poet Geoffrey Chaucer (c. 1343-1400), called the "Father of English Literature," chiefly wrote long narrative poems, including *The Book of the Duchess, Anelida and Arcite, The House of Fame, The Parlement of Foules, The Legend of Good Women,* and *Troilus and Criseyde.* His most famous work is *The Canterbury Tales.* Its historical and cultural context is life during the Middle Ages, representing a cross-section of society—tradespeople, professionals, nobility, clergy, and housewives, among others—and religious pilgrimages, a common practice of the time. Its literary context is a frame-tale, a story within a story. Chaucer described a varied group of pilgrims on their way to Canterbury to visit the shrine of St. Thomas à Becket, taking turns telling stories to amuse the others. Tales encompass a broad range of subjects: bawdy comedy, chivalry, romance, and religion. These include *The Knight's Tale, The Miller's Tale, The Reeve's Tale, The Cook's Tale, The Man of Law's Tale, The Wife of Bath's Tale, The Friar's Tale, The Summoner's Tale, The Clerk's Tale, The Merchant's Tale, The Squire's Tale, The Franklin's Tale, The Physician's Tale, The Pardoner's Tale,* and *The Nun's Priest's Tale.*

The Parlement of Foules

In the brief preface to his poem "The Parlement of Foules," Chaucer refers to classic Roman author Cicero's "The Dream of Scipio," a dream-vision dialogue reflecting Stoic philosophy. Chaucer takes Cicero's broad scope of macrocosm (viewing the universe as a whole) and narrows it to a microcosm (individual focus) as he explores themes of order, disorder, and the role of humanity in nature. By using animals as characters, he is able to both parody and probe human nature for the reader.

Sir Thomas Browne

Sir Thomas Browne (1605-1682) had an immeasurable influence on the development of English literature. Both his writing style and thought process were highly original. The Oxford English Dictionary credits Browne with coining over 100 new words (and quotes him in over 3,000 other entries), such as approximate, literary, and ultimate. His creativity and vision have inspired other authors over the past four centuries and were instrumental in developing much of the vocabulary used in today's prose and poetry. In 1671 he was knighted by Charles II in recognition of his accomplishments, which continue to affect literature today.

Metaphysical Poets

Dr. Samuel Johnson, a famous 18th-century figure, who wrote philosophy, poetry, and authoritative essays on literature, coined the term "Metaphysical Poets" to describe a number of mainly 17th-century lyric poets who shared certain elements of content and style in common. The poets included John Donne (considered the founder of the Metaphysical Poets), George Herbert, Andrew Marvell, Abraham Cowley, John Cleveland, Richard Crashaw, Thomas Traherne, and Henry Vaughan. These poets encouraged readers to see the world from new and unaccustomed perspectives by shocking and surprising them with paradox; contradictory imagery; original syntax; combinations of religious, philosophical, and artistic images; subtle argumentation; and extended metaphors called conceits. Unlike their contemporaries, they did not allude to classical mythology or nature imagery in their poetry, but to current geographical and scientific discoveries. Some, like Donne, showed Neo-Platonist influences—like the idea that a lover's beauty reflected Eternity's perfect beauty. They were called metaphysical for their transcendence—Donne in particular—of typical 17th-century rationalism's hierarchical organization through their adventurous exploration of religion, ideas, emotions, and language.

Romanticism

The height of the Romantic movement occurred in the first half of the 19th century. It identified with and gained momentum from the French Revolution (1789) against the political and social standards of the aristocracy and its overthrowing of them. Romanticism was also part of the Counter-Enlightenment, a reaction of backlash against the Enlightenment's insistence on rationalism, scientific treatment of nature, and denial of emotionalism. Though expressed most overtly in the creative arts, Romanticism also affected politics, historiography, natural sciences, and education. Though often associated with radical, progressive, and liberal politics, it also included conservatism, especially in its influences on increased nationalism in many countries. The Romantics championed individual heroes, artists, and pioneers; freedom of expression; the exotic; and the power of the individual imagination. American authors Edgar Allan Poe and Nathaniel Hawthorne, Laurence Sterne in England, and Johann Wolfgang von Goethe in Germany were included among well-known Romantic authors. The six major English Romantic poets were William Blake, William Wordsworth, Samuel Taylor Coleridge, Lord Byron, Percy Bysshe Shelley, and John Keats.

William Blake

William Blake (1757-1827) is considered one of the earliest and foremost English Romantic poets. He was also an artist and printmaker. In addition to his brilliant poetry, he produced paintings, drawings, and engravings, impressive for their technical expertise, artistic beauty, and spiritual subject matter. Because he held many idiosyncratic opinions, and moreover because he was subject to visions, reporting that he saw angels in the trees and other unusual claims, Blake was often thought crazy by others during his life. His work's creative, expressive character, and its mystical

- 40 -

and philosophical elements, led people to consider him both precursor to and member of Romanticism, and a singular, original, unclassifiable artist at the same time. Blake illustrated most of his poetry with his own hand-colored, illuminated printing. His best-known poetry includes *Songs of Innocence and of Experience*, *The Book of Thel*, *The Marriage of Heaven and Hell*, and *Jerusalem*.

William Wordsworth

William Wordsworth (1770-1850) was instrumental in establishing Romanticism when he and Samuel Taylor Coleridge collaboratively published *Lyrical Ballads* (1798). Wordsworth's "Preface to Lyrical Ballads" is considered a manifesto of English Romantic literary theory and criticism. In it, Wordsworth described the elements of a new kind of poetry, which he characterized as using "real language of men" rather than traditional 18th-century poetic style. In this Preface he also defined poetry as "the spontaneous overflow of powerful feelings [which] takes its origin from emotion recollected in tranquility." *Lyrical Ballads* included the famous works "The Rime of the Ancient Mariner" by Coleridge, and "Tintern Abbey" by Wordsworth. His semi-autobiographical poem, known during his life as "the poem to Coleridge," was published posthumously, entitled *The Prelude* and regarded as his major work. Wordsworth was England's Poet Laureate from 1843-1850. Among many others, his poems include "I Wandered Lonely as a Cloud" (often called "Daffodils"), "Ode: Intimations of Immortality," "Westminster Bridge," and "The World Is Too Much with Us."

Samuel Taylor Coleridge

Samuel Taylor Coleridge (1772-1834) was also a philosopher and literary critic and collaborated with William Wordsworth in launching the Romantic movement. He wrote very influential literary criticism, including the major two-volume autobiographical, meditative discourse *Biographia Literaria* (1817). Coleridge acquainted English-language intellectuals with German idealist philosophy. He also coined many now familiar philosophical and literary terms, like "the willing suspension of disbelief," meaning that readers would voluntarily withhold judgment of implausible stories if their authors could impart "human interest and a semblance of truth" to them. He strongly influenced the American Transcendentalists, including Ralph Waldo Emerson. Coleridge's poem *Love,* a ballad (written to Sara Hutchinson), inspired John Keats' poem "La Belle Dame Sans Merci." He is credited with the origin of "Conversational Poetry" and Wordsworth's adoption of it. Some of his best-known works include "The Rime of the Ancient Mariner," "Christabel," "Kubla Khan," "The Nightingale," "Dejection: An Ode," and "To William Wordsworth."

George Gordon, Lord Byron

George Gordon Byron, commonly known as Lord Byron (1788-1824) is known for long narrative poems "Don Juan," "Childe Harold's Pilgrimage," and the shorter lyric poem "She Walks in Beauty." The aristocratic Byron travelled throughout Europe, living in Italy for seven years. He fought in the Greek War of Independence against the Ottoman Empire, making him a national hero in Greece, before dying a year later from a fever contracted there. He was the most notoriously profligate and flamboyant Romantic poet, with reckless behaviors including multiple bisexual love affairs, adultery, rumored incest, self-exile, and enormous debts. He became friends with fellow Romantic writers Percy Bysshe Shelley, the future Mary Shelley, and John Polidori. Their shared fantasy writing at a Swiss villa the summer of 1816 resulted in Mary Shelley's *Frankenstein*, Byron's *Fragment of a Novel*, and was the inspiration for Polidori's *The Vampyre*, establishing the romantic vampire genre. Byron also wrote linguistic volumes on American and Armenian grammars. His name is synonymous today with the mercurial Romantic.

<u>Percy Bysshe Shelley</u>

Percy Bysshe Shelley (1792-1822) was not famous during life but became so after death, particularly for his lyric poetry. His best-known works include "Ozymandias," "Ode to the West Wind," "To a Skylark," "Music," "When Soft Voices Die," "The Cloud," "The Masque of Anarchy"; longer poems "Queen Mab"/"The Daemon of the World" and "Adonaïs"; and the verse drama *Prometheus Unbound.* Shelley's second wife, Mary Shelley, was the daughter of his mentor William Godwin and the famous feminist Mary Wollstonecraft (*A Vindication of the Rights of Woman*), and became famous for her Gothic novel *Frankenstein.* Early in his career Shelley was influenced by William Wordsworth's Romantic poetry, and wrote the long poem *Alastor, or the Spirit of Solitude.* Soon thereafter he met Lord Byron, and was inspired to write "Hymn to Intellectual Beauty". He composed "Mont Blanc," inspired by touring the French Alpine commune Chamonix-Mont-Blanc. Shelley also encouraged Byron to compose his epic poem *Don Juan.* Shelley inspired Henry David Thoreau, Mahatma Gandhi, and others to civil disobedience, nonviolent resistance, vegetarianism, and animal rights.

<u>John Keats</u>

John Keats (1795-1821), despite his short life, was a major English Romantic poet. He is known for his six Odes: "Ode on a Grecian Urn," "Ode on Indolence," "Ode on Melancholy," "Ode to a Nightingale," "Ode to Psyche," and "To Autumn." Other notable works include the sonnet "O Solitude," "Endymion," "La Belle Dame Sans Merci," "Hyperion," and the collection *Lamia, Isabella, The Eve of St. Agnes and Other Poems.* The intensity and maturity he achieved in only six years are often praised since his death, though during life he felt he accomplished nothing lasting. He wrote a year before dying, "I have left no immortal work behind me—nothing to make my friends proud of my memory—but I have lov'd the principle of beauty in all things, and if I had had time I would have made myself remember'd." He was proven wrong. His verse from "Ode on a Grecian Urn" is renowned: "'Beauty is truth, truth beauty'—that is all / Ye know on earth, and all ye need to know."

Modernism in Yeats' Poetry

William Butler Yeats (1865-1939) was among the greatest influences in 20th-century English literature and was believed transitional from Romanticism to Modernism. His earlier verses were lyrical, but later became realistic, symbolic, and apocalyptic. He was fascinated with Irish legend, occult subjects, and historical cycles—"gyres." He incorporated Irish folklore, mythology, and legends in "The Stolen Child," "The Wanderings of Oisin," "The Death of Cuchulain," "Who Goes with Fergus?" and "The Song of Wandering Aengus." Early collections included *The Secret Rose* and *The Wind Among the Reeds.* His later, most significant poetry collections include *The Green Helmet, Responsibilities, The Tower,* and *The Winding Stair.* Yeats's visionary, apocalyptic poem "The Second Coming" (1920) reflects his belief that his times were the anarchic end of the Christian cycle/gyre: "what rough beast, its hour come round at last, / Slouches toward Bethlehem to be born?"

Major Forms of Poetry

From man's earliest days, he expressed himself with poetry. A large percentage of the surviving literature from ancient times is in epic poetry, utilized by Homer and other Greco-Roman poets. Epic poems typically recount heroic deeds and adventures, using stylized language and combining dramatic and lyrical conventions. Epistolary poems also developed in ancient times: poems that are written and read as letters. In the fourteenth and fifteenth centuries, the ballad became a popular convention. Ballads are often structured with rhyme and meter and focus on subjects such as love, death, and religious topics. From these early conventions, numerous other poetic forms developed, such as elegies, odes, and pastoral poems. Elegies are mourning poems written in three parts:

lament, praise of the deceased, and solace for loss. Odes evolved from songs to the typical poem of the Romantic time period, expressing strong feelings and contemplative thoughts. Pastoral poems idealize nature and country living. Poetry can also be used to make short, pithy statements. Epigrams (memorable rhymes with one or two lines) and limericks (two lines of iambic dimeter followed by two lines of iambic dimeter and another of iambic trimeter) are known for humor and wit.

Haiku

Haiku was originally a Japanese poetry form. In the 13th century, haiku was the opening phrase of renga, a 100-stanza oral poem. By the 16th century, haiku diverged into a separate short poem. When Western writers discovered haiku, the form became popular in English, as well as other languages. A haiku has 17 syllables, traditionally distributed across three lines as 5/7/5, with a pause after the first or second line. Haiku are syllabic and unrhymed. Haiku philosophy and technique are that brevity's compression forces writers to express images concisely, depict a moment in time, and evoke illumination and enlightenment. An example is 17th-century haiku master Matsuo Basho's classic: "An old silent pond… / A frog jumps into the pond, / splash! Silence again." Modern American poet Ezra Pound revealed the influence of haiku in his two-line poem "In a Station of the Metro"—line 1 has 5+7 syllables, line 2 has 7, but it still preserves haiku's philosophy and imagistic technique: "The apparition of these faces in the crowd; / Petals on a wet, black bough."

Sonnets

The sonnet traditionally has 14 lines of iambic pentameter, tightly organized around a theme. The Petrarchan sonnet, named for 14th-century Italian poet Petrarch, has an eight-line stanza, the octave, and a six-line stanza, the sestet. There is a change or turn, known as the volta, between the eighth and ninth verses, setting up the sestet's answer or summary. The rhyme scheme is ABBA/ABBA/CDECDE or CDCDCD. The English or Shakespearean sonnet has three quatrains and one couplet, with the rhyme scheme ABAB/CDCD/EFEF/GG. This format better suits English, which has fewer rhymes than Italian. The final couplet often contrasts sharply with the preceding quatrains, as in Shakespeare's sonnets—for example, Sonnet 130, "My mistress' eyes are nothing like the sun…And yet, by heaven, I think my love as rare / As any she belied with false compare." Variations on the sonnet form include Edmund Spenser's Spenserian sonnet in the 16th century, John Milton's Miltonic sonnet in the 17th century, and sonnet sequences. Sonnet sequences are seen in works such as John Donne's *La Corona* and Elizabeth Barrett Browning's *Sonnets from the Portuguese*.

> **Review Video: Forms of Poetry**
> Visit mometrix.com/academy and enter code: 451705

Prose

Major Forms

Historical fiction is set in particular historical periods, including prehistoric and mythological. Examples include Walter Scott's *Rob Roy* and *Ivanhoe*; Leo Tolstoy's *War and Peace;* Robert Graves' *I, Claudius;* Mary Renault's *The King Must Die* and *The Bull from the Sea* (an historical novel using Greek mythology); Virginia Woolf's *Orlando* and *Between the Acts;* and John Dos Passos's *U.S.A* trilogy. Picaresque novels recount episodic adventures of a rogue protagonist or *pícaro,* like Miguel de Cervantes' *Don Quixote* or Henry Fielding's *Tom Jones.* Gothic novels originated as a reaction against 18th-century Enlightenment rationalism, featuring horror, mystery, superstition, madness,

- 43 -

supernatural elements, and revenge. Early examples include Horace Walpole's *Castle of Otranto*, Matthew Gregory Lewis' *Monk*, Mary Shelley's *Frankenstein*, and Bram Stoker's *Dracula*. In America, Edgar Allan Poe wrote many Gothic works. Contemporary novelist Anne Rice has penned many Gothic novels under the pseudonym A. N. Roquelaure. Psychological novels, originating in 17th-century France, explore characters' motivations. Examples include Abbé Prévost's *Manon Lescaut;* George Eliot's novels; Fyodor Dostoyevsky's *Crime and Punishment;* Tolstoy's *Anna Karenina;* Gustave Flaubert's *Madame Bovary;* and the novels of Henry James, James Joyce, and Vladimir Nabokov.

Novel of Manners

Novels of manners are fictional stories that observe, explore, and analyze the social behaviors of a specific time and place. While deep psychological themes are more universal across different historical periods and countries, the manners of a particular society are shorter-lived and more varied; the novel of manners captures these societal details. Novels of manners can also be regarded as symbolically representing, in artistic form, certain established and secure social orders. Characteristics of novels of manners include descriptions of a society with defined behavioral codes; the use of standardized, impersonal formulas in their language; and inhibition of emotional expression, as contrasted with the strong emotions expressed in romantic or sentimental novels. Jane Austen's detailed descriptions of English society and characters struggling with the definitions and restrictions placed on them by society are excellent models of the novel of manners. In the 20th century, Evelyn Waugh's *Handful of Dust* is a novel of social manners, and his *Sword of Honour* trilogy is a novel of military manners. Another 20th-century example is *The Unbearable Bassington* by Saki (the pen name of writer H. H. Munro), focusing on Edwardian society.

Western-World Sentimental Novels

Sentimental love novels originated in the movement of Romanticism. Eighteenth-century examples of novels that depict emotional rather than only physical love include Samuel Richardson's *Pamela* (1740) and Jean-Jacques Rousseau's *Nouvelle Héloïse* (1761). Also in the 18th century, Laurence Sterne's novel *Tristram Shandy* (1760-1767) is an example of a novel with elements of sentimentality. The Victorian era's rejection of emotionalism caused the term "sentimental" to have undesirable connotations. Even non-sentimental novelists such as William Makepeace Thackeray and Charles Dickens incorporated sentimental elements in their writing. A 19th-century author of genuinely sentimental novels was Mrs. Henry Wood (e.g., *East Lynne,* 1861). In the 20th century, Erich Segal's sentimental novel *Love Story* (1970) was a popular bestseller.

Epistolary Novels

Epistolary novels are told in the form of letters written by their characters rather than in narrative form. Samuel Richardson, the best-known author of epistolary novels like *Pamela* (1740) and *Clarissa* (1748), widely influenced early Romantic epistolary novels throughout Europe that freely expressed emotions. Richardson, a printer, published technical manuals on letter-writing for young gentlewomen; his epistolary novels were natural fictional extensions of those nonfictional instructional books. Nineteenth-century English author Wilkie Collins' *The Moonstone* (1868) was a mystery written in epistolary form. By the 20th century, the format of well-composed written letters came to be regarded as artificial and outmoded. A 20th-century evolution of letters was tape-recording transcripts in French playwright Samuel Beckett's drama *Krapp's Last Tape.* Though evoking modern alienation, Beckett still created a sense of fictional characters' direct communication without author intervention as Richardson had.

Pastoral Novels

Pastoral novels lyrically idealize country life as idyllic and utopian, akin to the Garden of Eden. *Daphnis and Chloe*, written by Greek novelist Longus around the second or third century, influenced Elizabethan pastoral romances like Thomas Lodge's *Rosalynde* (1590), which inspired Shakespeare's *As You Like It*, and Philip Sidney's *Arcadia* (1590). Jacques-Henri Bernardin de St. Pierre's French work *Paul et Virginie* (1787) demonstrated the early Romantic view of the innocence and goodness of nature. Though the style lost popularity by the 20th century, pastoral elements can still be seen in novels like *The Rainbow* (1915) and *Lady Chatterley's Lover* (1928), both by D. H. Lawrence. Growing realism transformed pastoral writing into less ideal and more dystopian, distasteful and ironic depictions of country life in George Eliot's and Thomas Hardy's novels. Saul Bellow's novel *Herzog* (1964) may demonstrate how urban ills highlight an alternative pastoral ideal. The pastoral style is commonly thought to be overly idealized and outdated today, as seen in Stella Gibbons' pastoral satire, Cold Comfort Farm (1932).

Bildungsroman

Bildungsroman is German for "education novel." This term is also used in English to describe "apprenticeship" novels focusing on coming-of-age stories, including youth's struggles and searches for things such as identity, spiritual understanding, or the meaning in life. Johann Wolfgang von Goethe's *Wilhelm Meisters Lehrjahre* (1796) is credited as the origin. Charles Dickens' two novels *David Copperfield* (1850) and *Great Expectations* (1861) also fit this form. H. G. Wells wrote *bildungsromans* about questing for apprenticeships to address modern life's complications in *Joan and Peter* (1918), and from a Utopian perspective in *The Dream* (1924). School *bildungsromans* include Thomas Hughes' *Tom Brown's School Days* (1857) and Alain-Fournier's *Le Grand Meaulnes* (1913). Many Hermann Hesse novels, including *Demian, Steppenwolf, Siddhartha, Magister Ludi*, and *Under the Wheel* are *bildungsromans* about struggling, searching youth. Samuel Butler's *The Way of All Flesh* (1903) and James Joyce's *A Portrait of the Artist as a Young Man* (1916) are two modern examples. Variations include J. D. Salinger's *The Catcher in the Rye* (1951), set both within and beyond school, and William Golding's *Lord of the Flies* (1955), a novel not set in a school but one that is a coming-of-age story nonetheless.

Roman à Clef

Roman à clef, French for "novel with a key," refers to books that require a real-life frame of reference, or key, for full comprehension. In Geoffrey Chaucer's *Canterbury Tales,* the Nun's Priest's Tale contains details that confuse readers unaware of history about the Earl of Bolingbroke's involvement in an assassination plot. Other literary works fitting this form include John Dryden's political satirical poem "Absalom and Achitophel" (1681), Jonathan Swift's satire "A Tale of a Tub" (1704), and George Orwell's political allegory *Animal Farm* (1945), all of which cannot be understood completely without knowing their camouflaged historical contents. *Roman à clefs* disguise truths too dangerous for authors to state directly. Readers must know about the enemies of D. H. Lawrence and Aldous Huxley to appreciate their respective novels: Aaron's Rod (1922) and Point Counter Point (1928). Marcel Proust's *Remembrance of Things Past (À la recherché du temps perdu,* 1871-1922) is informed by his social context. James Joyce's *Finnegans Wake* is an enormous *roman à clef* containing multitudinous personal references.

Realism

Realism is a literary form with the goal of representing reality as faithfully as possible. Its genesis in Western literature was a reaction against the sentimentality and extreme emotionalism of the works written in the literary movement of Romanticism, which championed feelings and their expression. Realists focused in great detail on immediacy of time and place, on specific actions of their characters, and the justifiable consequences of those actions. Some techniques of realism include writing in the vernacular (conversational language), using specific dialects and placing an emphasis on character rather than plot. Realistic literature often addresses ethical issues. Historically, realistic works have often concentrated on the middle classes of the authors' societies. Realists eschew treatments that are too dramatic or sensationalistic as exaggerations of the reality that they strive to portray as closely as they are able. Influenced by his own bleak past, Fyodor Dostoevsky wrote several novels, such as *Crime and Punishment* (1866) that shunned romantic ideals and sought to portray a stark reality. Henry James was a prominent writer of realism in novels such as *Daisy Miller* (1879). Samuel Clemens (Mark Twain) skillfully represented the language and culture of lower-class Mississippi in his novel *Huckleberry Finn* (1885).

Satire

Satire uses sarcasm, irony, and/or humor as social criticism to lampoon human folly. Unlike realism, which intends to depict reality as it exists without exaggeration, satire often involves creating situations or ideas deliberately exaggerating reality to be ridiculous to illuminate flawed behaviors. Ancient Roman satirists included Horace and Juvenal. Alexander Pope's poem "The Rape of the Lock" satirized the values of fashionable members of the 18th-century upper-middle class, which Pope found shallow and trivial. The theft of a lock of hair from a young woman is blown out of proportion: the poem's characters regard it as seriously as they would a rape. Irishman Jonathan Swift satirized British society, politics, and religion in works like "A Tale of a Tub." In "A Modest Proposal," Swift used essay form and mock-serious tone, satirically "proposing" cannibalism of babies and children as a solution to poverty and overpopulation. He satirized petty political disputes in *Gulliver's Travels.*

Drama

Early Development

English drama originally developed from religious ritual. Early Christians established traditions of presenting pageants or mystery plays, traveling on wagons and carts through the streets to depict biblical events. Medieval tradition assigned responsibility for performing specific plays to the different guilds. In Middle English, "mystery" meant both religious ritual/truth, and craft/trade. Historically, mystery plays were to be reproduced exactly the same every time like religious rituals. However, some performers introduced individual interpretations of roles and even improvised. Thus drama was born. Narrative detail and nuanced acting were evident in mystery cycles by the Middle Ages. As individualized performance evolved, plays on other subjects also developed. Middle English mystery plays extant include the York Cycle, Coventry Cycle, Chester Mystery Plays, N-Town Plays, and Towneley/Wakefield Plays. In recent times, these plays began to draw interest again, and several modern actors such as Dame Judi Dench began their careers with mystery plays.

> **Review Video: Dramas**
> Visit mometrix.com/academy and enter code: 216060

Defining Characteristics

In the Middle Ages, plays were commonly composed in verse. By the time of the Renaissance, Shakespeare and other dramatists wrote plays that mixed prose, rhymed verse, and blank verse. The traditions of costumes and masks were seen in ancient Greek drama, medieval mystery plays, and Renaissance drama. Conventions like asides, in which actors make comments directly to the audience unheard by other characters, and soliloquies (dramatic monologues) were also common

- 46 -

during Shakespeare's Elizabethan dramatic period. Monologues dated back to ancient Greek drama. Elizabethan dialogue tended to use colloquial prose for lower-class characters' speech and stylized verse for upper-class characters. Another Elizabethan convention was the play-within-a-play, as in *Hamlet*. As drama moved toward realism, dialogue became less poetic and more conversational, as in most modern English-language plays. Contemporary drama, both onstage and onscreen, includes a convention of breaking the fourth wall, as actors directly face and address audiences.

Comedy

Today, most people equate the idea of comedy with something funny, and of tragedy with something sad. However, the ancient Greeks defined these differently. Comedy needed not be humorous or amusing: it needed only a happy ending. The classical definition of comedy, as included in Aristotle's works, is any work that tells the story of a sympathetic main character's rise in fortune. According to Aristotle, protagonists needed not be heroic or exemplary: he described them as not evil or worthless, but as ordinary people—"average to below average" morally. Comic figures who were sympathetic were usually of humble origins, proving their "natural nobility" through their actions as their characters were tested, rather than characters born into nobility— who were often satirized as self-important or pompous.

Shakespearean Comedy

William Shakespeare lived in England from 1564-1616. He was a poet and playwright of the Renaissance period in Western culture. He is generally considered the foremost dramatist in world literature and the greatest author to write in the English language. He wrote many poems, particularly sonnets, of which 154 survive today, and approximately 38 plays. Though his sonnets are greater in number and are very famous, he is best known for his plays, including comedies, tragedies, tragicomedies and historical plays. His play titles include: *All's Well That Ends Well, As You Like It, The Comedy of Errors, Love's Labour's Lost, Measure for Measure, The Merchant of Venice, The Merry Wives of Windsor, A Midsummer Night's Dream, Much Ado About Nothing, The Taming of the Shrew, The Tempest, Twelfth Night, The Two Gentlemen of Verona, The Winter's Tale, King John, Richard II, Henry IV, Henry V, Richard III, Romeo and Juliet, Coriolanus, Titus Andronicus, Julius Caesar, Macbeth, Hamlet, Troilus and Cressida, King Lear, Othello, Antony and Cleopatra,* and *Cymbeline.* Some scholars have suggested that Christopher Marlowe wrote several of Shakespeare's works. While most scholars reject this theory, Shakespeare did pay homage to his contemporary, alluding to several of his characters, themes, or verbiage, as well as borrowing themes from several of his plays: Marlowe's *Jew of Malta* influenced Shakespeare's *Merchant of Venice,* etc.

When Shakespeare was writing, during the Elizabethan period of the Renaissance, Aristotle's version of comedies was popular. While some of Shakespeare's comedies were humorous and others were not, all had happy endings. *A Comedy of Errors* is a farce. Based and expanding on a Classical Roman comedy, it is lighthearted and includes slapstick humor and mistaken identity. *Much Ado About Nothing* is a romantic comedy. It incorporates some more serious themes, including social mores; perceived infidelity; marriage's duality as both trap and ideal; and honor and its loss, public shame, and deception, but also much witty dialogue and a happy ending.

Dramatic Comedy

Three types of dramas classified as comedy include the farce, the romantic comedy, and the satirical comedy.

Farce

The farce is a zany, goofy type of comedy that includes pratfalls and other forms of slapstick humor. The characters appearing in a farce tend to be ridiculous or fantastical in nature. The plot also tends to contain highly improbable events, featuring complications and twists that continue throughout, and incredible coincidences that could never occur in reality. Mistaken identity, deceptions, and disguises are common devices used in farcical comedies. Shakespeare's play *The Comedy of Errors,* with its cases of accidental mistaken identity and slapstick, is an example of farce. Contemporary examples of farce include the Marx Brothers' movies, the Three Stooges movies and TV episodes, and the *Pink Panther* movie series.

Romantic Comedy

Romantic comedies are probably the most popular of the types of comedy, in both live theater performances and movies. They include not only humor and a happy ending, but also love. In the typical plot of a romantic comedy, two people well suited to one another are either brought together for the first time, or reconciled after being separated. They are usually both sympathetic characters, and seem destined to be together yet separated by some intervening complication—such as ex-lovers, interfering parents or friends, or differences in social class. The happy ending is achieved through the lovers' overcoming all these obstacles. William Shakespeare's *Much Ado About Nothing;* Walt Disney's version of *Cinderella* (1950); Broadway musical *Guys and Dolls* (1955); and movies *Princess Bride* (1987), directed by Rob Reiner; *Sleepless in Seattle* (1993) and *You've Got Mail* (1998), both directed by Nora Ephron and starring Tom Hanks and Meg Ryan; and *Forget Paris* (1995), co-written, produced, directed by and starring Billy Crystal, are examples of romantic comedies.

Satirical Comedy and Black Comedy

Satires generally mock and lampoon human foolishness and vices. Satirical comedies fit the classical definition of comedy by depicting a main character's rise in fortune, but they also fit the definition of satire by making that main character either a fool, morally corrupt, or cynical in attitude. All or most of the other characters in the satirical comedy display similar foibles. These include cuckolded spouses, dupes, and other gullible types; tricksters, con artists, and criminals; hypocrites; fortune seekers; and other deceptive types who prey on the latter, who are their willing and unwitting victims. Some classical examples of satirical comedies include *The Birds* by ancient Greek comedic playwright Aristophanes, and *Volpone* by 17th-century poet and playwright Ben Jonson, who made the comedy of humors popular. When satirical comedy is extended to extremes, it becomes black comedy, wherein the comedic occurrences are grotesque or terrible.

Tragedy

The opposite of comedy is tragedy, portraying a hero's fall in fortune. While by classical definitions, tragedies could be sad, Aristotle went further, requiring that they depict suffering and pain to cause "terror and pity" in audiences. Additionally, he decreed that tragic heroes be basically good, admirable, and/or noble, and that their downfalls be through personal action, choice, or error, not by bad luck or accident.

Aristotle's Criteria for Tragedy

In his *Poetics,* Aristotle defined five critical terms relative to tragedy. (1) *Anagnorisis:* Meaning tragic insight or recognition, this is a moment of realization by a tragic hero(ine) when s/he suddenly understands how s/he has enmeshed himself/herself in a "web of fate." (2) *Hamartia:* This is often called a "tragic flaw," but is better described as a tragic error. *Hamartia* is an archery term meaning a shot missing the bull's eye, used here as a metaphor for a mistake—often a simple

- 48 -

one—which results in catastrophe. (3) *Hubris:* While often called "pride," this is actually translated as "violent transgression," and signifies an arrogant overstepping of moral or cultural bounds—the sin of the tragic hero who over-presumes or over-aspires. (4) *Nemesis:* translated as "retribution," this represents the cosmic punishment or payback that the tragic hero ultimately receives for committing hubristic acts. (5) *Peripateia:* Literally "turning," this is a plot reversal consisting of a tragic hero's pivotal action, which changes his/her status from safe to endangered.

Hegel's Theory of Tragedy

Georg Wilhelm Friedrich Hegel (1770-1831) proposed a different theory of tragedy than Aristotle (384-322 BCE), which was also very influential. Whereas Aristotle's criteria involved character and plot, Hegel defined tragedy as a dynamic conflict of opposite forces or rights. For example, if an individual believes in the moral philosophy of the conscientious objector, i.e., that fighting in wars is morally wrong, but is confronted with being drafted into military service, this conflict would fit Hegel's definition of a tragic plot premise. Hegel theorized that a tragedy must involve some circumstance in which two values, or two rights, are fatally at odds with one another and conflict directly. Hegel did not view this as good triumphing over evil, or evil winning out over good, but rather as one good fighting against another good unto death. He saw this conflict of two goods as truly tragic. In ancient Greek playwright Sophocles' tragedy *Antigone,* the main character experiences this tragic conflict between her public duties and her family and religious responsibilities.

Revenge Tragedy

Along with Aristotelian definitions of comedy and tragedy, ancient Greece was the origin of the revenge tragedy. This genre became highly popular in Renaissance England, and is still popular today in contemporary movies. In a revenge tragedy, the protagonist has suffered a serious wrong, such as the assault and murder of a family member. However, the wrongdoer has not been punished. In contemporary plots, this often occurs when some legal technicality has interfered with the miscreant's conviction and sentencing, or when authorities are unable to locate and apprehend the criminal. The protagonist then faces the conflict of suffering this injustice, or exacting his or her own justice by seeking revenge. Greek revenge tragedies include *Agamemnon* and *Medea.* Playwright Thomas Kyd's *The Spanish Tragedy* (1582-1592) is credited with beginning the Elizabethan genre of revenge tragedies. Shakespearean revenge tragedies include *Hamlet* (1599-1602) and *Titus Andronicus* (1588-1593). A Jacobean example is Thomas Middleton's *The Revenger's Tragedy* (1606, 1607).

Hamlet's "Tragic Flaw"

Despite virtually limitless interpretations, one way to view Hamlet's tragic error generally is as indecision: He suffers the classic revenge tragedy's conflict of whether to suffer with his knowledge of his mother's and uncle's assassination of his father, or to exact his own revenge and justice against Claudius, who has assumed the throne after his crime went unknown and unpunished. Hamlet's famous soliloquy, "To be or not to be" reflects this dilemma. Hamlet muses "Whether 'tis nobler in the mind to suffer the slings and arrows of outrageous fortune, / Or to take arms against a sea of troubles, / And by opposing end them?" Hamlet both longs for and fears death, as "the dread of something after death … makes us rather bear those ills we have / Than fly to others that we know not … Thus conscience does make cowards of us all." For most of the play, the protagonist struggles with his responsibility in avenging his father, who was killed by Hamlet's uncle Claudius. So Hamlet's tragic error at first might be considered a lack of action. But he then makes several attempts at revenge, each of which end in worse tragedy, until his efforts are ended by the final tragedy – Hamlet's own murder.

Making Predictions

When we read literature, making predictions about what will happen in the writing reinforces our purpose(s) for reading and prepares us mentally. We can make predictions before we begin reading and during our reading. As we read on, we can test the accuracy of our predictions, revise them in light of additional reading, and confirm or refute our predictions. A reader can make predictions by observing the title and illustrations; noting the structure, characters, and subject; drawing on existing knowledge relative to the subject; and asking "why" and "who" questions. Connecting reading to what we already know enables us to learn new information and construct meaning. For example, before third-graders read a book about Johnny Appleseed, they may start a KWL chart—a list of what they *Know*, what they *Want* to know or learn, and what they have *Learned* after reading. Activating existing background knowledge and thinking about the text before reading improves comprehension.

> **Review Video: Predictions**
> Visit mometrix.com/academy and enter code: 437248

Drawing Inferences

Inferences about literary text are logical conclusions that readers make based on their observations and previous knowledge. By inferring, readers construct meanings from text relevant to them personally. By combining their own schemas or concepts and their background information pertinent to the text with what they read, readers interpret it according to both what the author has conveyed and their own unique perspectives. Authors do not always explicitly spell out every meaning in what they write; many meanings are implicit. Through inference, readers can comprehend implied meanings in the text, and also derive personal significance from it, making the text meaningful and memorable to them. Inference is a natural process in everyday life. When readers infer, they can draw conclusions about what the author is saying, predict what may reasonably follow, amend these predictions as they continue to read, interpret the import of themes, and analyze the characters' feelings and motivations through their actions.

> **Review Video: Identifying Logical Conclusions**
> Visit mometrix.com/academy and enter code: 281653

Making Connections to Enhance Comprehension

Reading involves thinking. For good comprehension, readers make text-to-self, text-to-text, and text-to-world connections. Making connections helps readers understand text better and predict what might occur next based on what they already know, such as how characters in the story feel or what happened in another text. Text-to-self connections with the reader's life and experiences make literature more personally relevant and meaningful to readers. Readers can make connections before, during, and after reading—including whenever the text reminds them of something similar they have encountered in life or other texts. The genre, setting, characters, plot elements, literary structure and devices, and themes an author uses allow a reader to make connections to other works of literature or to people and events in their own lives. Venn diagrams and other graphic organizers help visualize connections. Readers can also make double-entry notes: key content, ideas, events, words, and quotations on one side, and the connections with these on the other.

Summarizing Literature to Support Comprehension

When reading literature, especially demanding works, summarizing helps readers identify important information and organize it in their minds. They can also identify themes, problems, and solutions, and can sequence the story. Readers can summarize before, during, and after they read. They should use their own words, as they do when describing a personal event or giving directions. Previewing a text's organization before reading by examining the book cover, table of contents, and illustrations also aids summarizing. So does making notes of key words and ideas in a graphic organizer while reading. Graphic organizers are another useful method: readers skim the text to determine main ideas and then narrow the list with the aid of the organizer. Unimportant details should be omitted in summaries. Summaries can include description, problem-solution, comparison-contrast, sequence, main ideas, and cause-and-effect.

> **Review Video: Summarizing Text**
> Visit mometrix.com/academy and enter code: 172903

Evaluation of Summaries

A summary of a literary passage is a condensation in the reader's own words of the passage's main points. Several guidelines can be used in evaluating a summary. The summary should be complete yet concise. It should be accurate, balanced, fair, neutral, and objective, excluding the reader's own opinions or reactions. It should reflect in similar proportion how much each point summarized was covered in the original passage. Summary writers should include tags of attribution, like "Macaulay argues that" to reference the original author whose ideas are represented in the summary. Summary writers should not overuse quotations: they should only quote central concepts or phrases they cannot precisely convey in words other than those of the original author. Another aspect in evaluating a summary is whether it can stand alone as a coherent, unified composition. In addition, evaluation of a summary should include whether its writer has cited the original source of the passage so that readers can find it.

Textual Evidence to Analyze Literature

Knowing about the historical background and social context of a literary work, as well as the identity of that work's author, can help to inform the reader about the author's concerns and intended meanings. For example, George Orwell published his novel *1984* in the year 1949, soon after the end of World War II. At that time, following the defeat of the Nazis, the Cold War began between the Western Allied nations and the Eastern Soviet Communists. People were therefore concerned about the conflict between the freedoms afforded by Western democracies versus the oppression represented by Communism. Author Orwell had also previously fought in the Spanish Civil War against a Spanish regime that he and his fellows viewed as oppressive. From this information, readers can infer that Orwell was concerned about oppression by totalitarian governments. This informs *1984*'s story of Winston Smith's rebellion against the oppressive "Big Brother" government of the fictional dictatorial state of Oceania and his capture, torture, and ultimate conversion by that government.

Textual Evidence to Evaluate Predictions

Textual evidence to evaluate reader predictions about literature includes specific synopses of the work, paraphrases of the work or parts of it, and direct quotations from it. The best literary analysis shows special insight into a theme, character trait, or change. The best textual evidence is strong, relevant, and accurate. Analysis that is not best, but enough, shows reasonable understanding of

- 51 -

theme, character trait, or change; contains supporting textual evidence that is relevant and accurate, if not strong; and shows a specific and clear response. Analysis that partially meets criteria also shows reasonable understanding, but the textual evidence is generalized, incomplete, only partly relevant or accurate, or connected only weakly. Inadequate analysis is vague, too general, or incorrect; it may give irrelevant or incomplete textual evidence, or may simply summarize the plot rather than analyzing the work.

> **Review Video: Textual Evidence for Predictions**
> Visit mometrix.com/academy and enter code: 261070

Conflict

A conflict is a problem to be solved. Literary plots typically include one conflict or more. Characters' attempts to resolve conflicts drive the narrative's forward movement. Conflict resolution is often the protagonist's primary occupation. Physical conflicts like exploring, wars, and escapes tend to make plots most suspenseful and exciting. Emotional, mental, or moral conflicts tend to make stories more personally gratifying or rewarding for many audiences. Conflicts can be external or internal. A major type of internal conflict is some inner personal battle, or "man against himself." Major types of external conflicts include "man against nature," "man against man," and "man against society." Readers can identify conflicts in literary plots by identifying the protagonist and antagonist and asking why they conflict, what events develop the conflict, where the climax occurs, and how they identify with the characters.

> **Review Video: Conflict**
> Visit mometrix.com/academy and enter code: 559550

Mood and Tone

Mood is a story's atmosphere, or the feelings the reader gets from reading it. The way authors set the mood in writing is comparable to the way filmmakers use music to set the mood in movies. Instead of music, though, writers judiciously select descriptive words to evoke certain moods. The mood of a work may convey joy, anger, bitterness, hope, gloom, fear, an ominous feeling, or any other emotion the author wants the reader to feel. In addition to vocabulary choices, authors also use figurative expressions, particular sentence structures, and choices of diction that project and reinforce the moods they want to create. Whereas mood is the reader's emotions evoked by reading what is written, tone is the emotions and attitudes of the writer that s/he expresses in the writing. Authors use the same literary techniques to establish tone as they do to establish mood. An author may use a humorous tone, an angry or sad tone, a sentimental or unsentimental tone, or something else entirely.

> **Review Video: Style, Tone, and Mood**
> Visit mometrix.com/academy and enter code: 416961

Analysis of Character Development

To understand the meaning of a story, it is vital to understand the characters as the author describes them. We can look for contradictions in what a character thinks, says, and does. We can notice whether the author's observations about a character differ from what other characters in the story say about that character. A character may be dynamic (changing significantly during the story) or static (remaining the same from beginning to end). Characters may be two-dimensional, not fully developed, or may be well developed with characteristics that stand out vividly. Characters may also symbolize universal properties. Additionally, readers can compare and contrast characters to analyze how they were developed.

Dialogue

Effectively written dialogue serves at least one but usually several purposes. It advances the story and moves the plot. It develops the characters. It sheds light on the work's theme(s) or meaning(s). It can, often subtly, account for the passage of time not otherwise indicated. It can alter the direction that the plot is taking, typically by introducing some new conflict(s) or changing (an) existing one(s). Dialogue can establish a work's narrative voice and the characters' voices and set the tone of the story or of particular characters. When fictional characters display enlightenment or realization, dialogue can give readers an understanding of what those characters have discovered and how. Dialogue can illuminate the motivations and wishes of the story's characters. By using consistent thoughts and syntax, dialogue can support character development. Skillfully created, it can also represent real-life speech rhythms in written form. Via conflicts and ensuing action, dialogue also provides drama.

In fictional works, effectively written dialogue should not only have the effect of breaking up or interrupting sections of narrative. While dialogue may supply exposition for readers, it must nonetheless be believable. Dialogue should be dynamic, not static, and it should not resemble regular prose. Authors should not use dialogue to write clever similes or metaphors, or to inject their own opinions. Nor should they use dialogue at all when narrative would be better; dialogue should not slow the plot movement. Dialogue must seem natural, which means careful construction of phrases rather than actually duplicating natural speech, which does not necessarily translate well to the written word. Finally, all dialogue must be pertinent to the story rather than just added conversation.

First-Person Narration

First-person narratives let narrators express inner feelings and thoughts, especially when the narrator is the protagonist as Lemuel Gulliver is in Jonathan Swift's *Gulliver's Travels.* The narrator may be a close friend of the protagonist, like Dr. Watson in Arthur Conan Doyle's *Sherlock Holmes.* Or the narrator can be less involved with the main characters and plot, like Nick Carraway in F. Scott Fitzgerald's *The Great Gatsby.* When a narrator reports others' narratives secondhand or more, s/he is a "frame narrator," like the nameless narrator of Joseph Conrad's *Heart of Darkness* or Mr. Lockwood in Emily Brontë's *Wuthering Heights.* First-person plural is unusual but can be effective, as in Isaac Asimov's *I, Robot;* William Faulkner's *A Rose for Emily;* Maxim Gorky's *Twenty-Six Men and a Girl;* or Jeffrey Eugenides' *The Virgin Suicides.* Author Kurt Vonnegut is the first-person narrator in his semi-autobiographical novel *Timequake.* Also unusual but effective is a first-person omniscient (rather than the more common third-person omniscient) narrator, like Death in Markus Zusak's *The Book Thief* and the ghost in Alice Sebold's *The Lovely Bones.*

Second-Person Narration

While second-person address is very commonplace in popular song lyrics, it is the least used form of narrative voice in literary works. Popular serial books of the 1980s like *Fighting Fantasy* or *Choose Your Own Adventure* employed second-person narratives. In some cases, a narrative combines both second-person and first-person voices, speaking of "you" and "I." This can draw readers into the story, and it can also enable the authors to compare directly "your" and "my" feelings, thoughts, and actions. When the narrator is also a character in the story, as in Edgar Allan Poe's short story "The Tell-Tale Heart" or Jay McInerney's novel *Bright Lights, Big City,* the narrative is better defined as first-person despite its also addressing "you."

Third-Person Narration

Narration in the third person is the most prevalent type, as it allows authors the most flexibility. It is so common that readers simply assume without needing to be informed that the narrator is not a character in, or involved in the story. Third-person singular is used more frequently than third-person plural, though some authors have also effectively used plural. However, both singular and plural are most often included in stories according to which character(s) is/are being described. The third-person narrator may be either objective or subjective, and either omniscient or limited. Objective third-person narration does not include what the characters described are thinking or feeling, while subjective third-person narration does. The third-person omniscient narrator knows everything about all characters, including their thoughts and emotions, and all related places, times, and events, whereas the third-person limited narrator may know everything about a particular character of focus, but is limited to that character; in other words, the narrator cannot speak about anything that character does not know.

Alternating-Person Narration

Although authors more commonly write stories from one point of view, there are also instances wherein they alternate the narrative voice within the same book. For example, they may sometimes use an omniscient third-person narrator and a more intimate first-person narrator at other times. In J. K. Rowling's series of *Harry Potter* novels, she often writes in a third-person limited narrative, but sometimes changes to narration by characters other than protagonist Harry Potter. George R. R. Martin's series *A Song of Ice and Fire* changes the point of view to coincide with divisions between chapters. The same technique is used by Erin Hunter (a pseudonym for several authors of the *Warriors, Seekers,* and *Survivors* book series). Authors using first-person narrative sometimes switch to third-person to describe significant action scenes, especially those where the narrator was absent or uninvolved, as Barbara Kingsolver does in her novel *The Poisonwood Bible.*

Literary Devices and Analysis

Literal and Figurative Meaning

When language is used literally, the words mean exactly what they say and nothing more. When language is used figuratively, the words mean something more and/or other than what they say. For example, "The weeping willow tree has long, trailing branches and leaves" is a literal description. But "The weeping willow tree looks as if it is bending over and crying" is a figurative description—specifically, a simile or stated comparison. Another figurative language form is metaphor, or an implied comparison. A good example is the metaphor of a city, state, or city-state as a ship, and its governance as sailing that ship. Ancient Greek lyrical poet Alcaeus is credited with first using this metaphor, and ancient Greek tragedian Aeschylus then used it in *Seven Against Thebes,* and then Plato used it in the *Republic.* Henry Wadsworth Longfellow later famously referred to it in his poem, "O Ship of State" (1850), which has an extended metaphor with numerous nautical references throughout.

Figurative Language

Figurative language extends past the literal meanings of words. It offers readers new insight into the people, things, events, and subjects covered in a work of literature. Figurative language also enables readers to feel they are sharing the authors' experiences. It can stimulate the reader's senses, make comparisons that readers find intriguing or even startling, and enable readers to view the world in different ways. Seven specific types of figurative language include: alliteration, personification, imagery, similes, metaphors, onomatopoeia, and hyperbole.

> **Review Video: Figurative Language**
> Visit mometrix.com/academy and enter code: 584902

Alliteration, Personification, and Imagery

Alliteration is using a series of words containing the same sounds—assonance with vowels, and consonance with consonants. Personification is describing a thing or animal as a person. Imagery is description using sensory terms that create mental images for the reader of how people, animals, or things look, sound, feel, taste, and/or smell. Alfred Tennyson's poem "The Eagle" uses all of these types of figurative language: "He clasps the crag with crooked hands." Tennyson used alliteration, repeating /k/ and /kr/ sounds. These hard-sounding consonants reinforce the imagery giving visual and tactile impressions of the eagle.

Tennyson also used personification, describing a bird as "he" and calling its talons "hands." In *Romeo and Juliet*, Shakespeare uses personification to describe the changing of the seasons: "When well-appareled April on the heel / Of limping winter treads...." Here "April" and "winter" are given the human characteristics of walking, dressing, and aging.

> **Review Video: Alliteration**
> Visit mometrix.com/academy and enter code: 462837
>
> **Review Video: Personification**
> Visit mometrix.com/academy and enter code: 260066

Similes

Similes are stated comparisons using "like" or "as." Similes can be used to stimulate readers' imaginations and appeal to their senses. By comparing fictional characters to well-known objects or experiences, the reader can better relate to them. William Wordsworth's poem about "Daffodils" begins, "I wandered lonely as a cloud." This simile compares his loneliness to that of a cloud. It is also personification, giving a cloud the human quality loneliness. In his novel *Lord Jim* (1900), Joseph Conrad writes in Chapter 33, "I would have given anything for the power to soothe her frail soul, tormenting itself in its invincible ignorance like a small bird beating about the cruel wires of a cage." Conrad uses the word "like" to compare the girl's soul to a small bird. His description of the bird beating at the cage shows the similar helplessness of the girl's soul to gain freedom.

> **Review Video: Simile**
> Visit mometrix.com/academy and enter code: 642949

Metaphors and Onomatopoeia

Metaphor is an implied comparison that does not use "like" or "as" the way a simile does. Henry Wadsworth Longfellow echoes the ancient Greeks in "O Ship of State": the metaphor compares the state and its government to a nautical ship and its sailing. Onomatopoeia uses words imitating the

- 55 -

sounds of things they name or describe. For example, in his poem "Come Down, O Maid," Alfred Tennyson writes of "The moan of doves in immemorial elms, / And murmuring of innumerable bees." The word "moan" sounds like some sounds doves make, "murmuring" represents the sounds of bees buzzing.

Ted Hughes' Animal Metaphors

Hughes frequently used animal metaphors in his poetry. In "The Thought Fox," a model of concise, structured beauty, Hughes characterizes the poet's creative process with succinct, striking imagery of an idea entering his head like a wild fox. Repeating "loneliness" in the first two stanzas emphasizes the poet's lonely work: "Something else is alive / Beside the clock's loneliness." He treats an idea's arrival as separate from himself. Three stanzas detail in vivid images a fox's approach from the outside winter forest at starless midnight —its nose, "Cold, delicately" touching twigs and leaves; "neat" paw prints in snow; "bold" body; brilliant green eyes; and self-contained, focused progress—"Till, with a sudden sharp hot stink of fox," he metaphorically depicts poetic inspiration as the fox's physical entry into "the dark hole of the head." Hughes ends by summarizing his vision of poet as an interior, passive idea recipient, with the outside world unchanged: "The window is starless still; the clock ticks, / The page is printed."

Literary Examples of Metaphor

A metaphor is an implied comparison, i.e. it compares something to something else without using "like", "as", or other comparative words. For example, in "The Tyger" (1794), William Blake writes, "Tyger Tyger, burning bright, / In the forests of the night." Blake compares the tiger to a flame not by saying it is like a fire, but by simply describing it as "burning." Henry Wadsworth Longfellow's poem "O Ship of State" (1850) uses an extended metaphor by referring consistently throughout the entire poem to the state, union, or republic as a seagoing vessel, referring to its keel, mast, sail, rope, anchors, and to its braving waves, rocks, gale, tempest, and "false lights on the shore". Within the extended metaphor, Wordsworth uses a specific metaphor: "the anchors of thy hope!"

> **Review Video: Metaphor**
> Visit mometrix.com/academy and enter code: 133295

Hyperbole

Hyperbole is excessive exaggeration used for humor or emphasis rather than for literal meaning. For example, in *To Kill a Mockingbird*, Harper Lee narrated, "People moved slowly then. There was no hurry, for there was nowhere to go, nothing to buy and no money to buy it with, nothing to see outside the boundaries of Maycomb County." This was not literally true; Lee exaggerates the scarcity of these things for emphasis. In "Old Times on the Mississippi," Mark Twain wrote, "I... could have hung my hat on my eyes, they stuck out so far." This is not literal, but makes his description vivid and funny. In his poem "As I Walked Out One Evening", W. H. Auden wrote, "I'll love you, dear, I'll love you / Till China and Africa meet, / And the river jumps over the mountain / And the salmon sing in the street." He used things not literally possible to emphasize the duration of his love.

> **Review Video: Hyperbole and Understatement**
> Visit mometrix.com/academy and enter code: 308470

Literary Irony

In literature, irony demonstrates the opposite of what is said or done. Three types are verbal irony, situational irony, and dramatic irony. Verbal irony uses words opposite to the meaning. Sarcasm may use verbal irony. An everyday example is describing something confusing as "clear as mud." In his 1986 movie *Hannah and Her Sisters,* author/director/actor Woody Allen says to his character's date, "I had a great evening; it was like the Nuremburg Trials." Notice these employ similes. In situational irony, what happens contrasts with what was expected. In dramatic irony, narrative informs audiences of more than its characters know. O. Henry's short story *The Gift of the Magi* uses situational irony: a husband and wife each sacrifice their most prized possession to buy each other a Christmas present. The irony is that she sells her long hair to buy him a watch fob, while he sells his heirloom pocket-watch to buy her the jeweled combs for her hair she had long wanted; in the end, neither of them can use their gifts.

Literary Terminology

In works of prose such as novels, a group of connected sentences covering one main topic is termed a paragraph. In works of poetry, a group of verses similarly connected is called a stanza. In drama, when early works used verse, these were also divided into stanzas or couplets. Drama evolved to use predominantly prose. Overall, whether prose or verse, the conversation in a play is called dialogue. Large sections of dialogue spoken by one actor are called soliloquies or monologues. Dialogue that informs audiences but is unheard by other characters is called an aside. Novels and plays share certain common elements, such as characters (the people in the story), plot (the action of the story), climax (when action and/or dramatic tension reaches its highest point), and denouement (the resolution following the climax). Sections dividing novels are called chapters, while sections of plays are called acts. Subsections of plays' acts are called scenes. Novel chapters are usually not subdivided, although some novels have larger sections divided into groups of chapters.

Poetry

Unlike prose, which traditionally (except in forms like stream of consciousness) consists of complete sentences connected into paragraphs, poetry is written in verses. These may form complete sentences, clauses, or phrases. Poetry may be written with or without rhyme. It can be metered, following a particular rhythmic pattern such as iambic, dactylic, spondaic, trochaic, or anapestic, or may be without regular meter. The terms iamb and trochee, among others, identify stressed and unstressed syllables in each verse. Meter is also described by the number of beats or stressed syllables per verse: dimeter (2), trimeter (3), tetrameter (4), pentameter (5), and so forth. Using the symbol ⌣ to denote unstressed and / to denote stressed syllables, iambic = ⌣/; trochaic = /⌣; spondaic =//; dactylic =/⌣⌣; anapestic =⌣⌣/. Rhyme schemes identify which lines rhyme, such as ABAB, ABCA, AABA, and so on. Poetry with neither rhyme nor meter is called free verse. Poems may be in free verse, metered but unrhymed, rhymed but without meter, or using both rhyme and meter. In English, the most common meter is iambic pentameter. Unrhymed iambic pentameter is called blank verse.

Literary Theories and Criticism and Interpretation

Literary theory gives a rationale for the literary subject matter of criticism, and also for the process of interpreting literature. For example, Aristotle's *Poetics'* requirement of unity underlies any discussion of unity in Sophocles' *Oedipus Rex.* Postcolonial theory, assuming historical racism and exploitation, informs Nigerian novelist and critic Chinua Achebe's contention that in *Heart of Darkness,* Joseph Conrad does not portray Africans with complete humanity. Gender and feminist theories support critics' interpretation of Edna Pontellier's drowning at the climax of Kate Chopin's novel *The Awakening* (1899) as suicide. Until the 19th century, critics largely believed literature referenced objective reality, holding "a mirror up to nature" as William Shakespeare wrote.

Twentieth-century Structuralism and New Historicism were predated and influenced by non-traditional, historicized, cross-cultural comparative interpretations of biblical text in 19th-century German "higher criticism." Literary critic Charles Augustin Saint-Beuve maintained that biography could completely explain literature; contrarily, Marcel Proust demonstrated in narrative that art completely transformed biography. A profound 19th-century influence on literary theory was Friedrich Nietzsche's idea that facts must be interpreted to become facts.

Theme and Plot

Literary Theme

When we read parables, their themes are the lessons they aim to teach. When we read fables, the moral of each story is its theme. When we read fictional works, the authors' perspectives regarding life and human behavior are their themes. Unlike in parables and fables, themes in literary fiction are not meant to preach or teach the readers a lesson. Hence themes in fiction are not as explicit as they are in parables or fables. Instead they are implicit, and the reader only infers them. By analyzing the fictional characters through thinking about their actions and behavior, and understanding the setting of the story and reflecting on how its plot develops, the reader comes to infer the main theme(s) of the work. When writers succeed, they communicate with their readers such that common ground is established between author and audience. While a reader's individual experience may differ in its details from the author's written story, both may share universal underlying truths which allow author and audience to connect.

> **Review Video: Theme**
> Visit mometrix.com/academy and enter code: 732074

Determining Theme

In well-crafted literature, theme, structure, and plot are interdependent and inextricable: each element informs and reflects the others. The structure of a work is how it is organized. The theme is the central idea or meaning found in it. The plot is what happens in the story. (Plots can be physical actions or mental processes—e.g., Marcel Proust.) Titles can also inform us of a work's theme. For instance, Edgar Allan Poe's title "The Tell-Tale Heart" informs us of its theme of guilt before we even read about the repeated heartbeat the protagonist begins hearing immediately before and constantly after committing and hiding a murder. Repetitive patterns of events or behaviors also give clues to themes. The same is true of symbols: in F. Scott Fitzgerald's *The Great Gatsby,* for Jay Gatsby the green light at the end of the dock symbolizes Daisy Buchanan and his own dreams for the future. More generally, it symbolizes the American Dream, and narrator Nick Carraway explicitly compares it to early settlers' sight of America rising from the ocean.

Thematic Development

In *The Great Gatsby*, F. Scott Fitzgerald portrayed 1920s America as greedy, cynical, and rife with moral decay. Jay Gatsby's lavish weekly parties symbolize the reckless excesses of the Jazz Age. The growth of bootlegging and organized crime in reaction to Prohibition is symbolized by the character of Meyer Wolfsheim and by Gatsby's own ill-gotten wealth. Fitzgerald symbolized social divisions using geography: the "old money" aristocrats like the Buchanans lived on East Egg, while the "new money" bourgeois like Gatsby lived on West Egg. Fitzgerald also used weather, as many authors have, to reinforce narrative and emotional tones in the novel. Just as in *Romeo and Juliet*, William Shakespeare set the confrontation of Tybalt and Mercutio and its deadly consequences on the hottest summer day under a burning sun, in *The Great Gatsby*, Fitzgerald did the same with Tom

- 58 -

Wilson's deadly confrontation with Gatsby. Both works are ostensible love stories carrying socially critical themes about the destructiveness of pointless and misguided behaviors—family feuds in the former, pursuit of money in the latter.

In Victor Hugo's novel *Les Misérables*, the overall metamorphosis of protagonist Jean Valjean from a cynical ex-convict into a noble benefactor demonstrates Hugo's theme of the importance of love and compassion for others. Hugo also reflects this in more specific plot events. For example, Valjean's love for Cosette sustains him through many difficult periods and trying events. Hugo illustrates how love and compassion for others beget the same in them: Bishop Myriel's kindness to Valjean eventually inspires him to become honest. Years later, Valjean, as M. Madeleine, has rescued Fauchelevent from under a fallen carriage, Fauchelevent returns the compassionate act by giving Valjean sanctuary in the convent. M. Myriel's kindness also ultimately enables Valjean to rescue Cosette from the Thénardiers. Receiving Valjean's father-like love enables Cosette to fall in love with and marry Marius. And the love between Cosette and Marius enables the couple to forgive Valjean for his past crimes when they are revealed.

In one of his shortest stories, "The Tell-Tale Heart," Poe used economy of language to emphasize the murderer-narrator's obsessive focus on bare details like the victim's cataract-milky eye, the sound of a heartbeat, and insistence he is sane. The narrator begins by denying he is crazy, even citing his extreme agitation as proof of sanity. Contradiction is then extended: the narrator loves the old man, yet kills him. His motives are irrational—not greed or revenge, but to relieve the victim of his "evil eye." Because "eye" and "I" are homonyms, readers may infer that eye/I symbolizes the old man's identity, contradicting the killer's delusion that he can separate them. The narrator distances himself from the old man by perceiving his eye as separate, and dismembering his dead body. This backfires in another body part when he imagines the victim's heartbeat, which is really his own. Guilty and paranoid, he gives himself away. Poe predated Freud in exploring the paradox of killing those we love and the concept of projecting our own processes onto others.

William Faulkner contrasts the traditions of the antebellum South with the rapid changes of post-Civil War industrialization in his short story "A Rose for Emily." Living inside the isolated world of her house, Emily Grierson denies the reality of modern progress. Contradictorily, she is both a testament to time-honored history and a mysterious, eccentric, unfathomable burden. Faulkner portrays her with deathlike imagery even in life, comparing her to a drowned woman and referring to her skeleton. Emily symbolizes the Old South; as her social status is degraded, so is the antebellum social order. Like Miss Havisham in Charles Dickens' *Great Expectations,* Emily preserves her bridal bedroom, denying change and time's passage. Emily tries to control death through denial, shown in her necrophilia with her father's corpse and her killing of Homer Barron to stop him from leaving her, then also denying his death. Faulkner uses the motif of dust throughout to represent not only the decay of Emily, her house, and Old Southern traditions, but also how her secrets are obscured from others.

The great White Whale in *Moby-Dick* plays various roles to different characters. In Captain Ahab's obsessive, monomaniacal quest to kill it, the whale represents all evil, and Ahab believes it his duty and destiny to rid the world of it. Ishmael attempts through multiple scientific disciplines to understand the whale objectively, but fails—it is hidden underwater and mysterious to humans— reinforcing Melville's theme that humans can never know everything; here the whale represents the unknowable. Melville reverses white's usual connotation of purity in Ishmael's dread of white, associated with crashing waves, polar animals, albinos—all frightening and unnatural. White is often viewed as an absence of color, yet white light is the sum total of all colors in the spectrum. In the same way, white can signify both absence of meaning, and totality of meaning incomprehensible to humans. As a creature of nature, the whale also symbolizes how 19th-century white men's exploitative expansionistic actions were destroying the natural environment.

Because of the old fisherman Santiago's struggle to capture a giant marlin, some people characterize Ernest Hemingway's *The Old Man and the Sea* as telling of man against nature. However, it can more properly be interpreted as telling of man's role as part of nature. Both man and fish are portrayed as brave, proud, and honorable. In Hemingway's world, all creatures, including humans, must either kill or be killed. Santiago reflects, "man can be destroyed but not defeated," following this principle in his life. As heroes are often created through their own deaths, Hemingway seems to believe that while being destroyed is inevitable, destruction enables living beings to transcend it by fighting bravely with honor and dignity. Hemingway echoes Romantic poet John Keats' contention that only immediately before death can we understand beauty as it is about to be destroyed. He also echoes ancient Greek and Roman myths and the Old Testament with the tragic flaw of overweening pride or overreaching. Like Icarus, Prometheus, and Adam and Eve, the old man "went out too far."

Universal Themes

The Old Testament book of Genesis, the Quran, and the Epic of Gilgamesh all contain flood stories. Versions differ somewhat: Genesis describes a worldwide flood, attributing it to God's decision that mankind, his creation, had become incontrovertibly wicked in spirit and must be destroyed for the world to start anew. The Quran describes the flood as regional, caused by Allah after sending Nuh (notice the similarity in name to Noah) as a messenger to his people to cease their evil. The Quran stipulates that Allah only destroys those who deny or ignore messages from his messengers. Marked similarities also exist: in the Gilgamesh poems Utnapishtim, like Noah, is instructed to build a ship to survive the flood. Both men send out birds afterward as tests, and both include doves and a raven, though with different outcomes. Historians and archeologists believe a Middle Eastern tidal wave was a real basis for these stories. However, their universal themes remain the same: the flood was seen as God's way of wiping out humans whose behavior had become ungodly.

Theme of Overreaching

A popular theme throughout literature is the human trait of reaching too far or presuming too much. In Greek mythology, Daedalus constructed wings of feathers and wax that men might fly like birds. He permitted his son Icarus to try them, but cautioned the boy not to fly too close to the sun. The impetuous youth (in what psychologist David Elkind later named adolescence's myth of invincibility) ignored this, flying too close to the sun: the wax melted, the wings disintegrated, and Icarus fell into the sea and perished. In the Old Testament, God warned Adam and Eve not to eat fruit from the tree of knowledge of good and evil. Because they ignored this command, they were banished from Eden's eternal perfection, condemning them to mortality and suffering. The Romans were themselves examples of overreaching in their conquest and assimilation of most of the then-known world and ultimate demise. In Christopher Marlowe's *Dr. Faustus* and Johann Wolfgang von Goethe's *Faust,* the protagonist sells his soul to the Devil for unlimited knowledge and success, ultimately leading to his own tragic end.

Story Vs. Discourse

In terms of plot, "story" is the characters, places, and events originating in the author's mind, while "discourse" is how the author arranges and sequences events—which may be chronological or not. Story is imaginary; discourse is words on the page. Discourse allows story to be told in different ways. One element of plot structure is relating events differently from the order in which they occurred. This is easily done with cause-and-effect; for example, in the sentence, "He died following a long illness," we know the illness preceded the death, but the death precedes the illness in words. In Kate Chopin's short story "The Story of an Hour" (1894), she tells some of the events out of chronological order, which has the effect of amplifying the surprise of the ending for the reader. Another element of plot structure is selection. Chopin omits some details, such as Mr. Mallard's trip home; this allows readers to be as surprised at his arrival as Mrs. Mallard is.

Plot and Meaning

Novelist E. M. Forster has made the distinction between story as relating a series of events, such as a king dying and then his queen dying, versus plot as establishing motivations for actions and causes for events, such as a king dying and then his queen dying from grief over his death. Thus plot fulfills the function of helping readers understand cause-and-effect in events and underlying motivations in characters' actions, which in turn helps them understand life. This affects a work's meaning by supporting its ability to explain why things happen, why people do things, and ultimately the meaning of life. Some authors find that while story events convey meaning, they do not tell readers there is any one meaning in life or way of living, but rather are mental experiments with various meanings, enabling readers to explore. Hence stories may not necessarily be constructed to impose one definitive meaning, but rather to find some shape, direction, and meaning within otherwise random events.

Classic Analysis of Plot Structure

In *Poetics,* Aristotle defined plot as "the arrangement of the incidents." He meant not the story, but how it is structured for presentation. In tragedies, Aristotle found results driven by chains of cause-and-effect preferable to those driven by the protagonist's personality/character. He identified "unity of action" as necessary for a plot's wholeness; its events must be internally connected, not episodic or relying on *deus ex machina* or other external intervention. A plot must have a beginning, middle, and end. Gustav Freytag adapted Aristotle's ideas into his Triangle/Pyramid (1863). The beginning, today called the exposition/incentive/inciting moment, emphasizes causes and de-emphasizes effects. Aristotle called the ensuing cause-and-effect *desis*, or tying up, today called complication(s) which occur during the rising action. These culminate in a crisis or climax, Aristotle's *peripateia.* This occurs at the plot's middle, where cause and effect are both emphasized. The falling action, which Aristotle called the *lusis* or unraveling, is today called the dénouement. The resolution comes at the catastrophe/outcome or end, when causes are emphasized and effects de-emphasized.

> ## Review Video: Plot Line
> Visit mometrix.com/academy and enter code: 944011

Analysis of Plot Structures Through Recurring Patterns

Authors of fiction select characters, places, and events from their imaginations and arrange them in ways that will affect their readers. One way to analyze plot structure is to compare and contrast different events in a story. For example, in Kate Chopin's "The Story of an Hour," a very simple but key pattern of repetition is the husband's leaving and then returning. Such patterns fulfill the symmetrical aspect that Aristotle said was required of sound plot structure. In James Baldwin's short story, "Sonny's Blues," the narrator is Sonny's brother. In an encounter with one of Sonny's old friends early in the story, the brother initially disregards his communication. In a subsequent flashback, Baldwin informs us that this was the same way he had treated Sonny. In Nathaniel Hawthorne's "Young Goodman Brown," a pattern is created by the protagonist's recurrent efforts

- 61 -

not to go farther into the wood; in Herman Melville's "Bartleby the Scrivener," by Bartleby's repeated refusals; and in William Faulkner's "Barn Burning," by the history of barn-burning episodes.

Carpe Diem Tradition in Poetry

Carpe diem is Latin for "seize the day." A long poetic tradition, it advocates making the most of time because it passes swiftly and life is short. It is found in multiple languages, including Latin, Torquato Tasso's Italian, Pierre de Ronsard's French, and Edmund Spenser's English, and is often used in seduction to argue for indulging in earthly pleasures. Roman poet Horace's Ode 1.11 tells younger woman Leuconoe to enjoy the present, not worrying about inevitable aging. Two Renaissance Metaphysical Poets, Andrew Marvell and Robert Herrick, treated *carpe diem* more as a call to action. In "To His Coy Mistress," Marvell points out that time is fleeting, arguing for love, and concluding that because they cannot stop time, they may as well defy it, getting the most out of the short time they have. In "To the Virgins, to Make Much of Time," Herrick advises young women to take advantage of their good fortune in being young by getting married before they become too old to attract men and have babies.

"To His Coy Mistress" begins, "Had we but world enough, and time, / This coyness, lady, were no crime." Using imagery, Andrew Marvell describes leisure they could enjoy if time were unlimited. Arguing for seduction, he continues famously, "But at my back I always hear/Time's winged chariot hurrying near; / And yonder all before us lie / Deserts of vast eternity." He depicts time as turning beauty to death and decay. Contradictory images in "amorous birds of prey" and "tear our pleasures with rough strife / Through the iron gates of life" overshadow romance with impending death, linking present pleasure with mortality and spiritual values with moral considerations. Marvell's concluding couplet summarizes *carpe diem*: "Thus, though we cannot make our sun / Stand still, yet we will make him run." "To the Virgins, to Make Much of Time" begins with the famous "Gather ye rosebuds while ye may." Rather than seduction to live for the present, Robert Herrick's experienced persona advises young women's future planning: "Old time is still a-flying / And this same flower that smiles today, / Tomorrow will be dying."

Couplets and Meter to Enhance Meaning in Poetry

When a poet uses a couplet—a stanza of two lines, rhymed or unrhymed—it can function as the answer to a question asked earlier in the poem, or the solution to a problem or riddle. Couplets can also enhance the establishment of a poem's mood, or clarify the development of a poem's theme. Another device to enhance thematic development is irony, which also communicates the poet's tone and draws the reader's attention to a point the poet is making. The use of meter gives a poem a rhythmic context, contributes to the poem's flow, makes it more appealing to the reader, can represent natural speech rhythms, and produces specific effects. For example, in "The Song of Hiawatha," Henry Wadsworth Longfellow uses trochaic (/ ◡) tetrameter (four beats per line) to evoke for readers the rhythms of Native American chanting: "*By* the *shores* of *Gitche* Gumee, / *By* the *shin*ing *Big*-Sea-*Wat*er / *Stood* the *wig*wam *of* No*kom*is." (Italicized syllables are stressed; non-italicized syllables are unstressed.)

Effects of Figurative Devices on Meaning in Poetry

Through exaggeration, hyperbole communicates the strength of a poet's or persona's feelings and enhances the mood of the poem. Imagery appeals to the reader's senses, creating vivid mental pictures, evoking reader emotions and responses, and helping to develop themes. Irony also aids thematic development by drawing the reader's attention to the poet's point and communicating the poem's tone. Thematic development is additionally supported by the comparisons of metaphors and similes, which emphasize similarities, enhance imagery, and affect readers' perceptions. The use of mood communicates the atmosphere of a poem, can build a sense of tension, and evokes the reader's emotions. Onomatopoeia appeals to the reader's auditory sense and enhances sound imagery even when the poem is visual (read silently) rather than auditory (read aloud). Rhyme connects and unites verses, gives the rhyming words emphasis and makes poems more fluent. Symbolism communicates themes, develops imagery, and evokes readers' emotional and other responses.

Poetic Structure to Enhance Meaning

The opening stanza of Romantic English poet, artist and printmaker William Blake's famous poem "The Tyger" demonstrates how a poet can create tension by using line length and punctuation independently of one another: "Tyger! Tyger! burning bright / In the forests of the night, / What immortal hand or eye / Could frame thy fearful symmetry?" The first three lines of this stanza are trochaic (/$\cup$), with "masculine" endings—that is, strongly stressed syllables at the ends of each of the lines. But Blake's punctuation contradicts this rhythmic regularity by not providing any divisions between the words "bright" and "In" or between "eye" and "Could." This irregular punctuation foreshadows how Blake disrupts the meter at the end of this first stanza by using a contrasting dactyl (/$\cup\cup$), with a "feminine" (unstressed) ending syllable in the last word, "symmetry." Thus Blake uses structural contrasts to heighten the intrigue of his work.

In enjambment, one sentence or clause in a poem does not end at the end of its line or verse, but runs over into the next line or verse. Clause endings coinciding with line endings give readers a feeling of completion, but enjambment influences readers to hurry to the next line to finish and understand the sentence. In his blank-verse epic religious poem "Paradise Lost," John Milton wrote: "Anon out of the earth a fabric huge / Rose like an exhalation, with the sound / Of dulcet symphonies and voices sweet, / Built like a temple, where pilasters round / Were set, and Doric pillars overlaid / With golden architrave." Only the third line is end-stopped. Milton, describing the palace of Pandemonium bursting from Hell up through the ground, reinforced this idea through phrases and clauses bursting through the boundaries of the lines. A caesura is a pause in mid-verse. Milton's commas in the third and fourth lines signal caesuras. They interrupt flow, making the narration jerky to imply that Satan's glorious-seeming palace has a shaky and unsound foundation.

Reflection of Content Through Structure

Wallace Stevens' short yet profound poem "The Snow Man" is reductionist: the snow man is a figure without human biases or emotions. Stevens begins, "One must have a mind of winter," the criterion for realizing nature and life does not inherently possess subjective qualities; we only invest it with these. Things are not as we see them; they simply are. The entire poem is one long sentence of clauses connected by conjunctions and commas, and modified by relative clauses and phrases. The successive phrases lead readers continually to reconsider as they read. Stevens' construction of the poem mirrors the meaning he conveys. With a mind of winter, the snow man, Stevens concludes, "nothing himself, beholds nothing that is not there, and the nothing that is" (ultimate reductionism).

Contrast of Content and Structure

Robert Frost's poem "Stopping by Woods on a Snowy Evening" (1923) is deceptively short and simple, with only four stanzas, each of only four lines, and short and simple words. Reinforcing this is Frost's use of regular rhyme and meter. The rhythm is iambic tetrameter throughout; the rhyme scheme is AABA in the first three stanzas and AAAA in the fourth. In an additional internal subtlety,

B ending "here" in the first stanza is rhymed with A endings "queer," "near," and "year" of the second; B ending "lake" in the second is rhymed in A endings "shake", "mistake," and "flake" of the third. The final stanza's AAAA endings reinforce the ultimate darker theme. Though the first three stanzas seem to describe quietly watching snow fill the woods, the last stanza evokes the seductive pull of mysterious death: "The woods are lovely, dark and deep," countered by the obligations of living life: "But I have promises to keep, / And miles to go before I sleep, / And miles to go before I sleep." The last line's repetition strengthens Frost's message that despite death's temptation, life's course must precede it.

Repetition to Enhance Meaning

A villanelle is a nineteen-line poem composed of five tercets and one quatrain. The defining characteristic is the repetition: two lines appear repeatedly throughout the poem. In Theodore Roethke's "The Waking," the two repeated lines are "I wake to sleep, and take my waking slow," and "I learn by going where I have to go." At first these sound paradoxical, but the meaning is gradually revealed through the poem. The repetition also fits with the theme of cycle: the paradoxes of waking to sleep, learning by going, and thinking by feeling represent a constant cycle through life. They also symbolize abandoning conscious rationalism to embrace spiritual vision. We wake from the vision to "Great Nature," and "take the lively air." "This shaking keeps me steady"—another paradox—juxtaposes and balances fear of mortality with ecstasy in embracing experience. The transcendent vision of all life's interrelationship demonstrates, "What falls away is always. And is near." Readers experience the poem holistically, like music, through Roethke's integration of theme, motion, and sound.

Sylvia Plath's villanelle "Mad Girl's Love Song" narrows the scope from universal to personal but keeps the theme of cycle. The two repeated lines, "I shut my eyes and all the world drops dead" and "(I think I made you up inside my head.)" reflect the existential viewpoint that nothing exists in any absolute reality outside of our own perceptions. In the first stanza, the middle line, "I lift my lids and all is born again," in its recreating the world, bridges between the repeated refrain statements—one of obliterating reality, the other of having constructed her lover's existence. Unlike other villanelles wherein key lines are subtly altered in their repetitions, Plath repeats these exactly each time. This reflects the young woman's love, constant throughout the poem as it neither fades nor progresses.

> **Review Video: Structural Elements of Poetry**
> Visit mometrix.com/academy and enter code: 265216

Reading for Information

Informational Texts and Rhetoric

Figurative vs. Literal Language, Denotation vs. Connotation, and Technical Language

As in fictional literature, informational text also uses both literal language, which means just what it says, and figurative language, which imparts more than literal meaning. For example, an informational text author might use a simile or direct comparison, such as writing that a racehorse "ran like the wind." Informational text authors also use metaphors or implied comparisons, such as "the cloud of the Great Depression." Similar to literal and figurative, denotation is the literal meaning or dictionary definition of a word whereas connotation is feelings or thoughts associated with a word not included in its literal definition. For example, "politician" and "statesman" have the same denotation, but in context, "politician" may have a negative connotation while "statesman" may have a positive connotation. Teachers can help students understand positive or negative connotations of words depending on their sentence contexts. For example, the word "challenge" has a positive connotation in this sentence: "Although I finished last, I still accomplished the challenge of running the race." Teachers can give students a multiple-choice game wherein they choose whether "challenge" here means (A) easy, (B) hard, (C) fun, or (D) taking work to overcome. The word "difficult" has a negative connotation in this sentence: "I finished last in the race because it was difficult." Students choose whether "difficult" here means (A) easy, (B) hard, (C) fun, or (D) lengthy. Positive and negative connotations for the same word can also be taught. Consider the following sentence: "When the teacher asked Johnny why he was in the restroom so long, he gave a *smart* answer." In this context, "smart" means disrespectful and carries a negative connotation. But in the sentence, "Johnny was *smart* to return to class from the restroom right away," the same word means wise and carries a positive connotation. Technical language is vocabulary related to a specific discipline, activity, or process, such as "itemize" when referring to organizing or "kindling" in fire-building instructions.

> **Review Video: Figurative Language**
> Visit mometrix.com/academy and enter code: 584902
>
> **Review Video: Denotation and Connotation**
> Visit mometrix.com/academy and enter code: 310092

Explicit and Implicit Information

When informational text states something explicitly, the reader is told by the author exactly what is meant, which can include the author's interpretation or perspective of events. For example, a professor writes, "I have seen students go into an absolute panic just because they weren't able to finish administering the Peabody [Picture Vocabulary Test] in the time they were allotted." This explicitly tells the reader that the students were afraid, and by using the words "just because," the writer indicates their fear was exaggerated out of proportion relative to what happened. However, another professor writes, "I have had students come to me, their faces drained of all color, saying 'We weren't able to finish the Peabody.'" This is an example of implicit meaning: the second writer did not state explicitly that the students were panicked. Instead, he wrote a description of their faces being "drained of all color." From this description, the reader can infer the students were so frightened that their faces paled.

Technical Language

Technical language, found in scientific texts, is more impersonal than literary and vernacular language. Passive voice tone makes tone impersonal. For example, instead of writing, "We found this a central component of protein metabolism," scientists write, "This was found a central component of protein metabolism." While science professors traditionally instructed students to avoid active voice because it leads to first-person ("I" and "we") usage, science editors today find passive voice dull and weak. Many journal articles combine both. Tone in technical science writing should be detached, concise, and professional. While one writes in the vernacular, "This chemical has to be available for proteins to be digested," professionals write technically, "The presence of this chemical is required for the enzyme to break the covalent bonds of proteins."

Making Inferences About Informational Text

With informational text, reader comprehension depends not only on recalling important statements and details, but also on reader inferences based on examples and details. Readers add information from the text to what they already know to draw inferences about the text. These inferences help the readers to fill in the information that the text does not explicitly state, enabling them to understand the text better. When reading a nonfictional autobiography or biography, for example, the most appropriate inferences might concern the events in the book, the actions of the subject of the autobiography or biography, and the message the author means to convey. When reading a nonfictional expository (informational) text, the reader would best draw inferences about problems and their solutions, and causes and their effects. When reading a nonfictional persuasive text, the reader will want to infer ideas supporting the author's message and intent.

Standards for Citing Textual Evidence

Reading standards for informational texts expect sixth-graders to cite textual evidence to support their inferences and analyses. Seventh-graders are expected additionally to identify several specific pieces of textual evidence to defend each of their conclusions. Eighth-graders are expected to differentiate strong from weak textual evidence. Ninth- and 10th-graders are expected to be able to cite thorough evidence as well as strong evidence from text. Eleventh- and 12th-graders are expected, in combination with the previous grade-level standards, to determine which things are left unclear in a text. Students must be able to connect text to their background knowledge and make inferences to understand text, judge it critically, draw conclusions about it, and make their own interpretations of it. Therefore, they must be able to organize and differentiate between main ideas and details in a text to make inferences about them. They must also be able to locate evidence in the text.

Paired Reading Strategy to Identify Main Ideas and Details

Students can support one another's comprehension of informational text by working in pairs. Each student silently reads a portion of text. One summarizes the text's main point, and then the other must agree or disagree and explain why until they reach an agreement. Then each person takes a turn at identifying details in the text portion that support the main idea that they have identified. Finally, they repeat each step with their roles reversed. Each pair of students can keep track of the central ideas and supporting details by taking notes in two columns: one for main ideas and the other for the details that support those main ideas.

Text Coding

Some experts (cf. Harvey and Daniels, 2009) recommend text coding or text monitoring as an active reading strategy to support student comprehension of informational texts. As they read, students make text code notations on Post-it Notes or in the margins of the text. Teachers should model text coding for students one or two codes at a time until they have demonstrated all eight codes: A check mark means "I know this." An X means "This is not what I expected." An asterisk (*) means "This is important." A question mark means "I have a question about this." Two question marks mean "I am really confused about this." An exclamation point means "I am surprised at this." An L means "I have learned something new from this." And RR means "I need to reread this part."

Two-Column Notes

When students read or listen to an informational text, it can help them find and note main ideas and supporting details by using the "two-column notes" strategy. Teachers should first introduce this strategy to students, model it, and have them practice using it. As students use two-column notes, they can better organize textual information, find data in text supporting conclusions, and evaluate whether textual evidence supports author claims. For example, in analyzing Abraham Lincoln's Gettysburg Address, students put in the Main Ideas column, "Our founding fathers created the U.S." Next to it in the Details column, they place "Conceived in liberty" and "Dedicated to all men being created equal." Under Main Ideas: "Now the U.S. is in a Civil War." Under Details: "Testing whether our nation as conceived can survive." Main Ideas: "We are here to dedicate the Gettysburg battlefield." Details: "The dedication is to those who died in the war," "This is their final resting place," and "This is a fitting and proper thing to do."

Structures or Organizational Patterns in Informational Texts

Informational text can be descriptive, invoking the five senses and answering the questions what, who, when, where, and why. Another structure of informational text is sequence and order: Chronological texts relate events in the sequence that they occurred, from start to finish, while how-to texts organize information into a series of instructions in the sequence in which the steps should be followed. Comparison-contrast structures of informational text describe various ideas to their readers by pointing out how things or ideas are similar and how they are different. Cause and effect structures of informational text describe events that occurred, and identify the causes or reasons that those events occurred. Problem and solution structures of informational text introduce and describe problems, and then offer one or more solutions for each problem described.

> **Review Video: Organizational Methods to Structure Text**
> Visit mometrix.com/academy and enter code: 606263

Connections and Distinctions Among Elements in Text

Students should be able to analyze how an informational text makes connections and distinctions among ideas, events, or individuals, such as by comparing them or contrasting them, making analogies between them, or dividing them into categories to show similarities and differences. For example, teachers can help eighth-graders analyze how to divide animals into categories of carnivores, which eat only meat; herbivores, which eat only plants; and omnivores, which eat both meat and plants. Teachers and students can identify the author's comparisons and contrasts of groups. Teachers can help students analyze these processes by supplying sentence frames. For example, "A _____ is a _____, so" and "A _____ is a _____ which means." The students fill these empty spaces in, such as, "A frog is a carnivore, so it eats only meat," and "A rabbit is an herbivore, which means it eats only plants."

Text Features in Informational Texts

The title of a text gives readers some idea of its content. The table of contents is a list near the beginning of a text, showing the book's sections and chapters and their coinciding page numbers. This gives readers an overview of the whole text, and helps them find specific chapters easily. An appendix, at the back of the book or document, adds important information not in the main text. Also at the back, an index lists the book's important topics alphabetically with their page numbers to help students find them easily. Glossaries, usually found at the backs of books, list technical terms alphabetically with their definitions to aid vocabulary learning and comprehension. Boldface print is used to emphasize certain words, often identifying words included in the text's glossary where readers can look up their definitions. Headings separate sections of text and show the topic of each. Subheadings divide subject headings into smaller, more specific categories to help readers organize information. Footnotes, at the bottom of the page, give readers more information, such as citations or links. Bullet points list items separately, making facts and ideas easier to see and understand. A sidebar is a box of information to one side of the main text giving additional information, often on a more focused or in-depth example of a topic.

Illustrations and photographs are pictures visually emphasizing important points in text. The captions below the illustrations explain what those images show. Charts and tables are visual forms of information that make something easier and faster to understand. Diagrams are drawings that show relationships or explain a process. Graphs visually show relationships of multiple sets of information plotted along vertical and horizontal axes. Maps show geographical information visually to help students understand the relative locations of places covered in the text. Timelines are visual graphics showing historical events in chronological order to help readers see their sequence.

> **Review Video: Informative Text**
> Visit mometrix.com/academy and enter code: 924964

Technical Material for Non-Technical Readers

Writing about technical subjects for non-technical readers differs from writing for colleagues in that authors begin with a different goal: it may be more important to deliver a critical message than to impart the maximum technical content possible. Technical authors also must assume that non-technical audiences do not have the expertise to comprehend extremely scientific or technical messages, concepts, and terminology. They must resist the temptation to impress audiences with their scientific knowledge and expertise, and remember that their primary purpose is to communicate a message that non-technical readers will understand, feel, and respond to. Non-technical and technical styles include similarities: both should formally cite references when used and acknowledge other authors' work utilized. Both must follow intellectual property and copyright regulations. This includes the author's protecting his/her own rights, or a public domain statement, as s/he chooses.

Writers of technical or scientific material may need to write for many non-technical audiences. Some readers have no technical or scientific background, and those who do may not be in the same field as the authors. Government and corporate policymakers and budget managers need technical information they can understand for decision-making. Citizens affected by technology and/or science are another audience. Non-governmental organizations can encompass many of the preceding groups. Elementary and secondary school programs also need non-technical language for presenting technical subject matter. Additionally, technical authors will need to use non-technical language collecting consumer responses to surveys, presenting scientific or para-scientific material to the public, writing about the history of science, and writing about science and technology in developing countries.

When authors of technical information must write about their subjects using non-technical language that readers outside their disciplinary fields can comprehend, they should not only use non-technical terms, they should also use normal, everyday language to accommodate non-native-language readers. For example, instead of writing that "eustatic changes" like "thermal expansion" causing "hazardous conditions" in the "littoral zone," an author would do better to write that a "rising sea level" is "threatening the coast." When technical terms cannot be avoided, authors should also define and/or explain them using non-technical language. Although authors must cite references and acknowledge others' work they use, they should avoid the kinds of references or citations that they would use in scientific journals—unless they reinforce author messages. They should not use endnotes, footnotes, or any other complicated referential techniques because non-technical journal publishers usually do not accept them. Including high-resolution illustrations, photos, maps, or satellite images and incorporating multimedia into digital publications will enhance public non-technical writing about technical subjects. Technical authors may publish using non-technical language in e-journals, trade journals, specialty newsletters, and daily newspapers.

Evaluating Arguments Made by Informational Text Writers

When evaluating an informational text, the first step is to identify the argument's conclusion. Then identify the author's premises that support the conclusion. Try to paraphrase premises for clarification and make the conclusion and premises fit. List all premises first, sequentially numbered, then finish with the conclusion. Identify any premises or assumptions not stated by the author but required for the stated premises to support the conclusion. Read word assumptions sympathetically, as the author might. Evaluate whether premises reasonably support the conclusion: For inductive reasoning, the reader should ask if the premises are true, if the support the conclusion, and how strongly. For deductive reasoning, the reader should ask if the argument is valid or invalid. If all premises are true, the argument is valid unless the conclusion can be false. If it can, then the argument is invalid. Alter an invalid argument to become valid, adding any premises needed.

Determining an Informational Author's Purpose

Informational authors' purposes are why they wrote texts. Readers must determine authors' motivations and goals. Readers gain greater insight into text by considering the author's motivation. This develops critical reading skills. Readers perceive writing as a person's voice, not simply printed words. Uncovering author motivations and purposes empowers readers to know what to expect from the text, read for relevant details, evaluate authors and their work critically, and respond effectively to the motivations and persuasions of the text. The main idea of a text is what the reader is supposed to understand from reading it; the purpose of the text is why the author has written it and what the author wants readers to do with its information. Authors state some purposes clearly, while others may be unstated but equally significant. When purposes stated contradict other parts of text, authors may have hidden agendas. Readers can better evaluate a text's effectiveness, whether they agree or disagree with it, and why they agree or disagree through identifying unstated author purposes.

Identifying Author's Point of View or Purpose

In some informational texts, readers find it easy to identify the author's point of view and/or purpose, as when the author explicitly states his or her position and/or reason for writing. But other texts are more difficult, either because of the content or because the authors give neutral or balanced viewpoints. This is particularly true in scientific texts, in which authors may state the purpose of their research in the report, but never state their point of view except by interpreting evidence or data. To analyze text and identify point of view or purpose, readers should ask themselves the following four questions: (1) With what main point or idea does this author want to persuade readers to agree? (2) How do this author's choices of words affect the way that readers consider this subject? (3) How do this author's choices of examples and/or facts affect the way that readers consider this subject? And (4) What is it that this author wants to accomplish by writing this text?

Use of Rhetoric

There are many ways authors can support their claims, arguments, beliefs, ideas, and reasons for writing informational texts. For example, authors can appeal to readers' sense of logic by communicating their reasoning through a carefully sequenced series of logical steps to help "prove" the points made. Authors can appeal to readers' emotions by using descriptions and words that evoke feelings of sympathy, sadness, anger, righteous indignation, hope, happiness, or any other emotion to reinforce what they express and share with their audience. Authors may appeal to the moral or ethical values of readers by using words and descriptions that can convince readers that something is right or wrong. By relating personal anecdotes, authors can supply readers with more accessible, realistic examples of points they make, as well as appealing to their emotions. They can provide supporting evidence by reporting case studies. They can also illustrate their points by making analogies to which readers can better relate.

Rhetorical Devices

An anecdote is a brief story authors may relate, which can illustrate their point(s) in a more real and relatable way. Aphorisms concisely state common beliefs and may rhyme. For example, Benjamin Franklin's "Early to bed and early to rise / Make a man healthy, wealthy, and wise" is an aphorism. Allusions refer to literary or historical figures to impart symbolism to a thing or person, and/or create reader resonance. In John Steinbeck's *Of Mice and Men,* protagonist George's last name is Milton, alluding to John Milton who wrote *Paradise Lost*, to symbolize George's eventual loss of his dream. Satire ridicules or pokes fun at human foibles or ideas, as in the works of Jonathan Swift and Mark Twain. A parody is a form of satire that imitates another work to ridicule its topic and/or style. A paradox is a statement that is true despite appearing contradictory. Hyperbole is overstatement using exaggerated language. An oxymoron combines seeming contradictions, such as "deafening silence."

- 70 -

Analogies compare two things that share common elements. Similes (stated comparisons using the words "like" or "as") and metaphors (implied comparisons) are considered forms of analogy. When using logic to reason with audiences, syllogism refers either to deductive reasoning or a deceptive, very sophisticated, or subtle argument. Deductive reasoning moves from general to specific, inductive reasoning from specific to general. Diction is author word choice establishing tone and effect. Understatement achieves effects like contrast or irony by downplaying or describing something more subtly than warranted. Chiasmus uses parallel clauses, the second reversing the order of the first. Examples include T. S. Eliot's "Has the Church failed mankind, or has mankind failed the Church?" and John F. Kennedy's "Ask not what your country can do for you; ask what you can do for your country." Anaphora regularly repeats a word or phrase at the beginnings of consecutive clauses or phrases to add emphasis to an idea. A classic example of anaphora was Winston Churchill's emphasis of determination: "We shall fight in the trenches. We shall fight on the oceans. We shall fight in the sky."

Evaluating Media Information Sources

With the wealth of media in different formats available today, users are more likely to take media at face value. However, to understand the content of media, consumers must critically evaluate each source. Users should ask themselves about media sources: Who is delivering this message, and why? What methods do a media source's publishers employ to gain and maintain users' attention? Which points of view is the media source representing? What are the various ways a message could be interpreted? And what information is missing from the message? Is the source scholarly, i.e., peer-reviewed? Does it include author names and their credentials pertinent to the information? Who publishes it, and why? Who is the target audience? Is the language technically specific or non-technical/public? Are sources cited, research claims documented, conclusions based on furnished evidence, and references provided? Is the publication current? All of these questions and more can and should be asked of media sources.

For books, consider whether information is up-to-date and whether historical perspectives apply. Content is more likely to be scholarly if publishers are universities, government, or professional organizations. Book reviews can also provide useful information. For articles, identify the author, publisher, frequency of periodical publication, and what kind of advertising, if any, is included. Looking for book reviews also informs users. For articles, look for biographical author information; publisher name; frequency of periodical publication; and whether advertising is included and, if so, whether for certain occupations/disciplines. For web pages, check their domain names, identify publishers or sponsors (strip back URLs to uncover), look for author/publisher contact information, check dates of most recent page updates, and be alert to biases and verify information's validity. Quality and accuracy of web pages located through search engines rather than library databases ranges widely, requiring careful user inspection. Web page recommendations from reliable sources like university faculties can help indicate quality and accuracy. Citations of websites by credible or scholarly sources also show reliability. Authors' names, relevant credentials, affiliations, and contact information support their authority. Site functionality, such as ease of navigation, ability to search, site maps and/or indexes, are also criteria to consider.

Persuasive Media

Some media using persuasion are advertising, public relations, and advocacy. Advertisers use persuasion to sell goods and services. The public relations field uses persuasion to give good impressions of companies, governments, or organizations. Advocacy groups use persuasion to garner support or votes. Persuasion can come through commercials, public service announcements, speeches, websites, and newsletters, among others. Activists, lobbyists, government officials, and politicians use political rhetoric involving persuasive techniques. Basic techniques include using celebrity spokespersons, whom consumers admire or aspire to resemble; or, conversely, "everyday people" (albeit often portrayed by actors) with whom consumers identify. Using expert testimonials lends credibility. Explicit claims of content, effectiveness, quality, and reliability—which often cannot be proven or disproven—are used to persuade. While news and advocacy messages mostly eschew humor for credibility's sake (except in political satire), advertising often persuades via humor, which gets consumer attention and associates its pleasure with advertised products and services. "Weasel words," such as qualifiers, are often combined with exaggerated claims. Intensifiers—hyperbole, superlatives, and repetition—and sentimental appeals are also persuasive.

Intermediate Techniques

Dangerous propagandist Adolf Hitler said people suspect little lies more than big ones; hence the "Big Lie" is a persuasion method requiring consumers' keen critical thinking to identify. A related method is charisma, which can induce people to believe messages they would otherwise reject. Euphemism substitutes abstract, vague, or bland terms for more graphic, clear, and unpleasant ones. For example, the terms "layoffs" and "firing" are replaced by "downsizing," and "torture" is replaced with "intensive interrogation techniques." Extrapolation bases sweeping conclusions on small amounts of minor information to appeal to what consumers wish or hope. Flattery appeals to consumer self-esteem needs, such as L'Oreal's "You're worth it." Flattery is sometimes accomplished through contrast, like ads showing others' mistakes to make consumers feel superior and smarter. "Glittering generalities" are "virtue" concepts, such as beauty, love, health, democracy, freedom, and science. Persuaders hope these gain consumer acceptance without questioning what they mean. The opposite is name-calling to persuade consumers to reject someone or something.

American citizens love new ideas and technology. Persuaders exploit this by emphasizing the newness of products, services, and candidates. Conversely, they also use nostalgia to evoke consumers' happy memories, which they often remember more than unhappy ones. Citing "scientific evidence" is an intermediate version of the basic technique of expert testimonials. Consumers may accept this as proof, but some advertisers, politicians, and other persuaders may present inaccurate or misleading "evidence." Another intermediate technique is the "simple solution." Although the natures of people and life are complex, when consumers feel overwhelmed by complexity, persuaders exploit this by offering policies, products, or services they claim will solve complicated problems with simple means. Persuaders also use symbols—images, words, and names we associate with more general, emotional concepts like lifestyle, country, family, religion, and gender. While symbols have power, their significance also varies across individuals: for example, some consumers regard the Hummer SUV as a prestigious status symbol, while others regard it as environmentally harmful and irresponsible.

Advanced Techniques

Ad hominem, Latin for "against the man"—also called "shoot the messenger"—attacks someone delivering a message, not the message itself. It operates by association: problems with the messenger must indicate problems with the message. "Stacking the deck" misleads by presenting only selected information that supports one position. Denial evades responsibility, either directly or indirectly, for controversial or unpopular subjects: A politician saying, "I won't mention my opponent's tax evasion issues" manages to mention them while seeming less accusatory. Persuaders use majority belief, such as "Four out of five dentists recommend this brand" or the ubiquitous "[insert number] people can't be wrong." In an intensified version, persuaders exploit group dynamics at rallies, speeches, and other live-audience events where people are vulnerable to surrounding crowd influences. Scapegoating—blaming one person or group for complex problems, is a form of the intermediate "simple solution" technique, a practice common in politics. Timing also persuades, like advertising flowers and candy preceding Valentine's Day, ad campaigns preceding new technology rollouts, and politician speeches following big news events.

Writing

Essays

The basic format of an essay can be said to have three major parts: the introduction, the body, and the conclusion. The body is further divided into the writer's main points. Short and simple essays may have three main points, while essays covering broader ranges and going into more depth can have almost any number of main points, depending on length.

An essay's introduction should answer three questions: (1) What is the subject of the essay? If a student writes an essay about a book, the answer would include the title and author of the book and any additional information needed—such as the subject or argument of the book. (2) How does the essay address the subject? To answer this, the writer identifies the essay's organization by briefly summarizing main points and/or evidence supporting them. (3) What will the essay prove? This is the thesis statement, usually the opening paragraph's last sentence, clearly stating the writer's message.

The body elaborates on all the main points related to the thesis and supporting evidence, introducing one main point at a time. Each body paragraph should state the point, explain its meaning, support it with quotations or other evidence, and then explain how this point and the evidence are related to the thesis. The writer should then repeat this procedure in a new paragraph for each additional main point. In addition to relating each point to the thesis, clearly restating the thesis in at least one sentence of each paragraph is also advisable.

The conclusion reiterates the content of the introduction, including the thesis, to review them for the reader. The essay writer may also summarize the highlights of the argument or description contained in the body of the essay, following the same sequence originally used in the body. For example, a conclusion might look like: Point 1 + Point 2 + Point 3 = Thesis, or Point 1 → Point 2 → Point 3 → Thesis Proof. Good organization makes essays easier for writers to compose and provides a guide for readers to follow. Well-organized essays hold attention better, and are more likely to get readers to accept their theses as valid.

> **Review Video: Reading Essays**
> Visit mometrix.com/academy and enter code: 169166

Informative/Explanatory vs. Argumentative Writing

Informative/explanatory writing begins with the basis that something is true or factual, while argumentative writing strives to prove something that may or may not be true or factual. Whereas argument is intended to persuade readers to agree with the author's position, informative/explanatory text merely provides information and insight to readers. Informative/explanatory writing concentrates on informing readers about why or how something is as it is. This includes offering new information, explaining how a process works, and/or developing a concept for readers. In accomplishing these objectives, the writing may emphasize naming and differentiating various things within a category; providing definitions of things; providing details about the parts of something; explaining a particular function or behavior; and giving readers explanations for why a fact, object, event, or process exists or occurs.

Necessary Skills for Informative/Explanatory Writing

For students to write in informative/explanatory mode, they must be able to locate and select pertinent information from primary and secondary sources. They must also combine their own experiences and existing knowledge with this new information they find. They must not only select facts, details, and examples relevant to their topics, but also learn to incorporate this information into their writing. Students need at the same time to develop their skills in various writing techniques, such as comparing and contrasting, making transitions between topics/points, and citing scenarios and anecdotes related to their topics. In teaching explanatory/informative writing, teachers must "read like writers" to use mentor texts to consider author craft and technique. They can find mentor texts in blogs, websites, newspapers, novels, plays, picture books, and many more. Teachers should know the grade-level writing standards for informative/explanatory writing to select classroom-specific, appropriate mentor texts.

> **Review Video: Informative Text**
> Visit mometrix.com/academy and enter code: 924964

Narrative Writing

Put simply, narrative writing tells a story. The most common examples of literary narratives are novels. Non-fictional biographies, autobiographies, memoirs, and histories also use narrative. Narratives should tell stories in such a way that the readers learn something, or gain insight or understanding. Students can write more interesting narratives by relating events or experiences that were meaningful to them. Narratives should not begin with long descriptions or introductions, but start with the actions or events. Students should ensure that there is a point to each story by describing what they learned from the experience they narrate. To write effective description, students should include sensory details, asking themselves what they saw, heard, felt/touched, smelled, and tasted during the experiences they describe. In narrative writing, the details should be concrete rather than abstract. Using concrete details enables readers to imagine everything that the writer describes.

> **Review Video: Narratives**
> Visit mometrix.com/academy and enter code: 280100

Sensory Details and Concrete vs. Abstract Descriptions in Narrative

Students need vivid description to write descriptive essays. Narratives should also include description of characters, things, and events. Students should remember to describe not only the visual detail of what someone or something looks like, but details from other senses as well. For example, they can contrast the feelings of a sea breeze versus a mountain breeze, describe how they think something inedible would taste, and sounds they hear in the same location at different times of day and night. Readers have trouble visualizing images or imagining sensory impressions and feelings from abstract descriptions, so concrete descriptions make these more real.

Concrete language provides information that readers can grasp and may empathize with, while abstract language, which is more general, can leave readers feeling disconnected, empty, or even confused. "It was a lovely day" is abstract, but "The sun shone brightly, the sky was blue, the air felt warm, and a gentle breeze wafted across my skin" is concrete. "Ms. Couch was a good teacher" uses abstract language, giving only a general idea of the writer's opinion. But "Ms. Couch is excellent at helping us take our ideas and turn them into good essays and stories" uses concrete language, giving more specific examples of what makes Ms. Couch a good teacher. "I like writing poems but not essays" gives readers a general idea that the student prefers one genre over another, but not

- 75 -

why. But by saying, "I like writing short poems with rhythm and rhyme, but I hate writing five-page essays that go on and on about the same ideas," readers understand that the student prefers the brevity, rhyme, and meter of short poetry over the length and redundancy of longer prose.

Journals and Diaries

A journal is a personal account of events, experiences, feelings, and thoughts. Many people write journals to confide their feelings and thoughts or to help them process experiences they have had. Since journals are private documents not meant for sharing with others, writers may not be concerned with grammar, spelling, or other mechanics. However, authors may write journals that they expect or hope to publish someday; in this case, they not only express their thoughts and feelings and process their experiences, but they additionally attend to their craft in writing them. Some authors compose journals to document particular time periods or series of related events, such as a cancer diagnosis, treatment, surviving the disease, and how these experiences have changed/affected them; experiences in recovering from addiction; journeys of spiritual exploration and discovery; trips to or time spent in another country; or anything else someone wants to personally document. Journaling can also be therapeutic: some people use them to work through feelings of grief over loss or to wrestle with big decisions.

The Diary of a Young Girl by Dutch Jew Anne Frank (1947) contains her life-affirming, nonfictional diary entries from 1942-1944 while her family hid in an attic from World War II's genocidal Nazis. *Go Ask Alice* (1971) by Beatrice Sparks is a cautionary, fictional novel in the form of diary entries by an unhappy, rebellious teen who takes LSD, runs away from home and lives with hippies, and eventually returns home. Frank's writing reveals an intelligent, sensitive, insightful girl, raised by intellectual European parents—a girl who believes in the goodness of human nature despite surrounding atrocities. Character Alice, influenced by early 1970s counterculture, becomes less optimistic. However, similarities can be found: Frank dies in a Nazi concentration camp while the fictitious Alice dies in a drug overdose; both are unable to escape their surroundings. Additionally, adolescent searches for personal identity are evident in both books.

Letters

Letters are messages written to other people. In addition to letters written between individuals, some writers compose letters to the editors of newspapers, magazines, and other publications; some write "Open Letters" to be published and read by the general public. Open letters, while intended for everyone to read, may also identify a group of people or a single person whom the letter directly addresses. In everyday use, the most-used forms are business letters and personal or friendly letters. Both kinds share common elements: business or personal letterhead stationery; the writer's return address at the top; the addressee's address next; a salutation, such as "Dear [name]" or some similar opening greeting, followed by a colon in business letters or a comma in personal letters; the body of the letter, with paragraphs as indicated; and a closing, like "Sincerely/Cordially/Best regards/etc." or "Love," in intimate personal letters.

The Greek word for "letter" is *epistolē*, which became the English word "epistle." The earliest letters were called epistles, including the New Testament's Epistles from the Apostles to the Christians. In ancient Egypt, the writing curriculum in scribal schools included the epistolary genre. Epistolary novels frame a story in the form of letters. For example, 18th-century English novelist Samuel Richardson wrote the popular epistolary novels *Pamela* (1740) and *Clarissa* (1749). Henry Fielding's satire of *Pamela,* entitled *Shamela* (1741) mocked epistolary writing. French author Montesquieu wrote *Lettres persanes* (1721); Jean-Jacques Rousseau wrote *Julie, ou la nouvelle Héloïse* (1761); and Pierre Choderlos de Laclos penned *Les Liaisons dangereuses* (1782), which was adapted into a screenplay for the multiple Oscar-winning 1988 English-language movie *Dangerous Liaisons*. German author Johann Wolfgang von Goethe wrote *The Sorrows of Young Werther* in epistolary form. Frances Brooke also wrote the first North American novel, *The History of Emily Montague* (1769) using epistolary form. In the 19th century, epistolary novels included Honoré de Balzac's *Letters of Two Brides* (1842) and Mary Shelley's *Frankenstein* (1818).

Blogs

The word "blog" is derived from "web log" and refers to writing done exclusively on the Internet. Readers of reputable newspapers expect quality content and layouts that enable easy reading. These expectations also apply to blogs. For example, readers can easily move visually from line to line when columns are narrow; overly wide columns cause readers to lose their places. Blogs must also be posted with layouts enabling online readers to follow them easily. However, because the way people read on computer, tablet, and smartphone screens differs from how they read print on paper, formatting and writing blog content is more complex than writing newspaper articles. Two major principles are the bases for blog-writing rules: (1) While readers of print articles skim to estimate their length, online they must scroll down to scan; therefore, blog layouts need more subheadings, graphics, and other indications of what information follows. (2) Onscreen reading is harder than reading printed paper, so legibility is crucial in blogs.

Rules and Rationales for Writing Blogs

Expert web designer, copywriter, and blogger Annabel Cady (http://www.successfulblogging.com/) shares the following blog-posting rules: Format all posts for smooth page layout and easy scanning. Column width should be a maximum of 80 characters, including spaces, for easier reading. Headings and subheadings separate text visually, enable scanning or skimming, and encourage continued reading. Bullet-pointed or numbered lists enable quick information location and scanning. Punctuation is critical, so beginners should use shorter sentences until confident. Blog paragraphs should be far shorter—two to six sentences each—than paragraphs written on paper to enable "chunking" because reading onscreen is more difficult. Sans serif fonts are usually clearer than serif fonts, and larger font sizes are better. Highlight important material and draw attention with **boldface**, but avoid overuse. Avoid hard-to-read *italics* and ALL CAPITALS. Include enough blank spaces: overly busy blogs tire eyes and brains. Images not only break up text, but also emphasize and enhance text, and can attract initial reader attention. Use background colors judiciously to avoid distracting the eye or making it difficult to read. Be consistent throughout posts, since people read them in different orders. Tell a story with a beginning, middle, and end.

Considerations to Teach Students About Occasions, Purposes, and Audiences

Teachers can explain to students that organizing their ideas, providing evidence to support the points they make in their writing, and correcting their grammar and mechanics are not simply for following writing rules or correctness for its own sake, but rather for ensuring that specific reader audiences understand what they intend to communicate. For example, upper-elementary-grade students writing for lower-elementary-grade students should write in print rather than script, use simpler vocabulary, and avoid writing in long, complex, compound, or complex-compound sentences. The purpose for writing guides word choice, such as encouraging readers to question opposing viewpoints or stimulate empathy and/or sympathy. It also influences narrative, descriptive, expository, or persuasive/argumentative format. For instance, business letters require different form and language than parent thank-you notes. Persuasive techniques, like words that evoke certain reader emotions, description that appeals to reader beliefs, and supporting information can all affect reader opinions.

Questions to Determine Content and Format

When student writers have chosen a viewpoint or idea about which to write, teachers can help them select content to include and the writing format(s) most appropriate to their subject. They should have students ask themselves what their readers need to know to enable them to agree with the viewpoint in the writing, or to believe what the writer is saying. Students can imagine another person hearing them say what they will write about, and responding, "Oh, yeah? Prove that!" Teachers should have students ask themselves what kinds of evidence they need to prove their positions/ideas to skeptical readers. They should have students consider what points might cause the reader to disagree. Students should consider what knowledge their reading audience shares in common with them. They should also consider what information they need to share with their readers. Teachers can have students adapt various writing formats, organizing techniques, and writing styles to different purposes and audiences to practice with choosing writing modes and language.

Appropriate Kinds of Writing for Different Tasks, Purposes, and Audiences

Students who are writing to persuade their parents to grant some additional privilege, such as permission for a more independent activity, should use more sophisticated vocabulary and diction that sounds more mature and serious to appeal to the parental audience. Students who are writing for younger children, however, should use simpler vocabulary and sentence structure, as well as choosing words that are more vivid and entertaining. They should treat their topics more lightly, and include humor as appropriate. Students who are writing for their classmates may use language that is more informal, as well as age-appropriate. Students wanting to convince others to agree with them should use persuasive/argumentative form. Those wanting to share an experience should use descriptive writing. Those wanting to relate a story and what can be learned from it should write narratives. Students can use speculative writing to invite others to join them in exploring ideas.

Main Ideas, Supporting Details, and Outlining a Topic

A writer often begins the first paragraph of a paper by stating the main idea or point, also known as the topic sentence. The rest of the paragraph supplies particular details that develop and support the main point. One way to visualize the relationship between the main point and supporting information is as a table: the tabletop is the main point, and each of the table's legs is a supporting detail or group of details. Both professional authors and students can benefit from planning their writing by first making an outline of the topic. Outlines facilitate quick identification of the main point and supporting details without having to wade through the additional language that will exist in the fully developed essay, article, or paper. Outlining can also help readers to analyze a piece of existing writing for the same reason. The outline first summarizes the main idea in one sentence. Then, below that, it summarizes the supporting details in a numbered list. Writing the paper then consists of filling in the outline with detail, writing a paragraph for each supporting point and adding an introduction and conclusion.

> **Review Video: Topics and Main Ideas**
> Visit mometrix.com/academy and enter code: 407801

Words That Signal Introduction of Successive Details

When a paragraph opens with the topic sentence, the second sentence may begin with a phrase like "First of all," introducing the first supporting detail/example. The writer may introduce the second supporting item with words or phrases like "Also," "In addition," and "Besides." The writer might introduce succeeding pieces of support with wording like, "Another thing," "Moreover" "Furthermore," or "Not only that, but." The writer may introduce the last piece of support with "Lastly," "Finally," or "Last but not least." Writers get off the point by presenting "off-target" items not supporting the main point. For example, a main point "My dog is not smart" is supported by the statement, "He's six years old and still doesn't answer to his name." But "He cries when I leave for school" is not supportive, as it does not indicate lack of intelligence. Writers stay on point by presenting only supportive statements that are directly relevant to and illustrative of their main point.

Paragraphs

A paragraph is a group of sentences that forms a unit separate from (but connected to) other paragraphs. Typically, all of one paragraph's sentences relate to one main idea or point. Two major properties that make paragraphs effective or ineffective are focus and development, or lack thereof. Paragraphs with poor focus impede comprehension because the sentences seem unrelated. When writers attempt to include too many ideas in a paragraph rather than focusing on the most important idea, or fail to supply transitions between ideas, they produce unfocused paragraphs. Undeveloped or inadequately-developed paragraphs may use good writing, but are still not effective. When a writer misunderstands the audience, depends overly on generalization, and fails to offer specific details, paragraph development will be poor. S/he may omit key term definitions, supporting evidence, setting description, context for others' ideas, background, and other important details, falsely assuming that readers already know these things.

Writing Effective Paragraphs

The first thing a writer should do for a good paragraph is to focus on one main idea as the subject. A writer may introduce a paragraph by stating this main idea in a topic sentence. However, the main idea may be so obvious that writers can imply it rather than state it overtly and readers can easily infer it. Second, a writer should use specific details to develop the main idea. Details should capture readers' attention and also explain the author's ideas. Insufficient detail makes a paragraph too abstract, which readers find boring or confusing. Excessive detail makes a paragraph unfocused, which readers find overwhelming and also confusing. Third, a writer should develop paragraphs using structural patterns.

Structural Patterns

Paragraphs have a nearly limitless range of structures, but certain patterns appear more often, including narration, description, definition, example and illustration, division and classification, comparison and contrast, analogy, cause and effect, and process.

Narration, Description, Definition, Example and Illustration, and Division and Classification

In narration, a paragraph's main idea is developed with a story. Writers may use stories as anecdotal evidence to support the main point. In description, the writer constructs a clear image of a scene or event by including specific, sensory and other details that depict a person, thing, place, and/or time. Description shows readers instead of telling them. In definition, the writer provides a detailed explanation of a term that is central to the piece of writing. In example and illustration, the writer provides the readers with one or more examples that illustrate the point that the writer wants to make. Paragraphs using division divide a concept into its component parts—for example, body parts or experiment steps. Paragraphs using classification group separate things into categories by their similarities—such as mammals and insects, tragedies and comedies, and so on.

Comparison and Contrast, Analogy, Cause and Effect, and Process

Paragraphs that compare two or more things make note of their similarities. Paragraphs that contrast two or more things make note of how they differ. Another common paragraph technique is both comparing and contrasting two or more items within the same paragraph, showing both similarities and differences. Analogy compares two things in an unusual way, often things that belong to very different categories. This can afford new reader insight. Writers may use analogies to develop their ideas. Writers also develop their ideas in paragraphs through cause and effect, which either explains what caused some event or result, or shows the effects that something produced. Paragraphs may start with causes and proceed to effects, or begin with effects and then give causes. Process paragraphs describe and/or explain some process. They often sequence the stages, phases, or steps of the process using chronological order.

Coherence

When a paragraph is coherent, the details fit together so that readers can clearly understand the main point, and its parts flow well. Writers produce more coherent paragraphs when they select structural patterns appropriate to the conceptual content. There are several techniques writers can use to make paragraphs more coherent. Repetition connects sentences by repeating key words or phrases. This not only helps sentences flow together, but it also signals to readers the significance of the ideas these words and phrases communicate. Parallelism uses parallel structure, within or between sentences. Humorist Bill Maher once said, "We're feeding animals too sick to stand to people too fat to walk." His parallelism emphasized and connected two issues: the practice of using downed cows as food and the obesity epidemic. Consistency keeps the viewpoint, tone, and linguistic register consistent within the paragraph or piece. Finally, transitions via connective words and phrases aid coherence immensely.

Transitions

Transitions between sentences and paragraphs guide readers from idea to idea. They also indicate relationships between sentences and paragraphs. Writers should be judicious in their use of transitions, inserting them sparingly. They should also be selected to fit the author's purpose—transitions can indicate time, comparison, and conclusion, among other purposes.

> **Review Video: Transitions in Writing**
> Visit mometrix.com/academy and enter code: 233246

Transitional Words and Phrases

Transitional words and phrases indicating time include: afterward, immediately, earlier, meanwhile, recently, lately, now, since, soon, when, then, until, before, etc. Transitions indicating sequence include: too, first, second, further, moreover, also, again, and, next, still, too, besides, and finally. Transitions specifying comparison include: similarly, in the same way, likewise, also, again, and once more. Transitions that indicate contrast include: but, although, despite, however, instead, nevertheless, on the one hand... on the other hand, regardless, yet, and in contrast. Transitions indicating examples include: for example, for instance, such as, to illustrate, indeed, in fact, and specifically. Transitions indicating cause and effect include: because, consequently, thus, therefore, then, to this end, since, so, as a result, if... then, and accordingly.

Transitions indicating place include: near, far, here, there, to the left/right, next to, above, below, beyond, opposite, and beside. Transitions expressing concession include: granted that, naturally, of course, it may appear, and although it is true that. Transitions showing repetition, summary, or conclusion include: as mentioned earlier, as noted, in other words, in short, on the whole, to summarize, therefore, as a result, to conclude, and in conclusion. These tell readers how a sentence relates to the previous ones, and directs their thinking across ideas.

> **Review Video: Transitional Words and Phrases**
> Visit mometrix.com/academy and enter code: 197796

Introduction

Because readers encounter the introduction first, a writer should design the introductory paragraph to capture interest. Introductions should state the main point, thesis, or topic sentence soon and logically. Introductions should also prepare readers for the content of the body. To do this, the topic should first be narrowed to a main idea. The writer should then determine which main points support the main idea, and decide how to order those points. Supporting details can then be organized in sequential order. Some techniques for sequencing include strongest-to-weakest or weakest-to-strongest, logical progression, or sequencing by association. A writer should compose a thesis statement, which may contain the plan for the piece's structure and organization. Then it is time to write the first draft of the body of the document, including transitions between sentences and paragraphs. Finally, the writer creates the introduction, focusing on engaging the reader, integrating the thesis into the introduction, and maintaining the document's organization and structure.

> **Review Video: Introduction**
> Visit mometrix.com/academy and enter code: 961328

Body

In an essay's introduction, the writer establishes the thesis and may indicate how the rest of the piece will be structured. In the body of the piece, the writer elaborates upon, illustrates, and explains the thesis statement. How writers sequence supporting details and their choices of paragraph types are development techniques. Writers may give examples of the concept introduced in the thesis statement. If the subject includes a cause-and-effect relationship, the author may explain its causality. A writer will explain and/or analyze the main idea of the piece throughout the body, often by presenting arguments for the veracity or credibility of the thesis statement. Writers may use development to define or clarify ambiguous terms. Paragraphs within the body may be organized with natural sequences, like space and time. Writers may employ inductive reasoning, using multiple details to establish a generalization or causal relationship, or deductive reasoning, proving a generalized hypothesis or proposition through a specific example/case.

> **Review Video: Drafting Body Paragraphs**
> Visit mometrix.com/academy and enter code: 724590

Conclusion

Two important principles to consider when writing a conclusion are strength and closure. A strong conclusion gives the reader a sense that the author's main points are meaningful and important, and that the supporting facts and arguments are convincing, solid, and well developed. When a conclusion achieves closure, it gives the impression that the writer has stated what needed stating and completed the work, rather than simply stopping after a specified length. Some things to avoid when writing concluding paragraphs include: introducing a completely new idea, beginning with obvious or unoriginal phrases like "In conclusion" or "To summarize," apologizing for one's opinions or writing, repeating the thesis word for word rather than rephrasing it, and believing that the conclusion must always summarize the piece.

> **Review Video: Drafting Conclusions**
> Visit mometrix.com/academy and enter code: 209408

Coherence vs. Cohesion

Cohesive writing flows smoothly, helping readers move easily from sentence to sentence and holding all sentences together. Coherent writing contains sentences that are not only clear individually, but also combine into a unified paragraph or passage. While we are often warned against using passive voice, sometimes a paragraph or passage is more cohesive using a passive construction that allows sentences to flow together better. For example, "Scientists are studying black holes. A black hole is made when a dead star collapses." The passive voice allows repetition of "black hole" from the end of the first sentence to the beginning of the second, connecting this idea. Making one sentence follow from the previous one is the "old-to-new" technique. If the second sentence in active voice read, "When a dead star collapses, it becomes a black hole," the term "black hole" would be farther away from the first sentence and they would not connect or flow as well.

Writers can make text cohesive with the old-to-new principle: starting sentences with familiar information and ending them with new or unexpected information. A paragraph can be cohesive, with ideas flowing smoothly from one sentence to the next, but still not coherent. For example, a writer may connect words or ideas between sentences, but change the subject with each new sentence. When writing is coherent, readers can make sense of paragraphs or passages because sentence ideas integrate into a unified whole with interrelated concepts. Coherent writing enables readers to easily recognize individual sentence topics and understand how they combine into a group of connected ideas. Readers feel more comfortable when sentence topics appear earlier in sentences, and when a sequence of sentences indicates the import of the entire paragraph or passage.

Beginning sentences with familiar information in short and simple phrases, keeping topics consistent, and making obvious transitions between ideas will help produce cohesive and coherent writing.

> **Review Video: Methods to Obtain Coherence in Writing**
> Visit mometrix.com/academy and enter code: 831344

Writing Style and Linguistic Form

Linguistic form encodes the literal meanings of words and sentences. It comes from the phonological, morphological, syntactic, and semantic parts of a language. Writing style consists of different ways of encoding the meaning and indicating figurative and stylistic meanings. Writers' stylistic choices accomplish three basic effects on their audiences: (1) they communicate meanings beyond linguistically dictated meanings, (2) they communicate the author's attitude, such as persuasive/argumentative effects accomplished through style, and (3) they communicate or express feelings. Within style, component areas include: narrative structure; viewpoint; focus; sound patterns; meter and rhythm; lexical and syntactic repetition and parallelism; writing genre;

representational, realistic, and mimetic effects; representation of thought and speech; meta-representation (representing representation); irony; metaphor and other indirect meanings; representation and use of historical and dialectal variations; gender-specific and other group-specific speech styles, both real and fictitious; and analysis of the processes for inferring meaning from writing.

Rubric for Assessing Student Writing

A rubric is a checklist to verify what students have learned or accomplished. Teachers can take lesson objectives to form the basis of a rubric. The teacher should explain the rubric to the students before they begin a writing assignment. During their writing exercise, the students can refer to the rubric to guide what and how they write. After the students have completed their writing assignments, the teacher can then apply the rubric to assess their work, checking to see if they have met all of the learning objectives. Students will be less confused and frustrated when teachers have given them well-planned, clearly expressed guidelines. In addition to clearly stating clearly their learning goals, objectives, and expectations for each assignment, teachers should model the kind of performance they expect. Teachers should connect lesson and assignment goals obviously and clearly with student achievement.

Summative and Formative Assessments

Summative assessments evaluate what a student can demonstrate s/he has learned at the end of a lesson, unit, course, or term. Final examinations are an example. Formative assessments are ongoing evaluations to demonstrate what a student is in the process of learning and has learned thus far. Formative assessments are not just for evaluation: they are also important for use in the classroom as a teaching tool. As teachers conduct ongoing evaluations via formative assessments, they should use both formal and informal assessment instruments. Teachers should never use only one formal or informal assessment of a class as a reason to group students on a permanent basis. They should only place students into groups after administering, scoring, and interpreting a number of different assessments. Teachers should also create student groups that take into account individual differences among the students in every group, and should accordingly make these groupings sufficiently flexible to accommodate individual student differences.

Observation

Observational assessment is appropriate for evaluating student progress and effectiveness of instruction. A teacher can create a checklist of skills, requirements, or competencies that students should attain. The teacher can then observe individuals or student groups and check off the skills or competencies demonstrated. For example, if a teacher has been instructing a class in listening carefully, s/he can compose a checklist with items such as paying attention, refraining from interrupting others, summarizing what ideas the other students have expressed, and asking questions of other students. The teacher can then initiate student discussion and observe, checking off the checklist items s/he observes the students performing. Or, when teaching interview skills, a teacher can make a checklist including confidence, personal appearance, mannerisms, and directly answering interviewer questions. S/he can also observe students participating in mock or real interviews and identify which items the students satisfy.

By observing students as they work on assignments or practice exercises, teachers can obtain valuable information. With kindergarten and first-grade classes, many school districts inform parents of children's progress by filling out "report cards" or inventories. Through experience, long-term teachers typically develop their own methods of making ongoing skills assessments of their students. Books about reading instruction typically include informal reading assessments. Experts recommend that teachers assess student progress in naturalistic ways on a continual basis. They find that teachers and parents continually observing students regarding their status and progress in the physical, cognitive, emotional, and social domains yields the most relevant assessment—particularly with young children. Experts also approve of portfolio assessments and performance assessments for more complete pictures of overall progress than standardized test scores. They also find that writing narrative reports about young children depicts the whole child better than giving them number and/or letter grades.

<u>Observational Checklists</u>

In informal assessment, using observational checklists to identify skills attained has an advantage over formal written tests because informal, naturalistic observation enables teachers to record behaviors that traditional written tests cannot include. For example, if teachers want to know whether students can follow all steps of a science experiment in the correct sequence, how many baskets they can make in free throws on the basketball court, or whether they can remember all of the significant parts to include in a speech they write and deliver to the class, they can record these by observing and marking such items on a checklist they have designed in advance—but they could not record any such behaviors through standard "pencil-and-paper" tests. The structure of checklists has the advantage of being consistent, but also the disadvantage of being inflexible. Teachers can remedy the latter by including a place at the end of the checklist to write open-ended comments on their observations of student performance.

Running Record

To identify what students are able and unable to do, one informal assessment measure teachers can use is a running record. For example, the teacher can listen to a student reading aloud from text such as an essay, a speech, a novel, or a class subject textbook. While listening, the teacher marks a copy of the text to show words the student mispronounces. The teacher draws a line through each word the student skips and draws an arrow under words the student repeats. Teachers may also mark student hesitations at certain words. If the teacher then calculates that the student correctly read 95 percent of the words, the student reads this text at the Independent level. If the student correctly reads 90-94 percent of the words, s/he reads this text at the Instructional level, indicating satisfactory performance with teacher assistance. Correctly reading 89 percent or fewer words indicates the Frustration level, where comprehension may be inadequate.

Anecdotal Records

Anecdotal records can provide good information for formative assessments. For example, when students conduct science experiments or complete class projects, teachers can use anecdotal records to instruct them in writing reports to explain the procedures they followed. When students in group learning activities solve a problem together, teachers can use anecdotal records to document the process used. Such anecdotal documents not only provide the teacher with formative assessment information, but teachers can also use them to give feedback to the group of students. Two disadvantages of using anecdotal records is that they can take more time for teachers to complete than other informal assessments and that it can be hard to use them for assigning grades. Two advantages are that anecdotal records can encompass all pertinent information, whereas other assessments may not, and that teachers may use them only for giving students feedback, which eliminates the need to base grades on them.

Portfolio Assessment

In portfolio assessment, teachers and/or students create a folder or box and deposit a student's best work products, accumulated over time. In language arts, teachers often collect student writing samples in portfolios for a whole year. Some language arts teachers additionally transmit year-long portfolios to the following year's teacher to aid in student assessment. Teachers can use portfolio assessments in any subject to enable students to assume greater responsibility for planning, organizing, and implementing what they learn. The combined products in the portfolio afford concise depictions of what students have achieved during specific time periods. Portfolios can include handwritten and/or printed essays, stories, and articles; videos; or computer files of multimedia presentations. Teachers should help students develop guidelines about which materials to place in portfolios, and how to self-assess their own work. The advantages of portfolios over tests include helping students develop self-assessment skills, giving clearer pictures of student progress, and learning from mistakes without the damage of a bad test grade.

Research-Based Strategies to Teach Effective Writing

Experts have reviewed multiple controlled, valid and reliable studies of writing instruction strategies that met research quality standards. These studies identify teaching strategies that improve overall writing performance. Some of these include: explicitly teaching students techniques to plan, revise, and edit their writing, and including activities such as brainstorming steps to follow for writing argumentation essays. Teacher modeling and independent student practice of strategies are recommended. Summarizing text is an effective strategy for helping students practice writing clearly, concisely, and accurately about main text ideas. Teachers can teach this explicitly or model it. Collaborative writing helps students plan, write, edit, and revise writing cooperatively. Teachers should supply structure and individual performance expectations within groups. Classmates can take turns reviewing each other's writing, giving both positive feedback for reinforcement and constructive feedback for improvement. Setting specific goals for writing assignments promotes motivation and accomplishment. Teachers and students can develop goals, such as incorporating certain genre elements or including more ideas in a paper.

A computer word processing program is a valuable student resource for planning, writing, and editing compositions. Another strategy is explicitly instructing students to produce more sophisticated and complex sentences via sentence combining. Teachers model combining two or more related sentences and encourage students to apply these skills when writing compositions. The process writing approach is a strategy in which teachers give students opportunities for extended practice with planning, writing, and review. Students interact throughout the process of writing, self-evaluating and taking personal responsibility for their writing. They are writing for authentic reader or listener audiences. Inquiry strategies include setting clear goals for writing and examining concrete data, such as observing others and documenting their own responses. Inquiry strategies may also include application of learning to compositions. Prewriting strategies help students generate and organize ideas, access background knowledge, research topics, and/or visualize their ideas graphically. Another strategy is giving students good models of expected writing types, analyzing models with students, and inviting students to emulate effective and critical model elements in their own writing.

Some researchers have found that students with writing challenges achieve strongly positive results when teachers explicitly model composition strategies and the writing process for them. When students collaborate with classmates and participate in conferences with teachers who give useful feedback, student writing improves. Using mnemonic devices, checklists, graphic organizers, outlines, and other procedural strategies can help students plan and revise their writing. Students who have difficulties with transcribing text benefit from dictation and other ways of limiting those obstacles. Teaching students to ask themselves questions and make self-statements enhances their self-regulation abilities, which also promotes writing improvement. Studies find that cognitive strategies aid students of all ability levels and ages. Teaching self-regulation increases maintenance and generalization of writing strategies by improving self-reflection and self-awareness of writing strengths and weaknesses. Additionally, it promotes more strategic writing efforts and better self-management of inhibiting emotions and behaviors, as well as empowerment to adapt strategies as needed. Explicit instruction, modeling, think-aloud sessions, and scaffolding are effective; exposure to writing processes alone is not enough.

Informative/Explanatory Writing

Instructional Methods to Guide Student Writing

Teachers can use mentor texts, which they can find from multiple everyday sources, and align them with the writing standards for their students' grade levels. Teachers can compose informative and/or explanatory text in front of their classes to model composition for them. They can use the "thinking out loud" technique for additional modeling. This demonstrates the process of defining and expressing ideas clearly in writing and supporting those ideas with details like explanations, descriptions, definitions, examples, anecdotes, and processes. Teachers should employ scaffolding with students: They begin with explicit instruction, proceed to modeling, and then provide activities for practice. These activities can include guided writing exercises, shared writing experiences, cooperative practice (collaborating with classmates), feedback that refers to the learning objectives that the teachers have established, or peer conferences.

Guidelines for Grades K-5

Teachers can pose questions related to the content area subjects they are teaching for students to answer, and they can invite and make use of interesting elementary-grade student questions like, "Why did immigrants come to America?" "Why does my face turn red in cold weather?" or "Why does my dog drool?" In lower elementary grades, students may choose or be assigned topics, give some definitions and facts about the topics, and write concluding statements. Students in upper elementary grades should be able to introduce topics, focus them, group information logically, develop topics with enough details, connect ideas, use specific academic vocabulary, and write conclusions. To develop these skills, students must have many opportunities for researching information and writing informative/explanatory text. Experts on writing standards recommend that roughly one-third of elementary student writing be informative/explanatory text. Children must read informational texts with depth and breadth, and use writing as a learning tool, to fulfill the objective of building knowledge through reading and writing.

Expectations and Recommendations for Grades 6-12

Standards expect high school students to use informative/explanatory text to communicate and investigate complex concepts, information, and ideas. They should be able to effectively choose, analyze, and organize content and to write accurately and clearly. Informative/explanatory text is recommended to comprise approximately 40 percent of high school students' writing across curriculum content subjects. Teachers can present brief mentor texts that use informative writing in creative, engaging form to students as demonstrations. Using mentor texts as templates, teachers can model composing similar texts about other topics. Teachers then have students apply this format to write about topics the students select, giving them support and/or scaffolding. Thereafter, teachers can have students write short texts on various topics that necessitate using prior knowledge and doing research. "Thinking aloud" to model the cognitive writing process is also important. Some experts also recommend that teachers assign frequent short research instead of traditional longer library-research term papers. Authentic writing tasks include conducting and reporting survey/interview research, producing newspaper front pages, and composing web pages.

Research-Based Assessment Techniques

Assessment of Student Learning

To assess student attitudes, educators can create various situations and observe and document their responses, requiring students to make choices among behaviors to demonstrate. To assess cognitive strategies, teachers can give students learning tasks, require them to select useful strategies for learning new information independently, and expect them to explain and discuss what methods they use for different learning tasks. To assess student comprehension, teachers give them topics and ask them to restate and summarize information. Or teachers may have students apply information in new contexts, such as giving statements with different words than the original lesson and asking students to identify the meanings. To assess student concept understanding, teachers give students new examples and "non-examples," having students classify these into the right categories. To assess student creativity, teachers can give students new problems—including products, presentations, or performances—to study, resolve, or "turn upside down." They can also have students fit solutions and products into specified resources and functions and give them situations that require novel responses or approaches.

Assessment of Different Student Outcomes

To assess student critical thinking, teachers can ask students to evaluate outcomes or information and have them perform research and analysis. To assess student insight, teachers should give opportunities to engage in inquiry and discovery activities, and offer situations for students to manipulate. To assess student metacognition, teachers should give a variety of problems or situations to address, and assign students to identify different kinds of thinking strategies for analysis and evaluation of their own thought processes. To assess multiple intelligences (cf. Gardner), teachers should give students learning experiences in each of the modalities they target, like verbal, musical, and physical. They should offer students choices of several different modalities. They should also require students to perform in the modalities selected. To assess motor skills, teachers must supply resources and situations in which students can perform the skills while the teachers evaluate, using checklists. To assess problem-solving, teachers ask students to choose appropriate strategies to solve different problem situations including simple, complex, structured, and unstructured.

Assessment of Procedural Knowledge, Scientific Inquiry, Thinking Skills, and Verbal Knowledge

To assess student knowledge of principles, rules, and procedures, teachers supply situations that require students to identify these correctly with everyday problems. Students are asked to state principles, rules, and procedures, and choose which apply to various scenarios. To assess student scientific inquiry skills, teachers give problems or situations that require students to speculate, inquire, and formulate hypotheses. Teachers should also give hands-on activities to conduct research and draw conclusions. To assess student thinking skills, teachers can ask students to give summaries of different kinds of thinking strategies. They provide situations in which students must select the best thinking strategies to apply. Teachers assign students to observe examples of open-mindedness versus closed-mindedness, accurate versus inaccurate, and responsible versus irresponsible applications of thinking methods. Teachers can design scenarios requiring student persistence for analyzing and discovering answers, as well as application of thinking strategies in real-life circumstances. To assess verbal knowledge, teachers require information recall, restatement, and comprehension.

Teaching Strategies to Address Student and Family Diversity

Teachers must recognize that each student is unique. When a teacher respects individual student differences, s/he communicates this attitude to the class. Research finds that cultural differences influence human behavior, and thus play a part in classrooms. Acknowledgement of cultural differences helps to prevent student isolation. To educate students from diverse backgrounds, teachers need to understand a student's culture and individual characteristics—as well as disabilities when these exist. Teacher and school involvement with students' families promotes student success during and after school. This requires educators to avoid ethnocentric approaches. Diverse families may need instruction in the school culture of collaboration and communication. Schools also must initially meet family needs physically, socially, and economically to enable involvement, requiring school knowledge of supportive community programs. Communications must be translated for families speaking different languages. Educators need willingness to interact outside of school hours and grounds. They can also recruit parent liaisons with similar cultural backgrounds. Teachers should open parent communications with positive feedback about children.

Inclusive educational programs require meaningful, effective collaboration of educators, students, and families. Teachers must not only meet student and family needs, but they must also communicate their own needs effectively and be willing to find solutions through team-based approaches. Collaboration allows outcomes that individuals cannot achieve alone. Researchers have discovered that despite the challenges of cooperation among staff members, the more teachers interact with each other, the greater educational change is achieved successfully. Understanding of cultural communication differences, respectful disagreement, respect for confidentiality, willingness to compromise, responsible communication of opinions and emotions (such as using "I" statements), tolerance for others' various perspectives, and careful listening to others are communication skills needed for effective communication and collaboration. Some educators advocate multicultural awareness days involving all school personnel, families, and community members when each school year starts. Culturally responsive standards-based instruction (CRSBI) incorporates caring, communication, and curriculum. Educators must also foster positive student-teacher relationships, and assure positive role models for every student.

Creating Safe Educational Environments

Teachers need to establish and sustain classroom environments for students in which they feel nurtured and know that the teacher is open to hearing their feelings, thoughts, and ideas. Teachers are responsible for developing respect for individual differences and openness to discussions in their classrooms. They may need to explain the difference between fairness and equality. For example, students who need eyeglasses cannot be deprived of them, but neither should all students be made to wear them. Teachers can use such examples to illustrate to students that fairness does not mean everybody gets the same treatment: while every student deserves help, that help will differ for different students. Teachers must create student-teacher relationships of mutual trust, and ensure that all students know the teachers care about them, both academically and personally. Teacher beliefs, attitudes, and performance expectations, and how teachers communicate these, establish this knowledge. Teachers must know student and family languages, communication styles, and home literacy practices, and build on these in their classrooms.

Speaking and Listening

Speaking

Speeches are written to be delivered in spoken language in public, to various groups of people, at formal or informal events. Some generic types include welcome speeches, thank-you speeches, keynote addresses, position papers, commemorative and dedication speeches, and farewell speeches. Speeches are commonly written in present tense. Speeches begin with an introduction, greeting the audience. At official functions, specific audience members are named ("Chairperson [name]," "Principal [name], teachers, and students," etc.) and when audiences include a distinguished guest, s/he is often named as well. Then the speaker introduces him/herself by name, position, and department or organization as applicable. After the greeting, the speaker then introduces the topic and states the purpose of the speech. The body of the speech follows, similarly to the body of an essay, stating its main points, their elaboration, and supporting evidence. Finally, in the conclusion, the speaker states his/her hope for accomplishing the speech's purpose and thanks the audience for attending and listening to the speech.

Educational Benefits of Digital Media

Digital media are powerful because they are flexible, versatile, and can be transformed, marked, and networked. For example, printed ink on paper and paint on canvas are permanent. However, digital images of these—while they sacrifice physical texture and some visual depth and tone—have the advantage that they can be displayed on anything from a giant public video screen, to a computer monitor, to a smartphone screen, around the world. Digital images can also be manipulated to sharpen, blur, darken/lighten, or alter portions. Images, text, and voice can be saved exactly and reliably over time periods, and also adapted or changed as needed for teaching. Digital media are not limited to text and pictures as books are: they also include video and audio, and can combine video and sound with text. Students can interact with multiple media at once, choose preferred formats, and adapt the media to help with learning difficulties.

Unlike hard copies, digitally-saved materials can be linked to each other. Embedded hyperlinks afford many learning supports to students, such as dictionaries, thesauruses, encyclopedias, reading comprehension prompts, supplementary materials to build student background knowledge, visual graphic organizers, and electronic notepads for keeping running notes. Students can rapidly navigate between words in a text and their dictionary definitions, images and their descriptions, videos and their captions, or passages of text and their audio recordings. Another advantage for teachers and students is that websites and pages are often constantly updated in real time. Educators and learners can access information and opinions contributed by a wide variety of peers, experts, and mentors—not just locally, but globally. Multimedia packages enable students to have multisensory experiences rather than simply reading print. Access is almost instantaneous. Networking affords teachers and students interconnected communication and information, plus formats and experiences that can be customized to the diversity of individual learners.

Transforming and Marking Digital Media

Students can use within-media transformations to change how website content is displayed by turning graphics or sound on or off, adjust volume, and change text and image appearance by using different browsers or adjusting browser settings. Cross-media transformations can use software to convert speech to text or text to speech, and can do so automatically by embedding into other software and browsers. This helps students with vision and hearing problems, auditory processing

- 89 -

deficits, and reading or learning disabilities. HTML (Hypertext Markup Language) and XML (Extensible Markup Language), both used in web design, enable students to adjust font, etc., to accommodate different learning needs. For example, students can underline all summary sentences in detailed texts, and teachers can italicize all English words with Greek or Latin roots, or boldface all metaphors. Unlike highlightings on paper, digital markups can be hidden, displayed, expanded, deleted, and changed as needed.

Instructional Videos

Instructional videos have potential for excellent two-way communication because questions and feedback can be built in. Videos can be targeted to particular audiences, and they can be paused for discussion or replayed to reinforce concepts. Students can see processes, including "before," "during," and "after" phases. Videos are accessible, because most communities have at least one DVD player or computer. Moreover, video players and computers are continually becoming less expensive to buy and use. Disadvantages include the necessity of editing software and equipment in some cases, as well as support from other print materials. There is also danger of overuse if other media or methods could be more appropriate, and higher up-front costs. Producers must account for the costs of script development and hiring local performers as needed.

DVDs and CDs

Interactive DVDs and CDs, such as games, give viewers the potential to participate, and are becoming increasingly popular. They are commonly used to target specific audiences, such as young people. Additionally, videos are considered to be a professional method of sharing information. Compared to many other media formats, discs are comparatively inexpensive to make, and are easy to transport due to their small size and weight. They are more resistant to damage and aging than older videotape technology, making them more durable. Some disadvantages include needing computer access to produce and play, and certain software programs to produce, especially if the producer wants to include video animation and audio commentary. Producers must also consider the time of paid staff and production and labeling expenses.

Media and Format Choices

Effective communication depends on choosing the correct method. Media and format choices are influenced by the target audience, the budget, and the needs of the audience.

> **Review Video: Media**
> Visit mometrix.com/academy and enter code: 785859

Television and Radio

Two media types are television and radio. Both are high-status mass media that reach many people. TV has the broadest reach: it can market to the general public or be customized for target audiences, while radio reaches specific target audiences. TV has the advantage of video plus audio, while audio only is one radio disadvantage. Both are useful for communicating simple slogans and messages, and both can generate awareness, interest, and excitement. However, television is more expensive than radio. Also, both TV and radio audiences can only interact directly during call-in programs. Programming times may be inconvenient, but tape, digital sound, and digital video recording (DVR) can remedy this.

Newspapers

Except for the occasional community columns, news releases, and letters to the editor, newspaper pages and features afford little opportunity for audience input or participation. However, they reach and appeal to the literate public, though the general public is unlikely to read them. Cost is an advantage: hiring a PR writer and paying for a news advertisement costs much less than a radio or TV spot. Additionally, newspaper features are high-status, and audiences can reread and review them as often as they like. However, newspaper ads may have difficulty affecting the reader as deeply without audio or video, and they require a literate audience. Their publication is also subject to editors' whims and biases. Newspaper pieces combining advertising and editorial— "advertorials"—afford inclusion of paid material, but are viewed as medium-status and cost more.

Internet Websites and Blogs, and Mobile Phones and Text Messaging

Computer literacy is required for online material, but participation potential is high via websites, e-networking, list-serves, and blogging. Mobile phones and text messaging have potential for enormous direct, public, two-way and one-on-one communication, with timely information and reminders. Web media need a literate public and can be tailored for specific audiences. They afford global information, are accessible by increasingly technology-literate populations, and are high-status. Web media disadvantages include the necessity of computers and people to design, manage, and supply content, as well as to provide technical support. Mobile and text media are globally popular, but appeal especially to certain demographics like teens and young adults. They are increasingly available, especially in rural regions, and are decreasing in cost. Mobile and text media disadvantages include required brevity in texts and provider messaging charges. List-serves can be inexpensive as well as reaching a broad audience through email. Links to related websites and pages within existing sites are also advantages.

Public Presentations and PowerPoint

Public presentations have great potential for audience participation and can directly target various audiences. They can encourage the establishment of partnerships and groups, stimulate local ownership of issues and projects, and make information public. A drawback to public presentations is that they are limited to nights, weekends, or whenever audiences are available, and do not always attract the intended audience.

Another method of presentation is to use PowerPoints. These presentations are best for sophisticated audiences like professionals, civil servants, and service organizations. Well-designed PowerPoint presentations are good for stimulating audience interest, selling ideas, and marketing purposes. Also, they are accessible online as well as in-person so can reach a broader audience. PowerPoint disadvantages include the necessity of projectors and other equipment. Also, they are limited to communicating more general points, outlines, and summaries rather than conveying a multitude of information in more detail.

Posters and Brochures

Both posters and brochures can target audiences of the general public and more specific public sectors. Posters are better for communicating simple slogans and messages, while brochures can include more detail and are better for printing instructional information. Both can be inexpensive to produce, especially if printed only as needed and in-house. Posters can often be printed in-house without using outside printing companies. However, it is difficult to get feedback on both posters and brochures—unless they have been broadly tested, or if their publication is accompanied by workshops and other participatory events. Disadvantages of posters include the simplicity required of their messages, and the requirement of literacy in written language and visual elements to understand them. Disadvantages of brochures include their limitations of distribution to specific groups or areas and, like posters, also requiring literacy.

<u>Flyers and Fact Sheets</u>

Flyers and fact sheets have one-way communication potential because readers cannot give feedback. Their target audiences are general. Some advantages of using this form of media include flexibility: people can distribute them at meetings or events, put them on car windshields in parking lots, leave them in stores or on bulletin boards at community agencies and schools, hand them out from booths and other displays, or mail them. When printed in black and white, they can be very inexpensive. They afford recipients the convenience of being able to review them at their leisure. Organizations and individuals can produce flyers and fact sheets in-house, or even at home with desktop publishing software. Disadvantages include their limitation to single facts or tips and specific information on specified topics.

Evaluating Speeches for Concise Information

To convince or persuade listeners and/or reinforce a message, speeches must be succinct. Audiences become confused by excessive anecdotes and details. If a speaker takes three minutes or more to get to the point, audience attention will flag, and will only worsen when details are off the subject. When answering a question, the asker and speaker may even forget the original question if the speaker takes too long. Speakers should practice not only rehearsing written speeches, but also developing skill for spontaneous question-and-answer sessions after speeches. Speakers should differentiate necessary from simply interesting information because brains will stop processing input beyond a certain limit, to prevent overload. Speakers should know what point(s) they wish to make. They should not be afraid to pause before responding to questions, which indicates thoughtfulness and control rather than lack of knowledge. Restating questions increases comprehension and appropriate responses, and allows time to form answers mentally.

Clearly Written Prose and Speeches

To achieve clarity, a writer or speaker must first define his/her purpose carefully. The speech should be organized logically, so that sentences make sense and follow each other in an understandable order. Sentences must also be constructed well, with carefully chosen words and structure. Organizing a speech in advance using an outline provides the writer/speaker with a blueprint, directing and focusing the composition to meet its intended purpose. Organized speeches enable audiences to comprehend and retain the presented information more easily. Humans naturally seek to impose order on the world by seeking patterns. Hence, when ideas in a speech are well-organized and adhere to a consistent pattern, the speaker communicates better with listeners and is more convincing. Speechwriters can use chronological patterns to organize events, sequential patterns to organize processes by their steps, and spatial patterns to help audiences visualize geographical locations and movements or physical scenarios. Also, comparison-contrast patterns give audiences insight about similarities and differences between and among topics, especially when listeners are more familiar with one than the other.

Organizational Patterns for Speeches

A speechwriter who uses an advantages-disadvantages pattern of organization presents the audience with the pros and cons of a topic. This aids writers in discussing two sides of an issue objectively without an argumentative position, enabling listeners to weigh both aspects. When a speechwriter uses a cause-and-effect pattern, it can help to persuade audiences to agree with an action or solution by showing significant relationships between factors. Writers may separate an outline into two main "cause" and "effect" sections, or separate it separate sections for each cause, including the effect for each. Persuasive writing also benefits from problem-solution patterns: by establishing the existence of a problem, writers induce audiences to realize a need for change. By supplying a solution and supporting its superiority above other solutions, the writer convinces audiences of the value of that solution. When none of these patterns—or chronological, sequential, spatial, or comparison-contrast patterns—applies, speechwriters often use topical patterns. These organize information by various subtopics and types within the main topic or category.

Effective Speech Delivery

Speakers should deliver speeches in a natural, conversational manner rather than being rigidly formal or theatrical. Effective delivery is also supported by confidence. Speakers should be direct, building audience rapport through personal connection and vivid imagery. Speakers should be mindful of the occasion, subject, and audience of their speeches and take care to use appropriate language. Good speakers learn vocal control, including loudness, speed, pitch, use of pauses, tonal variety, correct pronunciation, and clear articulation. They can express enthusiasm and emphasize important points with their voices. Nonverbal behaviors, such as eye contact, facial expressions, gestures, good posture and body movements clarify communication, stress important ideas, and influence perceptions that the speaker is trustworthy, competent, and credible. Nonverbal communications should seem as spontaneous and natural as vocal or verbal ones. Speakers should know their speeches well and practice frequently, taking care to avoid nervous or irrelevant movements such as tapping or pacing.

Techniques to Ensure Active Listening and Productive Participation

When assigning students to participate in cooperative learning projects and/or discussions, teachers should consider their cognitive, emotional, behavioral, and social developmental levels. If a teacher assigns a topic for age levels younger than the class, students will be bored and unengaged. If the topic assigned is for older age levels, they will be confused, overwhelmed, or lost. Before initiating class or group discussions, teachers should model and explain appropriate behaviors for discussions—particularly for students unfamiliar or inexperienced with these. For example, teachers can demonstrate active listening, including eye contact, affirming or confirming the speaker's message, and restating the speaker's message for confirmation or correction. Teachers should establish clear ground rules, such as not interrupting others when they are speaking, not monopolizing the conversation, not engaging in cross-talk, not insulting classmates verbally, and taking turns and waiting for appropriate times to make comment. For young children and students with behavioral issues, this would also include refraining from physical contact like hitting, kicking, and biting.

Active Student Listening

Active listening has multiple dimensions. It involves constructing meaning out of what is heard, being reflective and creative in considering and manipulating information, and making competent decisions rich in ideas. The natural properties of speech and thought are conducive to active listening: the typical speed of speaking is roughly 125 words per minute, whereas the estimated speed of thinking is roughly 500 words per minute. Therefore, students have around 375 words per minute of spare time to think about the speech they hear. As an educator (Carbone, in TILT Posts 2013-2014) points out, students' minds can wander during this extra time, so teachers should instruct them to use the time instead to summarize lecture information mentally—a form of active listening. Listening and learning are both social and reciprocal. They also both allow and require students to process and consider what they hear and stimulate their curiosity about subsequent information.

Whole-Class Learning Circles

Forming whole classes into learning circles requires student application of skills for listening to lectures, synthesizing information, and summarizing the information. Teachers can prepare students by articulating central discussion points; identifying next steps in thought, question forming, analysis, and action; guiding student analysis and construction of meaning from what they have read, observed, and experienced; and asking students questions beginning with "What?" "Why?" and "Now what?" Basic ground rules for learning circles include: (1) No student interrupts another. (2) Students may skip a turn until others have taken turns, but no student speaks out of turn. (3) Each student has a certain length of time for speaking. (4) Each student starts by restating what was said previously (e.g., summarizing shared points, differing points, missed points, or points not discussed fully). (5) After every student has had one turn, general discussion is open, possibly guided by teacher-provided questions.

Procedures and Ground Rules for Smaller Groups

Teachers can develop student discussion skills integrating listening, reading, and speaking skills by assigning small discussion groups to tackle assigned problems. Teachers may use established groups, assign new groups, or allow students to form groups of 4-5 students. Teachers read a text passage, describe a scenario, or pose a question for discussion. They give students several minutes to review homework/notes, briefly read new related material, and/or review essay drafts. Teachers then give each student in each group a specified number of uninterrupted minutes to speak in turn. After every student has taken a turn, the teacher opens general discussion, setting the following ground rules: (1) Students can only speak about others' ideas. (2) Teachers and classmates can ask students to clarify their ideas, give examples, connect them more closely to what they read, or elaborate. (3) Small groups can summarize overall points for other groups, including shared points, differences, and potential topics they missed.

Incorporating Active Student Listening into Lessons

At the beginning of each day (or class), teachers should clarify the "big picture" and identify the learning objectives incorporated into the day's activities. They should also give students a single word or phrase to summarize the prior day's subject and a single word or phrase to preview the current day's subject. Teachers should not only establish this recall, retrieval, prediction, and planning process as a daily habit, but should also encourage students to develop the same daily habit in their note-taking. Teachers should review main concepts and/or have students summarize the last lecture's main ideas to make connections with preceding lessons. By encouraging and guiding student listening, teachers supply spoken transitions analogously to those in written research. By cueing students to take notes with questions or summaries at the ends of sections, teachers also help students demonstrate their comprehension.

Teachers can allow students to take photos, videos, and audio recordings of lessons to review as needed. To encourage students to reword and recall instructional input, teachers can let students download class outlines from GoogleDocs, including hard-to-spell terminology or vocabulary words, jargon of specific disciplines, and links reminding students to follow up by accessing resources and readings to inform notes they take. Teachers should give outlines a two-column format: on the right, a wider column with teacher notes, to which students can add, and on the left, a narrower column for students to record notes and questions about previous lectures and reading. Teachers should advise students to take their own notes in similar formats. Students and teachers alike can learn through speaking, writing, listening, and reading when they contribute narratives to supplement visual graphics (photos, concept maps, charts, advance organizers, illustrations, diagrams, etc.) that support the concepts they analyze and explain.

Educator Techniques for Classroom Discussions

Students who feel comfortable with the teacher and the class are more likely to engage in open discussion. Teachers can encourage student openness and creativity by learning students' names and by posing questions rather than making comments. Lively discussions with all students participating are evidence that students are comfortable. A variety of student answers is evidence that the questioning technique works. When student discussions stray off the subject, learning goals will not be met. Teachers can redirect discussion by restating topics and questions previously announced, and by introducing new questions related to identified topics. When conversation refocuses on stated topics, teachers can identify specified learning goals/objectives students are meeting in their discussion. In most classes, a few students will dominate conversations. Teachers can pose less challenging questions, which can be answered even without preparation, to engage more reticent students, and then graduate to higher-level questions. They can evaluate all students' participation using attendance roll-based checklists.

Teaching Strategies to Encourage Discussion

During class discussions, students often contribute erroneous information. Teachers must be tactful in correcting them. If students withdraw from the conversation or cease further contributions, the teacher has not corrected them appropriately. If corrected students continue to contribute, the teacher has succeeded in providing positive reinforcement rather than punishment with the correction. Some ways to do this include acknowledging how the student came to a conclusion but explaining that it does not apply to the current context, or explaining how the student's response might be correct in another situation. Teachers can also provide incentives for students to contribute to class discussions. They may incorporate participation in the syllabus as part of the grade, keep records to tally when each student contributes to a discussion, or assign different students to lead class discussions in turn. These are some ways teachers can evaluate individual student participation in classroom discussions, as well as their own effectiveness in encouraging such participation.

Students often feel intimidated if "put on the spot" to answer questions without warning. Teachers can put them at ease by allowing time to prepare. They can announce topics and questions for class discussion, giving students five minutes to jot notes for responses and another five minutes for exchanging and reflecting on notes with classmates before beginning whole-class conversation. Teachers may distribute discussion topics at the end of one class for the next day's conversation or post questions online the night before class. One technique for evaluating discussion is asking students early in the term to write papers about the characteristics of good and bad class discussions, and then talk about these. Teachers then compose a list of classroom discussion goals and give copies to all students. Another technique is an informal survey: ask students midway through the semester to evaluate the overall quality of class discussions. Share responses with the class, and inform them of plans incorporating their feedback to enhance discussions.

Teachers can encourage in-class discussion by promoting group meetings and discussions outside the classroom. Interacting with students outside class also promotes a sense of community. Teachers demonstrate to students that they care about them as individuals and about their educational development by asking them about their holiday/summer plans, about how they are feeling during midterm and final exam periods, and about their other classes. Teachers can find

- 95 -

online articles related to class material and e-mail or text links to these for review. They can allow time at the beginnings of classes for announcements. They can also arrange classroom chairs in a semicircle to encourage conversation. These methods are all found effective in promoting a sense of community, which in turn encourages class discussions. To address different student learning styles and abilities, teachers can vary the levels and types of questions they ask them: asking them to give simple information, describe, compare, analyze, justify, compare, generalize, predict, or apply information.

Constructed Response

This section contains 10 example constructed response prompts to practice essay writing, along with sample responses. The specific examples or specific interpretations used in the sample responses should not be considered the only correct examples or interpretations that could be used to respond to such a prompt on the exam.

Using Examples from Dante's *Divine Comedy*, Explain the Role of Religious Allegory in Medieval/Renaissance Literature.

In allegory, authors use literal plot elements as symbols to represent more abstract subjects. For example, in *The Divine Comedy*, Dante symbolizes the human soul's efforts to achieve moral beliefs and behaviors and become united with God by narrating his persona's adventures as he travels through the kingdoms of Hell, Purgatory, and Heaven (*Inferno, Purgatorio,* and *Paradiso*). What appear to be literal stories of fantasy experiences are allegorical references to the human spiritual quest. The opening of *Inferno* sets the tone: "Midway on our life's journey, I found myself / In dark woods, the right road lost." By the plural first-person possessive in "*our* life's journey," Dante connects his persona's story to the universal human experience, reinforcing this by referring to "the right road" of which he has lost track. The "dark woods" are an allegorical symbol of a human being's sinful, unenlightened earthly existence and the "right road" symbolizes the life of virtue that unites people with God.

The Epigraph to T.S. Eliot's "The Love Song of J. Alfred Prufrock" is Taken from Dante's *Inferno*. Using this Example, Discuss How a Poet Might Inform his Work Using a Quote from Another Source.

In "The Love Song of J. Alfred Prufrock", Eliot's six-line epigraph is from Canto 27 of Dante's *Inferno.* Eliot quotes Dante's original Italian, spoken by Guido da Montefeltro: "*S'io credesse che mia risposta fosse / A persona che mai tornasse al mondo, / Questa fiamma staria senza piu scosse. /Ma percioche giammai di questo fondo/Non torno vivo alcun, s'i'odo il vero, / Senza tema d'infamia ti rispondo.*" Eliot omits translation: "If I believed my answer would be to a person who could return to the world, this flame would stay without more motion; but because nobody has ever come back alive from this abyss, if what I hear is true, without fear of infamy I can reply." In *Inferno*, Guido, fearing ill repute for his evil earthly deeds, believed he could confide these to Dante, who was also trapped in Hell and thus unable to repeat them. Guido's "flame" represents his disembodied form in Hell: if he had believed Dante could return to Earth (which he ultimately did), he would have spoken no more. This background adds a layer of meaning to "Prufrock," which echoes the hellish setting, depicting hypocrites pretending goodness. Prufrock's concern for his reputation echoes Guido's: his dramatic monologue is best safely addressed to nobody who would repeat it.

Explain the Use and Significance of Quotes and References in the First Section of T.S. Eliot's "The Wasteland."

In the first section of "The Waste Land," titled "The Burial of the Dead," Eliot refers to Chaucer's *Canterbury Tales* opening about April—but twists it from Chaucer's happy depiction of "sweet showers" to "the cruelest month, breeding / Lilacs out of the dead land, mixing / memory and desire." Eliot also quotes Wagner's opera *Tristan and Isolde* retelling the Arthurian story of adulterous lovers and the loss experienced through their actions. Eliot used his extensive knowledge of literature to reinforce his depiction of the fragmented, decayed "waste land" of post-World War I twentieth-century society. Two major influences Eliot took were *From Ritual to*

- 97 -

Romance by Jessie Weston and *The Golden Bough* by Sir James Frazier—both British contemporaries of Eliot. Both authors described ancient fertility rites reflected in both Arthurian legend and modern religion and thought—prominently, the Fisher King legend. His wounds, causing impotence, made his country a "waste land" that could only be reclaimed by healing the Fisher King. Eliot incorporates the Fisher King theme in "The Waste Land," yet his king is without healing potential, reinforcing the modern world's lack of mythological or religious narrative to unify it.

Using Emily Dickinson's "I Like to See it Lap the Miles," Explain the Concept of Extended Metaphor.

In her poem "I like to see it lap the Miles", Emily Dickinson describes a railroad train, a new invention during her time, via extended metaphor comparing it to a horse. She writes of seeing the train "lap the miles—/And lick the Valleys up—/And/...feed itself at Tanks..." She describes seeing it take a "prodigious step / Around a Pile of Mountains...And then a Quarry pare / To fit its Ribs..." She describes the train's whistle as "horrid—hooting stanza" and further characterizes it as a "neigh." She concludes the poem by describing how the train, like a horse, will "punctual as a Star / Stop—docile and omnipotent / At its own stable door," representing the train depot/station as a horse's "stable." Juxtaposing the opposites of docility and omnipotence, Dickinson alludes to the way horses are physically powerful, yet often gentle and obedient to much smaller, physically weaker humans. In the same way, she shows hrough the extended metaphor, trains have great power which is harnessed and controlled by humans.

Use Examples from Shakespeare's *Romeo and Juliet* and Keats' "To Autumn" to Explain the Use of Visual and Auditory Imagery in Literature.

In Act I, Scene V of *Romeo and Juliet,* Shakespeare uses visual imagery in Romeo's description of Juliet's beauty: "O, she doth teach the torches to burn bright! / It seems she hangs upon the cheek of night / Like a rich jewel in an Ethiope's ear..." By saying she "teaches" torches to burn brightly, Shakespeare makes the point that Juliet's radiance surpasses that of the flames, contrasting it with the darkness of night. Then, he compares night's darkness to an Ethiopian's skin, and Juliet's contrasting brilliance to a gem's glow in an earring against the dark skin. In "Ode to Autumn", Keats uses auditory imagery to bring the season's "music" alive: "in a wailful choir the small gnats mourn /...Or sinking as the light wind lives or dies; / And full-grown lambs loud bleat from hilly bourn; / Hedge-crickets sing; and now with treble soft / The redbreast whistles from a garden-croft, / And gathering swallows twitter in the skies." He appeals to readers' hearing, describing intermittent wind, small insects buzzing in chorus, lambs bleating, crickets singing, and robins and swallows twittering.

Explain the Difference Between Figures of Speech and Rhetorical Devices. Cite Examples of the Use of Anaphora as a Rhetorical Device in Whitman's "Crossing Brooklyn Ferry" and "Song of Myself."

Although figures of speech and rhetorical devices are very similar and overlap in many aspects of their definitions, one difference is that a figure of speech uses the effect of altering word meanings to express an idea more colorfully or vividly. For example, instead of saying that a woman is strong-willed, free-spirited, feisty, attractive, yet unpredictable and maybe dangerous, some people use the figure of speech, "She's a pistol." When the main purpose of a figure of speech is to convince or persuade the audience, then the figure of speech can be said to become a rhetorical device. One type of rhetorical device is anaphora: the repetition at regular intervals of the same word or phrase, which adds emphasis. Walt Whitman uses anaphora in his poem "Crossing Brooklyn Ferry":

"Flood-tide below me! I watch you, face to face; / Clouds of the west! sun there half an hour high! I see you also face to face." He also uses this device in "Song of Myself": "Do I contradict myself? / Very well then I contradict myself, / (I am large, I contain multitudes.)"

Summarize the Difference Between Figures of Speech and Rhetorical Devices, and Use Milton's *Paradise Lost* to Provide Examples Illustrating the Distinction.

Both figures of speech and rhetorical devices are used to create calculated effects and specific emphases. One main difference is that figures of speech change the meanings of words. For example, instead of writing, "She is brave", one writes "She is a tiger." This figure of speech employs a metaphor, conveying the same meaning with a different word. By contrast, one example of a rhetorical device is using repetition to create emphasis without changing word meanings: "I am never ever going to rob anyone for you and never, never ever give in to your sinful wish." In Book V of *Paradise Lost,* poet John Milton uses rhetoric: "...advise him of his happy state—/ Happiness in his power left free to will, / Left to his own free will, his will though free / Yet mutable..."

Describing Adam, Milton emphasized humanity's free will by repeating the words "free" and "will". But he also created ambiguity by writing "though free / Yet mutable," to show that free will was changeable: Adam could lose freedom by sinning/erring.

> **Review Video: <u>Figure of Speech</u>**
> Visit mometrix.com/academy and enter code: 111295

Using Donne's Holy Sonnet 10 –"Death, Be Not Proud," Describe the Use of Rhetoric in Poetry.

In Holy Sonnet 10 – "Death, be not proud" – metaphysical poet John Donne rhetorically berates Death. In the final sestet, Donne writes: "Thou art slave to fate, chance, kings, and desperate men, / And dost with poison, war, and sickness dwell, / And poppy or charms can make us sleep as well / And better than thy stroke; why swell'st thou then?" This illustrates the message stated in the first quatrain: "Death, be not proud, though some have called thee / Mighty and dreadful, for thou art not so; / For those whom thou think'st dost overthrow / Die not, poor Death, nor yet canst thou kill me." Donne opens by denying that Death is as powerful or horrible as some say, then adds that some whom Death thinks it kills do not die, and neither can Death kill him. He supports this argument by subsequently diminishing Death's reputed power, characterizing Death as a "slave" and associating it with the poor company of "poison, war, and sickness." Ultimately Donne asks the rhetorical question, "why swell'st thou then?" meaning Death has no reason to swell with pride—deflating Death's value and strength.

Describe the Use of Alliteration and Hyperbole as Rhetorical Devices. Consider Examples from "The Emperor of Ice Cream" by Wallace Stevens and "To His Coy Mistress" by Andrew Marvell.

Alliteration is both a literary and rhetorical device, using several words in sequence with the same initial sound. An example as literary device is in Wallace Stevens' (1922) poem "The Emperor of Ice Cream": "And bid him whip in kitchen cups concupiscent curds." Two examples of alliteration as rhetorical devices used by speakers for effect are Julius Caesar's "Veni, vidi, vici" ("I came, I saw, I conquered"), and John F. Kennedy's 1961 Inaugural Address: "Let us go forth to lead the land we love." Both repeated consonant sounds to make their speeches more memorable. Hyperbole is extreme exaggeration for emphasis or effect. An example is in Andrew Marvell's famous *carpe diem*-tradition poem "To His Coy Mistress": "My vegetable love should grow / Vaster than empires, and more slow; / An hundred years should go to praise / Thine eyes and on thine forehead gaze; / Two hundred to adore each breast, / But thirty thousand to the rest."

Marvell exaggerates his love—"Had we but world enough and time"—as potentially growing longer than empires, hundreds and thousands of years.

> **Review Video: Alliteration**
> Visit mometrix.com/academy and enter code: 462837
>
> **Review Video: Hyperbole and Understatement**
> Visit mometrix.com/academy and enter code: 308470

Describe the Use of Irony and Oxymoron as Rhetorical Devices in Shakespeare's *Julius Caesar* and *Hamlet*.

Irony is the literary and rhetorical device of expressing meaning by using words that have the opposite meaning. In everyday speech it is also called sarcasm. An example of irony in literature in Shakespeare's tragedy *Julius Caesar* is in Act 3, Scene 2, in Marc Antony's famous eulogy speech at Caesar's funeral: "He was my friend, faithful and just to me. / But Brutus says he was ambitious, / And Brutus is an honorable man." Antony is using irony when he calls Brutus "honorable" to mean he is not. Four lines earlier, he also says "For Brutus is an honorable man; / So are they all, all honorable men." Ironically and indirectly he is indicting the many dishonorable men involved. Oxymoron juxtaposes apparently contradictory words; some everyday speech examples include "deafening silence," "conspicuous absence," etc. A literary example is in Shakespeare's *Hamlet,* Act 3, Scene 4: "I must be cruel only to be kind." Shakespeare's phrasing was so popular that it has since been adopted into everyday expressions.

> **Review Video: Irony**
> Visit mometrix.com/academy and enter code: 374204

GACE Practice Test

Selected Response Practice Questions

Questions 1-3 refer to the following excerpts:

> Had we but world enough, and time,
> This coyness, lady, were no crime.
> We would sit down, and think which way
> To walk, and pass our long love's day.
> But at my back I always hear
> Time's winged chariot hurrying near;
> And yonder all before us lie
> Deserts of vast eternity.

1. Who is the author of this poem?
   a. John Donne
   b. Andrew Marvell
   c. George Herbert
   d. Henry Vaughan

2. This poem reflects a thematic tradition known as...
   a. Carpe diem.
   b. Classicism.
   c. Cinquain.
   d. Conceit.

3. What is the meter of the couplets in this poem?
   a. Pentameter
   b. Heptameter
   c. Hexameter
   d. Tetrameter

Questions 4-7 are based on the following excerpt:

> riverrun, past Eve and Adam's, from swerve of shore to bend of bay, brings us by a commodious vicus of recirculation back to Howth Castle and Environs.

4. This is the opening sentence of...
   a. *Ulysses.*
   b. *Finnegans Wake.*
   c. *Adventures in the Skin Trade.*
   d. *A Portrait of the Artist as a Young Man.*

5. In the excerpted sentence, the word "vicus" represents which of the following?
   a. Vicinity
   b. Vico Way
   c. Giambattista Vico
   d. All of the above

6. Why does this opening sentence begin with an uncapitalized word?

    a. This is to make it stand out to the reader.
    b. It is the continuation of the author's previous novel.
    c. It forms the completion of the novel's unfinished last sentence.
    d. A typesetting error in the original edition was preserved in perpetuity.

7. The author of the excerpted work is famous for using a literary technique known as...

    a. Stream-of-consciousness.
    b. The unreliable narrator.
    c. First-person narration.
    d. The author surrogate.

Questions 8-10 refer to the following excerpt:

> Call the roller of big cigars,
> The muscular one, and bid him whip
> In kitchen cups concupiscent curds.
> Let the wenches dawdle in such dress
> As they are used to wear, and let the boys
> Bring flowers in last month's newspapers.
> Let be be finale of seem.
> The only emperor is the emperor of ice-cream.

8. The excerpted poem was written in...

    a. The 17th century.
    b. The 18th century.
    c. The 19th century.
    d. The 20th century.

9. Which literary device is shown in the third line of the excerpted stanza?

    a. Alliteration
    b. Hyperbole
    c. Onomatopoeia
    d. Metonymy

10. The line "Let be be finale of seem" can be interpreted as reflecting a concept from which of the following?

    a. Ovid's *Metamorphoses*
    b. Dante's *Divine Comedy*
    c. Plato's *Dialogues*
    d. Homer's *Iliad*

Questions 11-13 refer to the following excerpt:

> I AM assured by our Merchants, that a Boy or a Girl before twelve Years old, is no saleable Commodity; and even when they come to this Age, they will not yield above [an amount of money] at most, on the Exchange; which cannot turn to Account...to the Parents...; the Charge of Nutriment and Rags, having been at least four Times that Value.

> I SHALL now therefore humbly propose my own Thoughts; which I hope will not be liable to the least Objection.

I HAVE been assured by a very knowing *American* of my Acquaintance in *London;* that a young healthy Child, well nursed, is, at a Year old, a most delicious, nourishing, and wholesome Food; whether *Stewed, Roasted, Baked,* or *Boiled;* and, I make no doubt, that it will equally serve in a *Fricasie,* or *Ragoust.*

11. The literary form used in the excerpted piece is...

    a. Persuasion.
    b. Satire.
    c. Exposition.
    d. Bathos.

12. The excerpted work was published in which century?

    a. 20th
    b. 19th
    c. 18th
    d. 17th

13. The author of the excerpted piece also wrote which of the following?

    a. *The Canterbury Tales*
    b. *The Faerie Queene*
    c. *Paradise Lost*
    d. *Gulliver's Travels*

Questions 14-17 refer to the following poem:

The Thought-Fox

I imagine this midnight moment's forest:
Something else is alive
Beside the clock's loneliness
And this blank page where my fingers move.
Through the window I see no star:
Something more near
Though deeper within darkness
Is entering the loneliness:
Cold, delicately as the dark snow
A fox's nose touches twig, leaf;
Two eyes serve a movement, that now
And again now, and now, and now
Sets neat prints into the snow
Between trees, and warily a lame
Shadow lags by stump and in hollow
Of a body that is bold to come
Across clearings, an eye,
A widening deepening greenness,
Brilliantly, concentratedly,
Coming about its own business
Till, with a sudden sharp hot stink of fox,
It enters the dark hole of the head.
The window is starless still; the clock ticks,

The page is printed.

14. The primary literary device used by the poet here is...

    a. Foreshadowing.
    b. Irony.
    c. Cliché.
    d. Metaphor.

15. Which of these does the poem really describe?

    a. The process of a fox's natural actions
    b. The process of being inspired by nature
    c. The process of being inspired to write
    d. The process of being attacked by a fox

16. Which of the following best characterizes how this poem portrays the creative process?

    a. The poet exercises tight control of a thought.
    b. The poet is a passive recipient of the thought.
    c. The poet carefully guides the thought to him.
    d. The poet imagines a fox to help him to write.

17. In which of the following forms is this poem written?

    a. In free verse
    b. Rhymed and metered
    c. Unrhymed and metered
    d. Rhymed and unmetered

Questions 18-20 refer to the following excerpts:

> I knew I should be grateful to Mrs. Guinea, only I couldn't feel a thing. If Mrs. Guinea had given me a ticket to Europe, or a round-the-world cruise, it wouldn't have made one scrap of difference to me, because wherever I sat—on the deck of a ship or at a street café in Paris or Bangkok—I would be sitting under the same glass bell jar, stewing in my own sour air.

> I sank back in the gray, plush seat and closed my eyes. The air of the bell jar wadded round me and I couldn't stir.

> [Following a successful shock treatment:]

> All the heat and fear had purged itself. I felt surprisingly at peace. The bell jar hung, suspended, a few feet above my head. I was open to the circulating air.

> "We'll take up where we left off, Esther," she [my mother] had said, with her sweet, martyr's smile. "We'll act as if all this were a bad dream."

> A bad dream.

> To the person in the bell jar, blank and stopped as a dead baby, the world itself is the bad dream.

Valerie's last, cheerful cry had been "So long! Be seeing you."

"Not if I know it," I thought.

But I wasn't sure. I wasn't sure at all. How did I know that someday—at college, in Europe, somewhere, anywhere—the bell jar, with its stifling distortions, wouldn't descend again?

From *The Bell Jar* by Sylvia Plath, copyright © 1971 by Harper & Row, Publishers, Inc.

18. The bell jar the author refers to is an example of which literary device?
    a. A simile
    b. An allusion
    c. A metaphor
    d. Personification

19. In this book, Plath uses a bell jar to symbolize…
    a. The strictures of reality.
    b. Her own mental illness.
    c. A case of writer's block.
    d. A disorder of breathing.

20. Which of the following statements is accurate about Sylvia Plath?
    a. *The Bell Jar* was her last in a long series of novels, all of them successful.
    b. She ultimately recovered, lived a long life, and wrote many more novels.
    c. Plath wrote only a few poems, but *The Bell Jar* was the first of her books.
    d. She wrote *The Bell Jar* about her initial breakdown almost a decade later.

21. William Shakespeare wrote during which historical and literary period?
    a. Medieval
    b. Renaissance
    c. Restoration
    d. Enlightenment

22. Which of the following was the author of *The Pilgrim's Progress?*
    a. John Bunyan
    b. William Congreve
    c. Daniel Defoe
    d. Samuel Butler

Questions 23-24 are based on the following excerpt:

Come live with me and be my love,
And we will all the pleasures prove
That valleys, groves, hills, and fields,
Woods, or steepy mountain yields.

23. This is the first stanza of a poem written by...

    a. Andrew Marvell.
    b. Christopher Marlowe.
    c. Sir Walter Raleigh.
    d. William Shakespeare.

24. The rhyme scheme of this stanza is...

    a. ABAB.
    b. ABBA.
    c. AABB.
    d. ABCD.

25. The legend of Faust has been treated in literature by which of the following?

    a. Christopher Marlowe
    b. Johann Wolfgang von Goethe
    c. Thomas Mann
    d. All of the above

26. Of the following works by Alexander Pope, which was written in prose?

    a. "An Essay on Criticism"
    b. "The Rape of the Lock"
    c. "The Universal Prayer"
    d. None of the above

Questions 27-29 refer to the following excerpts:

> [First stanza:] I wake to sleep, and take my waking slow.
> I feel my fate in what I cannot fear.
> I learn by going where I have to go.
> [Last stanza:] This shaking keeps me steady. I should know.
> What falls away is always. And is near.
> I wake to sleep, and take my waking slow.
> I learn by going where I have to go.

From *The Waking* by Theodore Roethke, in *Roethke: Collected Poems,* Doubleday & Company, Inc. copyright © 1937-1966 by Beatrice Roethke as Administratrix of the Estate of Theodore Roethke; copyright © 1932-1961 by Theodore Roethke.

> [First stanza:] I shut my eyes and all the world drops dead;
> I lift my lids and all is born again.
> (I think I made you up inside my head.)
> [Last stanza:] I should have loved a thunderbird instead;
> At least when spring comes they roar back again.
> I shut my eyes and all the world drops dead.
> (I think I made you up inside my head.)

From *Mad Girl's Love Song* by Sylvia Plath, copyright © 1954 by Sylvia Plath, in A Biographical Note, in *The Bell Jar,* Copyright © 1971 by Harper & Row, Publishers. *Mad Girl's Love Song* first appeared in *Mademoiselle,* August 1953 issue.

> [First stanza:] Do not go gentle into that good night,
> Old age should burn and rave at close of day;

Rage, rage against the dying of the light.
[Last stanza:] And you, my father, there on the sad height,
Curse, bless, me now with your fierce tears, I pray.
Do not go gentle into that good night.
Rage, rage against the dying of the light.

27. Which is true of all three excerpted poems?
    a. They are all ballads.
    b. They are all sonnets.
    c. They are all villanelles.
    d. They are all different forms.

28. Which of the excerpted poems focus on the nature of reality vs. the imagination?
    a. The second and third
    b. The first and second
    c. The first and third
    d. All three

29. Which of the excerpted poems deal(s) directly with the subject of death?
    a. The third
    b. The second and third
    c. The first and third
    d. All three

Questions 30-35 refer to the following poem:

> I like to see it lap the Miles —
> And lick the Valleys up —
> And stop to feed itself at Tanks —
> And then — prodigious step
> Around a pile of Mountains —
> And supercilious peer
> In Shanties — by the sides of Roads –
> And then a Quarry pare
> To fit its Ribs
> And crawl between
> Complaining all the while
> In horrid — hooting stanza —
> Then chase itself down Hill —
> And neigh like Boanerges —
> Then — punctual as a Star
> Stop — docile and omnipotent
> At its own stable door —

30. This poem describes which of the following?

    a. An aristocratic thoroughbred horse
    b. The recently invented railroad train
    c. An incredible mythological monster
    d. The subject cannot be determined

31. This poem was written around the time of...

    a. The American Revolution.
    b. The French Revolution.
    c. The War of 1812.
    d. The Civil War.

32. An amazing feat in this poem is that the structure of the subject described is mirrored in the poem's...

    a. Vocabulary.
    b. Rhythms.
    c. Syntax.
    d. Tone.

33. The adjectives "docile and omnipotent" in the penultimate line were chosen because they are...

    a. Synonymous.
    b. Nonsensical.
    c. Mechanical.
    d. Contrasting.

34. What is the source of the phrase "And neigh like Boanerges" in the last stanza?

    a. A Greek myth about a creature that inhabits Hades (the underworld)
    b. A New Testament reference to a fiery, strong-voiced preacher/orator
    c. An Old Testament reference to a wrathful prophet seeking vengeance
    d. A Roman name for a mythological animal that lived within a labyrinth

35. This poet famously used dashes for _____ and capitals for _____.

    a. Punctuation; honor
    b. Separation; names
    c. Prosody; emphasis
    d. Continuity; names

Questions 36-38 refer to the following poem:

> Because I could not stop for Death —
> He kindly stopped for me —
> The Carriage held but just Ourselves —
> And Immortality.
>
> We slowly drove — He knew no haste
> And I had put away
> My labor and my leisure too,
> For His Civility —
>
> We passed the School, where Children strove

At Recess — in the Ring —
We passed the Fields of Gazing Grain —
We passed the Setting Sun —

Or rather — He passed Us —
The Dews drew quivering and chill —
For only Gossamer, my Gown —
My Tippet — only Tulle —

We paused before a House that seemed
A Swelling of the Ground —
The Roof was scarcely visible —
The Cornice — in the Ground —

Since then — 'tis Centuries — and yet
Feels shorter than the Day
I first surmised the Horses' Heads
Were toward Eternity —

36. The descriptions of Death, of the "Fields of Gazing Grain," and of the setting sun all employ which literary device?

    a. Analogy
    b. Hyperbole
    c. Alliteration
    d. Personification

37. Irrespective of its topic, the tone of this poem would best be described as...

    a. Serious, grave, and portentously dark
    b. Detached, alienated, and numb of feeling
    c. Lighthearted, humorous, and gently ironic
    d. Frantic, agitated, and with a frenzy of fear

38. What is described in the fifth stanza?

    a. A home
    b. A grave
    c. A church
    d. A school

39. A distinguishing feature of the form known as haiku is...

    a. 5/7/5 syllables per line
    b. An ABA rhyme scheme
    c. Perfectly regular meter
    d. Lengthy epic narratives

40. Which of the following accurately identifies *The Diary of a Young Girl* by Anne Frank?

    a. A fictional novel of a 1920s American debutante's diary
    b. A non-fictional Dutch journal influenced by World War II
    c. A long, episodic poem depicting childhood schizophrenia
    d. A British record documenting a sociological diary project

Question 41 refers to the following excerpt:

> When I got to camp I warn't feeling very brash, there warn't much sand in my craw; but I says, this ain't no time to be fooling around. So I got all my traps into my canoe again so as to have them out of sight, and I put out the fire and scattered the ashes around to look like an old last-year's camp, and then clumb a tree.

41. This passage is taken from which of the following?

    a. *The Mysterious Stranger*
    b. *The Adventures of Tom Sawyer*
    c. *The Adventures of Huckleberry Finn*
    d. *The Prince and the Pauper*

42. Which of the following statements is most accurate regarding the characters of Drouet and Hurstwood in Theodore Dreiser's novel *Sister Carrie?*

    a. Drouet has the awareness to be decent, but he lacks the morality.
    b. Hurstwood has the morality, but not the awareness, for decency.
    c. Only one of these characters is representative of the middle class.
    d. Drouet is morally decent but unaware; Hurstwood is the opposite.

Questions 43- 45 refer to the following excerpt:

> I bequeath myself to the dirt to grow from the grass I love,
> If you want me again look for me under your boot-soles.

43. What is the title of the poem from which this is taken?

    a. "To You"
    b. "Thou Reader"
    c. "Song of Myself"
    d. "One's-Self I Sing"

44. Which of the following is the best interpretation of the excerpted lines?

    a. The poet means that he will be dead and buried in the future.
    b. The poet means he is one with and an integral part of nature.
    c. The poet means the person addressed is above him in station.
    d. The poet means the recipient stepped on/walked all over him.

45. The excerpted work was published in which century?

    a. 18th
    b. 19th
    c. 20th
    d. 21st

Questions 46-50 refer to the following excerpts:

> I should have been a pair of ragged claws
> Scuttling across the floors of silent seas.
> Shall I part my hair behind? Do I dare to eat a peach?
> I shall wear white flannel trousers, and walk upon the beach.
> I have heard the mermaids singing, each to each.
> I do not think that they will sing to me.

- 110 -

We have lingered in the chambers of the sea
By sea-girls wreathed with seaweed red and brown
Till human voices wake us, and we drown.

46. What is the title of the work from which these excerpts are taken?

    a. "The Waste Land"
    b. "The Love Song of J. Alfred Prufrock"
    c. "Notes Toward the Definition of Culture"
    d. "The Hollow Men"

47. The second excerpt is speaking about…

    a. Indecision.
    b. A vacation.
    c. Mortality.
    d. Drowning.

48. Which of the following is/are the best interpretation(s) of the meaning in the first excerpt?

    a. The speaker's existence is as significant as the life of a crab.
    b. The speaker loves the sea and wishes he could live under it.
    c. The scavenger can create beauty by reconstructing garbage.
    d. The answers choices in (A) and (C) are valid interpretations.

49. Why does the speaker say, "I do not think that they will sing to me"?

    a. Because he feels the despair of existence.
    b. Because he is becoming deaf with old age.
    c. Because he knows mermaids are not real.
    d. Because he is on the beach, not in the sea.

50. Which of the following is the best interpretation of the final line?

    a. Mermaids protect us from drowning; humans ruin it.
    b. The dream of art is ruined by the intrusion of reality.
    c. Dreaming of mermaids is part of death by drowning.
    d. Mermaids bewitch us from knowing that we drown.

51. Which of Chaucer's *Canterbury Tales* is an example of the literary form known as the fabliau?

    a. "The Physician's Tale"
    b. "The Wife of Bath's Tale"
    c. "The Miller's Tale"
    d. "The Pardoner's Tale"

52. Which of the following pairs are NOT both written in the form of frame tales?

    a. *The Canterbury Tales* by Geoffrey Chaucer and *The Decameron* by Giovanni Bocaccio
    b. The *Mahabharata* by Veda Vyasa and *The Parlement of Foules* by Geoffrey Chaucer
    c. *Frankenstein* by Mary W. Shelley and *Wuthering Heights* by Emily Brontë
    d. *The Great Gatsby* by F. Scott Fitzgerald and *To the Lighthouse* by Virginia Woolf

53. Which of the following works was the first ever published in vernacular Italian?

    a. *De re publica* (*On the Republic*) by Marcus Tullius Cicero
    b. *Il Decameron* (*The Decameron*) by Giovanni Bocaccio
    c. *La Divina Commedia (The Divine Comedy)* by Dante Alighieri
    d. *Il Nome della Rosa* (*The Name of the Rose*) by Umberto Eco

Questions 54-56 are based on the following poem:

Leda and the Swan

A sudden blow: the great wings beating still
Above the staggering girl, her thighs caressed
By the dark webs, her nape caught in his bill,
He holds her helpless breast upon his breast.
How can those terrified vague fingers push
The feathered glory from her loosening thighs?
And how can body, laid in that white rush,
But feel the strange heart beating where it lies?
A shudder in the loins engenders there
The broken wall, the burning roof and tower
And Agamemnon dead.
Being so caught up,
So mastered by the brute blood of the air,
Did she put on his knowledge with his power
Before the indifferent beak could let her drop?

William Butler Yeats, 1923

54. "The broken wall, the burning roof and tower/And Agamemnon dead" refer to...

    a. The Punic Wars.
    b. The Trojan War.
    c. The Peloponnesian War.
    d. A murder but no war.

55. In what form is this poem?

    a. A sonnet
    b. Villanelle
    c. Free verse
    d. A sestina

56. The poet's final question best suggests which of the following ideas?

    a. Humans get godlike knowledge and power from the gods.
    b. Human knowledge and power are necessarily incomplete.
    c. Humans in ancient Greece interacted differently with gods.
    d. Humans interacting with gods got power, not knowledge.

57. In the Three Cueing Systems model of word recognition in reading instruction, which system most relates to how words are assembled into meaningful language?

    a. Phonological
    b. Semantic
    c. Syntactic
    d. Pragmatic

58. In the word-recognition model of the Three Cueing Systems used in teaching reading, which of the following is most associated with the meanings of words?

    a. Using pragmatic cues
    b. Phonological system
    c. The syntactic system
    d. The semantic system

59. In the model known in reading instruction as the Three Cueing Systems, which of these relate most to how sounds are used to communicate meaning?

    a. Syntactic cues
    b. Semantic cues
    c. Phonological cues
    d. Pragmatic cues

60. In reading instruction, the Three Cueing Systems is one model used. Which of the following represent a valid reading strategy that is NOT a system in the Three Cueing Systems model?

    a. Syntactic cues
    b. Pragmatic cues
    c. Semantic cues
    d. Phonological cues

61. When should students be taught to activate their prior knowledge?

    a. Before reading
    b. During reading
    c. After reading
    d. All of the above

62. Which choice most appropriately fills the blanks in this statement? "Teaching children which thinking strategies are used by _____ and helping them use those strategies _____ creates the core of teaching reading." (*Mosaic of Thought,* Keene and Zimmerman, 1997)

    a. Reading teachers; in different ways
    b. Beginning students; with assistance
    c. Proficient readers; independently
    d. Published writers; more creatively

63. Scholars have identified three kinds of major connections that students make when reading: connecting text to self, text to the world, and text to text. Which of the following student statements best reflect(s) the connection of text to the world?

    a. "These mythic gods have more power, but feel and act like humans."
    b. "This novel is set during a period I learned about in my history class."
    c. "I can relate to how the main character felt about being controlled."
    d. All three statements equally reflect connection of text to the world.

64. When students are taught to use effective reading comprehension strategies, they not only achieve deeper understanding, but they also learn to think about how they think when reading. This is known as...

    a. Schemata.
    b. Scaffolding.
    c. Metacognition.
    d. Metamorphosis.

65. Activity settings (Tharp and Gallimore, 1988) are aspects of the sociocultural context that affect how students learn and read. Of five activity settings, one is participant identity, or who the students are. Of the other four, which is most related to motivation?

    a. When the activity is done
    b. Why the activity is done
    c. Where the activity is done
    d. How the activity is done

66. Some experts maintain that teaching reading comprehension entails not only the application of skills, but also the process of actively constructing meaning. This process they describe as *interactive*, *strategic,* and *adaptable*. Which of the following best defines the *interactive* aspect of this process?

    a. The process involves the text, the reader, and the context in which reading occurs.
    b. The process involves readers using a variety of strategies in constructing meaning.
    c. The process involves readers changing their strategies to read different text types.
    d. The process involves changing strategies according to different reasons for reading.

67. In first-language (L1) and second-language (L2) acquisition, which of the following is true about developmental stages?

    a. L2 learners do not undergo the first stage called the Silent Period as L1 learners do.
    b. L2 learners undergo all stages, but are urged to skip the first stage more than L1s.
    c. L2 learners do not undergo the second stage of Formulaic Speech as L1 learners do.
    d. L2 learners undergo the third stage of Structural and Semantic Simplifications later.

68. Which statement is most accurate about social contexts of L1 and L2 acquisition?

    a. Both L1 and L2 learning can occur in equally varied natural and educational contexts.
    b. L1s are only learned in natural contexts, while L2s are learned in educational contexts.
    c. Variations in L2 proficiency can result from the different contexts of learning the L2s.
    d. L2s are not a speaker's natural language and so are never learned in natural contexts.

69. Which of the following is unique to second-language learning?

    a. Zone of proximal development
    b. The critical period hypothesis
    c. Marked/unmarked features
    d. The process of fossilization

70. An ESL student whose L1 is Chinese tends to omit plural endings and articles before nouns. Of the following, which is the best explanation for these errors?

    a. The student has not yet learned these English grammatical forms.
    b. Omission avoids having to choose among irregular English forms.
    c. Incompatible nature and rules of the L1 are transferring to the L2.
    d. The student does not understand how the L1 and L2 forms relate.

71. Which of the following is the most accurate characterization of dialects?

    a. They are non-standard versions of any language.
    b. They are often seen as less socially acceptable.
    c. They include linguistic features that are incorrect.
    d. They indicate poor/incomplete language learning.

72. Of the following, which statement is correct regarding Standard English?

    a. The formal Standard English applies to written language.
    b. Standard English is universal in English-speaking nations.
    c. Speech communities use the Standard English of writing.
    d. The Standard English construct does not include dialects.

73. The Great Vowel Shift occurred during which time span?

    a. 10th to 13th centuries
    b. 12th to 15th centuries
    c. 15th to 18th centuries
    d. 16th to 19th centuries

74. The Great Vowel Shift caused the pronunciation of long vowels in English to shift:

    a. Farther back in the mouth.
    b. Higher in the mouth.
    c. Lower in the mouth.
    d. Farther to the front of the mouth.

75. Of the following authors, whose English existed *during* the Great Vowel Shift?

    a. William Shakespeare
    b. Geoffrey Chaucer
    c. Emily Dickinson
    d. The Pearl Poet

76. Linguists generally analyze the Great Vowel Shift as having transpired in _____ steps.

    a. Ten
    b. Eight
    c. Six
    d. Four

77. Which of the following areas has been affected in the long term by the Great Vowel Shift?

    a. Written spelling
    b. Teaching reading
    c. Text comprehension
    d. All the above

78. The source of the silent *b* in the English word *debt* was originally…

    a. A Middle English word.
    b. A voiced Old English *b.*
    c. From Latin etymology.
    d. From Greek etymology.

79. We are familiar with the modern English meanings of the word "disaster." But in the 16th century, this word meant…

    a. Catastrophe.
    b. Star-crossed.
    c. A misfortune.
    d. Unflowerlike.

80. The English word "salary" has a 2,000-year-old etymology to a word meaning…

    a. Salt.
    b. Celery.
    c. Money.
    d. Earnings.

81. Which of the following is an example of a portmanteau?

    a. Fax
    b. Brunch
    c. Babysitter
    d. Saxophone

82. The English language word "quark" is an example of the result of which linguistic process?

    a. Blending
    b. Conversion
    c. Neologisms
    d. Onomatopoeia

83. The questions in this test can give you an idea of what kinds of questions you might find on the actual test; however, they are not duplicates of the actual test questions, which cover the same subject material but may differ in form and content.

The preceding sentence is which of the following sentence types?

    a. Simple
    b. Complex
    c. Compound
    d. Compound-complex

84. A patient dies in surgery and the reporting doctor describes the death as a "negative patient outcome." This is *best* identified as an example of…

    a. Jargon.
    b. Ambiguity.
    c. Euphemism.
    d. Connotation.

85. Which of the following is NOT typically categorized as a prewriting process?

    a. Planning
    b. Reflection
    c. Visualization
    d. Brainstorming

86. Which of the following correctly represents the sequence of stages or steps in the writing process?

    a. Prewriting, drafting, revising, editing, publishing
    b. Prewriting, drafting, editing, publishing, revising
    c. Prewriting, editing, drafting, revising, publishing
    d. Prewriting, drafting, editing, revising, publishing

87. Research has found that which of the following occur for students during revision and rewriting?

    a. Students only correct their mechanical errors in revisions.
    b. Students often incorporate new ideas when they rewrite.
    c. Students retain their original writing goals during revision.
    d. Students' planning in prewriting is unaffected in rewriting.

88. Which of the following have researchers learned about children's writing?

    a. Children's writing reflects as much knowledge as they have on any given topic.
    b. Children stop writing when they have run out of things they want to articulate.
    c. Children stop writing when they cannot adequately articulate their knowledge.
    d. Children's writing commonly covers more than they actually know about a topic.

89. Arthur writes a paper. One classmate identifies ideas and words that resonated with her when she read it. Another describes how reading the paper changed his thinking. A third asks Arthur some questions about what he meant by certain statements in the paper. A fourth suggests that a portion of the paper needs more supporting information. This description is most typical of...

    a. A portfolio assessment.
    b. A holistic scoring.
    c. A scoring rubric.
    d. A peer review.

90. Which of the following is the best definition of Information Literacy?

    a. It is the set of skills required for reading and comprehending different information.
    b. It is the cognitive skill set necessary to amass a comprehensive base of knowledge.
    c. It is the skill set required for the finding, retrieval, analysis, and use of information.
    d. It is the set of skills necessary for effectively communicating information to others.

91. What is the primary reason the early 21st century has been referred to as the Information Age?

    a. Because educational and governmental agencies require greater information
    b. Because there are more sources and outputs of information than ever before
    c. Because students can now learn all they need to know in four years of college
    d. Because college students today are much more interested in new information

92. Of the following statements, which adheres to Information Literacy standards?

   a. Students accessing information must critically evaluate it and its sources before using it.
   b. Students accessing information can ascertain how much of it they need after they find it.
   c. Students accessing information efficiently sacrifice broader scope and incidental learning.
   d. Students accessing information ethically must eschew using it to attain specific purposes.

93. According to the MLA system for documenting sources in literature, which of the following typically combines signal phrases and parenthetical references?

   a. An MLA list of the works cited
   b. MLA in-text citations in a paper
   c. Adding MLA information notes
   d. All of the above

94. According to MLA guidelines for writing research papers, which of the following is correct regarding citations of web sources if you do not quickly see the author's name?

   a. Assume the author is not named, as this is a common occurrence on the Web.
   b. Do not name an agency or corporation as author if it is the sponsor of the source.
   c. Author names are often on websites, but need additional looking to discover.
   d. It is not permissible to cite the book or article title in lieu of an author's name.

95. When making in-text citations in a research paper, which of the following reflects MLA guidelines for citing Web sources with regard to page numbers?

   a. If a Web source does not include pagination, you are advised to avoid citing that source.
   b. If page numbers appear on a printout from a website, include these numbers in citations.
   c. In-text citations of online sources in research papers should never include page numbers.
   d. If the Web source is a PDF file, it is recommended to cite page numbers in your citations.

96. The MLA guidelines for citing multiple authors of the same source in the in-text citations of a research paper are to use the first author's name and "et al" for the other(s) in the case of...

   a. More than one author.
   b. Two or three authors.
   c. Three or more authors.
   d. Four or more authors.

97. A movie review is one example of what type and purpose of writing?

   a. Narration
   b. Description
   c. Persuasion
   d. Exposition

98. Of the following writing types and purposes, which can often be the hardest to write?

   a. Expository
   b. Persuasive
   c. Descriptive
   d. Narrative

99. Which of the following do *The Adventures of Huckleberry Finn* by Mark Twain, *The Diary of a Young Girl* by Anne Frank, and "The Fall of the House of Usher" by Edgar Allan Poe have in common?

   a. They are all examples of the narrative type and purpose of writing.
   b. They are all examples of a purely descriptive writing type/purpose.
   c. They are all examples of works of primarily expository writing type.
   d. They are all examples of writing of the persuasive type and purpose.

100. When you have a writing assignment, which of the following is true about your audience?

   a. You need not identify the audience because it is the teacher who gave the assignment.
   b. You should consider how your readers are likely to use what you write.
   c. You should know your writing purpose more than a reader's purposes.
   d. You are overthinking to wonder about readers' likely attitude/reaction.

101. Which statement is correct regarding the relationship of your audience profile to the decisions you make in writing?

   a. How much time you spend on research is unrelated to your audience.
   b. Your audience does not influence how much information you include.
   c. The writing style, tone and wording you use depend on your audience.
   d. How you organize information depends on structure, not on audience.

102. Which of the following statements is most accurate about writing the introduction to an essay?

   a. The introduction should use the technique of starting essays with dictionary definitions.
   b. The introduction should leave the most attention-getting material for later in the work.
   c. The introduction should move from the focused and specific to the broad and general.
   d. The introduction should move from the broad and general to the focused and specific.

103. When writing an essay, which part of the introduction should come first?

   a. Your thesis statement for the essay
   b Background on the essay's purpose
   c. Something original to engage reader attention
   d. A "road map" of how you will present the thesis

104. Which of the following is true about effective ways to open the introduction of an essay?

   a. You should summarize your position with your own words, not with a quote.
   b. Citing a surprising statistic related to the topic can grab readers' attention.
   c. Opening with a story or anecdote is counter to the purposes of an essay or paper.
   d. Asking rhetorical questions to open an essay or paper will only frustrate readers.

105. Which of the following is the *worst* way to view the conclusion of an essay?

   a. As a means of including all material that would not fit elsewhere
   b. As a means of reiterating the thesis you stated in the introduction
   c. As a means of synthesizing and/or summarizing your main points
   d. As a means of clarifying the context of your discussion/argument

106. In writing, _____ is the overall written expression of the writer's attitude, and _____ is the individual way in which the writer expresses the former.

    a. Voice; tone
    b. Tone; voice
    c. Style; tone
    d. Voice; style

107. _____ is the overall choice of language you make for your writing; _____ refers to the words that you use when writing within or about a specific discipline.

    a. Vocabulary; diction
    b. Vocabulary; jargon
    c. Diction; vocabulary
    d. Style; vocabulary

108. Which of the following is most accurate regarding writing style?

    a. The kind of diction you use does not affect style.
    b. Add style later in the writing process to give personality.
    c. Style is unrelated to your control of your content.
    d. Your purpose for writing guides your style.

109. When considering strategies for writing assignments, it helps to know the cognitive (or learning) objectives your teacher intends for an assignment. If the assignment asks you to "describe," "explain," "summarize," "restate," "classify," or "review" some material you read, what is the cognitive objective?

    a. Knowledge recall
    b. Application
    c. Comprehension
    d. Evaluation

110. Your writing assignment asks you to "organize," "plan," "formulate," "assemble," "compose," "construct," and/or "arrange" some material. Which of the following cognitive (learning) objectives is the teacher aiming to meet with this assignment?

    a. Analysis
    b. Synthesis
    c. Evaluation
    d. Application

111. Which of the following processes used in writing is the most complex?

    a. Evaluation
    b. Application
    c. Comprehension
    d. Knowledge recall

112. Of the following learning and writing processes, which strategy/strategies is (or are) the most common forms of analysis in college-level writing?

    a. Comparing and contrasting
    b. Explaining cause and effect
    c. Giving support to an opinion
    d. Options A and B

113. Which of the following writing strategies is (or are) among the most commonly used forms of synthesis in college-level writing?

    a. Explaining cause and effect
    b. Comparing and contrasting
    c. Proposing a solution
    d. Using persuasion

114. Among writing projects that can develop from research, which of the following discourse aims is represented by a white paper, an opinion survey, an annotated bibliography, and a problem solution?

    a. Expressive
    b. Exploratory
    c. Informative
    d. Persuasive

115. "This treatise developed from an initial idea about the way a plant develops from a seed." The preceding sentence is an example of which literary device and argument method?

    a. Analogy
    b. Allegory
    c. Allusion
    d. Antithesis

116. In the famous balcony scene of William Shakespeare's *Romeo and Juliet,* Romeo says:

> But soft! What light through yonder window breaks?
> It is the east, and Juliet is the sun.
> Arise, fair sun, and kill the envious moon,
> Who is already sick and pale with grief,
> That thou her maid art far more fair than she:
> Be not her maid, since she is envious;
> Her vestal livery is but sick and green
> And none but fools do wear it; cast it off.

The literary device Shakespeare used here is also used in all *except* which of the following?

    a. T. S. Eliot's description of the fog in "The Love Song of J. Alfred Prufrock" (1915)
    b. Robert Frost's entire poem "The Road Not Taken" (1916)
    c. Carl Sandburg's whole short poem "Fog" (1916)
    d. All of these use the same device as Shakespeare

117. Of the following sentences, which one appeals to emotion?

    a. It is dangerous to use a cell phone while driving because you steer one-handed.
    b. Statistics of accident risk show that cell-phone use while driving is dangerous.
    c. It is really stupid to use a cell phone when you drive because it is so dangerous.
    d. Many state laws ban cell-phone use when driving due to data on more accidents.

118. Which of the following gives an example of a fallacy of inconsistency?

    a. "There are exceptions to all general statements."
    b. "Please pass me; my parents will be upset if I fail."
    c. "He is guilty; there is no evidence that he is innocent."
    d. "Have you stopped cheating on your assignments?"

119. In the 1984 comedy movie *All of Me,* a character from another country, who has no experience with either telephones or flush toilets, flushes a toilet and then a phone rings. He flushes again and the phone rings again. After this occurs several times, the character concludes that pulling the toilet's flush handle causes the ringing. This is an example of which type of cognitive bias?

    a. An above-average effect
    b. A clustering illusion
    c. A confirmation bias
    d. A framing bias

120. Archie says, "Asian people are all terrible drivers." The *most precise* definition of this statement is...

    a. A stereotype.
    b. An inference.
    c. An assumption.
    d. A generalization.

Answers and Explanations

1. B: The author of the excerpted poem, "To His Coy Mistress," is Andrew Marvell. Marvell, Donne (A), Herbert (C), and Vaughan (D) were all members of a group of mainly 17th-century poets known as the Metaphysical Poets for their common time period, themes, content, and style.

2. A: Carpe diem is Latin for "seize the day." This tradition reflects the theme that time flies and that life is fleeting, and thus we should take advantage of the present moment. The tradition of classicism (B) reflects ancient Greek and Roman ideals of beauty and principles of form and discipline (as opposed to Romanticism's principles of emotional impact), as reflected in the works of Alexander Pope and John Dryden. The cinquain (C) is a five-line type of poem in which line 1 is a one-word title, line 2 contains two words describing the title, line 3 has three words telling the action, line 4 contains four words expressing the feeling, and line 5 reverts back to one word that recalls the title. The conceit (D) type of poetry uses a metaphor, simile, or image comparing two very dissimilar things, such as Shakespeare's Sonnet # 18, "Shall I compare thee to a summer's day?"

3. D: Tetrameter means four beats per line, which is the meter of the rhymed couplets in this poem. Pentameter (A) means five beats per line. Heptameter (B) means seven beats per line. Hexameter (C) means six beats per line. Also, beats are only the stressed syllables, not total syllables.

4. B: This is the opening sentence of James Joyce's last novel, *Finnegans Wake* (1939). He published *Ulysses* (A) previously, in 1922; and *A Portrait of the Artist as a Young Man* (D) even earlier, in 1916. *Adventures in the Skin Trade* (C) was not written by Joyce but by Dylan Thomas (1938).

5. D: Joyce used the word "vicus" because it means "vicinity" (A) or "lane" in Latin; to refer to Vico Way (B), the name of the shore road running alongside of Dublin Bay; and to allude to Giambattista Vico (C), an Italian philosopher (1688-1744) who espoused the cyclic theory of history, a theme in Joyce's novel.

6. C: The lower-case initial letter of the first word was not an error (D). It did not continue Joyce's previous novel (B). And he did not use it to make the opening stand out as different to the reader (A). Rather, it is uncapitalized to show that it completes the book's last sentence fragment, "A way a lone a last a loved a long the—." By writing the end of the book to be completed and continued only by the beginning, Joyce embodied the cyclical nature of history and of the novel within its sentence structure.

7. A: Joyce is famous for using stream-of-consciousness in his novels, as in *Ulysses* and *Finnegans Wake*. The unreliable narrator (B) is a technique used often in murder mysteries, as by Edgar Allan Poe in "The Tell-Tale Heart," "The Cask of Amontillado," and many other stories and by Agatha Christie in *The Murder of Roger Ackroyd*. Joyce is not famous for using it. He used third-person narration and often included soliloquies, but is not famous for using first-person narration (C). An example of the author surrogate (D) is Socrates in Plato's works; Joyce is not known for using this technique.

8. D: "The Emperor of Ice-Cream" was written by Wallace Stevens in 1922. The style of the excerpted stanza is typical of modern poetry and does not reflect the conventions of 17th-century (A), 18th-century (B), or 19th-century (C) poems.

9. A: "In kitchen cups concupiscent curds" makes use of alliteration, the repetition of the same initial sound and/or letter in adjoining or nearby words—in this case, the sound /k/ from the letter

- 123 -

"c." Hyperbole (B) is the device of exaggeration. Onomatopoeia (C) is the device of words sounding like what they mean (for example, "the clang of the bell" or "the gun went bang"). Metonymy (D) is the device of referring to a noun by an associated thing (such as using "the White House" to mean the U.S. government, or "Hollywood" to mean the American film and television industry).

10. C: Plato's *Dialogues* expound the philosophy of Socrates, including the concept that the mortal life of humanity and the world of the human senses and perception are an illusion, while the eternal life of the divine and the world of the ideal are reality, rather than vice versa. Stevens refers to this concept with "Let be be finale of seem"—meaning that "seem" is what we perceive, and is followed by "be," which is the reality found after life—as the first stanza's boys bringing flowers is continued in the second (final) stanza with references to shrouding a dead woman's body. A main theme in option (A) is the creation of the world; an allegorical journey through Hell, Purgatory, and Heaven in choice (B); and, in option (D), a journey home from war, which is also an allegory for every man's life journey.

11. B: The author, Jonathan Swift, wrote the excerpted piece, "A Modest Proposal," as a satire. He was not literally suggesting that children be cooked and eaten, but lampooning the way the British looked down on the Irish with his "proposal" as an ironic example of a "solution" to the poverty and overpopulation in Ireland. Persuasion (A) is a form of argument to sway the reader rather than make fun of something. Exposition (C) is also a straightforward method of giving information. Bathos (D) is a literary mood of overstated emotion that moves suddenly from the sublime to the ridiculous or pedestrian to create an anticlimactic effect.

12. C: "A Modest Proposal" was published in 1729, i.e., the 18th century. It does not have the modern style of the 20th (A) century. The bulk of Swift's work was published in the 1700s, with several pieces published in the late 1690s (D)—but not this one. Swift died in 1745 and even *A Journal to Stella,* published posthumously, was published in 1766, so the 19th century (B) is incorrect.

13. D: Jonathan Swift, author of the excerpted satirical essay "A Modest Proposal," also wrote *Gulliver's Travels* (1726, 1735), a novel satirizing human behavior and parodying the travel genre. *The Canterbury Tales* (A) were written by Geoffrey Chaucer in the 14th century. *The Faerie Queene* (B) was written by Edmund Spenser in the 16th century. *Paradise Lost* (C) was written by John Milton in the 17th century.

14. D: Hughes uses (extended) metaphor by describing the concrete presence of a fox to represent the abstract concept of a poet's inspiration. From beyond the blank window, starless sky, and dark forest, the fox, as a totem for the writer's imagination, approaches from without to inspire, its pawprints in the snow symbolizing print appearing on the blank page. Foreshadowing (A) is the literary device of hinting earlier in a work at something that will become more apparent later. Irony (B) is the device of creating a discrepancy between what is expected and what really occurs (verbal, dramatic, or situational irony). Hughes's work is notable for NOT including any overused expressions known as clichés (C).

15. C: The poem describes how the poet is inspired to write, using the fox to embody the thought that enters the poet's mind (hence the title "The Thought-Fox"). The fox's natural actions (A) are thus symbolic rather than literal. The poet is not inspired by nature (B); in this poem, he uses an element of nature (the fox) to represent the thought that he receives and writes. The fox's entering "the head" is not a literal attack (D) but a symbolic representation of having or getting that thought.

16. B: The poet's passivity and lack of control over the thought, or content, of his writing can be interpreted from Hughes's separation of the thought, which does not arise from within his head, but

approaches symbolically in the form of a fox from outside of his head, his body, and even his house. This separation is emphasized by the description of the Thought-Fox as "Coming about its own business." The poet as passive recipient is further shown in the last stanza, where the fox "enters the dark hole of the head." This passivity is further reflected in the last line, "The page is printed," as Hughes uses passive voice to represent the writing process, rather than saying that he himself prints the page.

17. A: This poem is written in free verse, meaning it has no regular rhyme scheme (options B and D) or metrical pattern (choices B and C). There is some partial rhyming, as in the sight rhyme of "snow" and "now" in stanza 3; the near rhymes of "star" with "near" in stanza 2 and "lame" with "come" in stanza 3; the rhymes of "darkness" and "loneliness" in stanza 2, "snow" and "hollow" in stanza 4, and "greenness" with "business" in stanza 5; and the off rhyme of "fox" with "ticks" in the last stanza. However, these are not regular, like the repeated rhymes of an established rhyme scheme. There is also no regular meter or number of beats per line. Hence the overall form of this poem is free verse.

18. C: The bell jar is a metaphor, an implied comparison between two things. A simile (A) is an overtly stated comparison; it would be a simile if she had written, "It was *like* a bell jar." An allusion (B) is an implied, indirect, or incidental reference, usually to a real or fictional person, place, or event. Personification (D) or anthropomorphism is attributing human characteristics to non-human animals or things.

19. B: The bell jar is Plath's metaphor for her mental illness. She describes feeling confined, not by reality (A), but by her own depression and its attendant alienated feelings and distorted perceptions. Writer's block (C) was not the bell jar but a symptom of it (her illness), as when she wrote about fearing she would never be able to write again. Moreover, though Plath did experience inability to write at times and her fear was genuine, she also produced many great poems as well as this novel during and in spite of her illness. Her references to "stewing in my own sour air," being unable to stir with the "air of the bell jar wadded round me," closed off from the "circulating air," being "blank and stopped as a dead baby," and "the bell jar, with its stifling distortions," do not signify any literal breathing disorder (D), but rather a metaphorical lack of the fresh air of reality and sanity.

20. D: Sylvia Plath underwent a serious breakdown and hospitalization in 1953; she wrote about this experience in *The Bell Jar* around 1961 (published in England in 1963 and America in 1971.) *The Bell Jar* was Plath's only novel (A). Plath wrote many poems, not a few (C). She did not recover to live a long life or write more novels (B); she committed suicide in 1963, a month after *The Bell Jar*'s London publication. (There is some evidence she intended to have the suicide attempt discovered and be rescued from it. She recounts a number of suicide attempts in *The Bell Jar*, which were either discovered in time or she found she could not complete.) While she wrote other prose pieces early in her career, *The Bell Jar* was, she wrote, "my world... as seen through the distorting lens of a bell jar." Before her death at age 30, she had intended to write a second novel about "that same world as seen through the eyes of health."

21. B: Shakespeare (1564-1616) wrote during the Renaissance. The Medieval (A) era (also known as the Middle Ages) was earlier, ending before the 16th century (circa 1485), and included authors like Geoffrey Chaucer, Dante Alighieri, the Pearl Poet and author of *Sir Gawain and the Green Knight*, and Sir Thomas Malory. The Restoration (C) period followed the Renaissance, circa 1660-1700, and included authors like John Dryden, who wrote poetry, satire, and criticism. The Enlightenment (D) occurred from 1700-1785, and included the authors Jonathan Swift, Alexander Pope, Dr. Samuel Johnson and James Boswell.

22. A: John Bunyan (1628-1688) was the author of *The Pilgrim's Progress*, a religious allegory. William Congreve (B) (1670-1729) wrote *The Way of the World,* originally a play not successful on the theatre stage, but subsequently highly regarded as a literary exemplar of the comedy of manners. Daniel Defoe (C) (circa 1660-1731) is known for *Robinson Crusoe* and other adventure novels. Samuel Butler (D) (1612-1680), one of the Augustan poets, wrote the burlesque poem "Hudibras."

23. B: This is the first stanza of "The Passionate Shepherd to His Love" by Christopher Marlowe (1564-1593). Andrew Marvell (A) also included poems on pastoral themes in his oeuvre, including "The Garden"; however, he lived later (1621-1678) than Marlowe and was one of the Metaphysical Poets. Sir Walter Raleigh (C) was more contemporary (1552-1618) with Marlowe and wrote "The Nymph's Reply to the Shepherd," among others. William Shakespeare (D) was a contemporary (1564-1616) of Raleigh and Marlowe and also included pastoral themes in his songs and sonnets, including "Shall I compare thee to a summer's day?"

24. C: The rhyme scheme of this stanza, and the rest of the poem, is AABB: The second line rhymes with the first, and the fourth line rhymes with the third. This use of rhyming couplets was popular in the poetry of the time.

25. D: All of the above. The legend of Faust, who sold his soul to the devil in exchange for knowledge (echoing Adam and Eve's fall from grace in Eden caused by their desire for knowledge), has been popular throughout the various literary eras. Marlowe (A) wrote *Dr. Faustus* near the end of the 1500s. Goethe (B) wrote his German dramatic masterpiece *Faust* in the 19th century. Mann (C), also German, wrote the novel *Doktor Faustus* in the 20th century.

26. D: None of the above. These are all titles of poems written by Pope. "An Essay on Criticism" (A) is a didactic poem discussing literary theory, modeled after the style, language, and tone of the ancient Roman poet Horace. "The Rape of the Lock" (B) is a satirical poem, like "The Dunciad" and many others; Pope became famous for his satires. "The Universal Prayer" (C) is also a poem from Pope's *Moral Essays,* stating his beliefs. Pope wrote in a variety of styles on diverse subjects, including romantic, philosophical, political, pastoral, and others as well as satires, but all of his works were poetry.

27. C: The poems excerpted are all villanelles (D). The villanelle has nineteen lines with five tercets (three-line stanzas) and an ending quatrain (four-line stanza). The first and third line of the first stanza are alternately quoted in the last line of each subsequent stanza and both lines are repeated as a refrain at the end of the last stanza. Villanelles typically have ABA rhyme schemes. The quoted excerpts are not in ballad (A) form, which often uses quatrains, and rhymes either all alternating lines or second and fourth lines. (A famous example is "The Rime of the Ancient Mariner" by Samuel Taylor Coleridge.) Sonnet (B) form also differs from villanelle form. The Petrarchan sonnet has 14 lines, with a major shift in thinking or *volta* between the octave and sestet. The Shakespearean sonnet's 14 lines are three quatrains with ABAB/CDCD/EFEF rhymes and ending with a pivotal GG couplet. Sonnets also lack the repetition characteristic of villanelles.

28. B: The first poem excerpted, "The Waking" by Theodore Roethke, is a meditation on the nature of waking reality vs. dreaming imagination and which is which; life vs. death, mortality vs. immortality, process/journey vs. product/destination, world vs. self; the constancy of change; and the inability to control or even understand the mysteries of life, nature, and eternity. The second poem excerpted, "Mad Girl's Love Song" by Sylvia Plath (options A and B), also contemplates the nature of reality vs. imagination via the existentialist argument that we construct and destroy our own realities, and nothing objective exists beyond these. The third excerpted poem, "Do not go

- 126 -

gentle into that good night" by Dylan Thomas (options A and C), focuses instead on how the dying should approach death.

29. A: Dylan Thomas' "Do not go gentle into that good night," addressed to his dying father, expresses the idea that death should be approached with spirited resistance rather than serene acceptance. The second poem, Sylvia Plath's "Mad Girl's Love Song," despite its use of the words "drops dead" and "born again," is not dealing with death but rather with the existentialist idea that reality is only what we perceive, imagine, or create and does not exist objectively outside of our own constructs. The first poem, Theodore Roethke's "The Waking," explores the nature of both reality vs. dreaming and life vs. death, but does not deal directly with the subject of death as Thomas' poem does.

30. B: This poem was written around 1862, during the Industrial Revolution when the railroad had recently been invented. (The poet's father was one of the owners of a local railroad.) The poet describes this "iron horse" by appropriately using the extended metaphor of a horse, but is not describing an actual horse (A) or a mythic monster (C). Thus it is not true that the subject of the poem cannot be determined (D).

31. D: This poem was written circa 1862. The American Revolution (A) was 1775-1783, the French Revolution (B) was 1789-1799, and the War of 1812 (C) was 1812-1815. The Civil War (D) was 1861-1865. Therefore, this poem was written during the Civil War period.

32. C: The poet performs an amazing structural feat in reflecting the composition of a railroad train in the composition of the poem's single, 17-line sentence. The first two words "I like" are the only subject and predicate; everything after the object "it" is a series of verbs complementing that object: "lap," "lick," "stop," "step," "peer," "pare," "crawl," "chase," "neigh," and "stop." This syntax mirrors the engine (subject and predicate) pulling the train behind it. The train's structure is not as specifically mirrored in vocabulary (A). The poem's rhythms (B) are typical of this poet, who very often wrote in iambic lines of alternating tetrameter and trimeter. The tone (D), a childlike kind of enthusiasm, is deliberately used to suggest its role as a powerful toy, satirizing the "progress" of the modern invention.

33. D: The poet, Emily Dickinson, chose these words because they both contrast with one another and typify characteristics of domesticated horses, thus carrying out her horse metaphor for the "iron horse" of the railroad train. In this sense, they are not contradictory: horses have great physical power, are larger than humans and could easily kill a human, but domesticated horses, when treated well, are also typically obedient and gentle with humans. Thus these words are contrasting rather than synonyms (A). They are not nonsense words (B). While they describe a mechanical object, they are not mechanical (C) words.

34. B: Dickinson compares the train's whistle, first metaphorically to a horse's neigh, and then in the simile "like Boanerges," the last name/nickname given by Jesus to disciples James and John, sons of Zebedee, in Mark 3:17. This name has since come to mean a fiery and/or vociferous preacher or orator, especially one with a powerful voice. One creature inhabiting Hades in Greek myth (A) was Cerberus, the three-headed guardian dog. A mythological animal in a labyrinth (D) was the Minotaur, slain by Theseus. This was a Greek myth, not a Roman one. (Like most Greek culture, it was later appropriated by the Romans.) One Old Testament prophet who was angry at opponents and prayed for vengeance (C) was Jeremiah.

35. C: Dickinson habitually used dashes as a kind of musical mechanism to establish the prosody of her poems and habitually capitalized the initials of certain words to lend them additional emphasis.

The dashes were not simply punctuation (A); she used other punctuation marks conventionally in places, and the dashes were more a rhythmic device. She did not capitalize to honor (A) the capitalized words. The dashes were not to separate words (B) and the capitals were not used only with names (B, D). The dashes added control to her prosody rather than providing continuity (D).

36. D: The author of this poem, Emily Dickinson, uses personification by attributing human qualities to nonhuman entities, a practice also known as anthropomorphism. She describes how Death "kindly stopped for me" and "knew no haste." She also describes the grain as "gazing," and notes that the setting sun "passed Us," using pronouns ("He") and human actions ("stopped," "drove," "knew," "gazing," "passed," "paused") to describe nonhumans. Analogy (A) is a comparison of different things, like saying that the human heart is like a pump. Hyperbole (B) is exaggeration. Alliteration (C) is repetition of sounds in adjacent or close words. Although "gazing grain" and "setting sun" both use brief alliteration in the poem, the descriptions of Death do not.

37. C: While the topic of this poem is death, it is treated with a lighthearted tone, finding humor in death with a gentle kind of irony. The diction, word choice, rhythms, and conclusion do not convey gravity, portent or darkness (A). The descriptive details of the journey to Eternity, slow yet seemingly over within a day in retrospect, do not convey detachment, alienation, or numbness (B). The deliberate, placid narrative has no frantic, agitated, frenzied, or fearful (D) qualities. Rather, the poet seems to welcome "Immortality" even as she quietly observes Death's "kindly" character and "Civility"—examples of the aforementioned gentle irony regarding death's inevitability, in that even if we cannot "stop for Death," death will still stop for us.

38. B: The fifth stanza about "a House that seemed/A Swelling of the Ground" is an oblique description of a grave. Its cornice is "in the Ground" and the roof is "scarcely visible," indicating that this "House" was underground. This is not a literal description of a home (A) or a church (C). A school (D) with children at recess is literally described as one of the aspects of life they pass in their journey, in the third stanza. The fifth stanza's description of a grave is in keeping with the whole poem's light, gentle, indirect, yet spiritually accepting treatment of death.

39. A: The haiku, originating in Japanese poetry and since adopted in English-language poetry, is a short poem of only three lines, often with 17 syllables, with the first and third lines having five syllables and the second line having seven syllables. (In Japanese there are many other rules, which become very complicated.) Haiku are typically unrhymed, so they do not have a rhyme scheme (B). Similarly, they do not employ any regular meter (C). Because haiku are typically 17 syllables or fewer, they do not involve long narratives (D).

40. B: This book was the actual diary kept by Anne Frank, a Dutch Jewish teenager whose family and others spent two years hiding in another family's attic before being sent to concentration camps by Nazis during World War II. Frank, 14-15 years old at the time, was intelligent and wrote articulately, depicting both the everyday details and the unusual difficulties of life in hiding and constant fear. The book is invaluable today, not only for its personal perspective on history and details of first-hand experiences with war and Nazism, but also as a testament to a young girl's unshakeable faith in human nature, even in the face of horrible inhumanity: she wrote near the end of her entries (July 15, 1944, only weeks before being arrested by Nazis) in one of the book's most often-quoted passages, "I still believe, in spite of everything, that people are truly good at heart."

41. C: All answer choices are novels by Mark Twain. However, while *The Mysterious Stranger* (A) is also a first-person narrative written in the literate language of its narrator, while *The Adventures of Huckleberry Finn* is written in its narrator's uneducated and Southern regional dialect. *The Adventures of Huckleberry Finn* followed and referred to *The Adventures of Tom Sawyer* (B), which is

a third-person narrative rather than in first person. *The Prince and the Pauper* (D) is also a third-person narrative. The use of a first-person narrative in dialect differentiates the correct choice from the others. (*Tom Sawyer* contains similar dialects as *Huckleberry Finn,* but only in dialogue spoken by characters, not in the actual narration, which is third-person and not narrated by a character.) Also, the subject matter of the excerpt does not fit choices A or D.

42. D: In *Sister Carrie* (1900), Drouet is basically a decent person but is deficient in the intelligence or awareness for moral behavior. Therefore, choice A is incorrect. Hurstwood, by contrast, has the intelligence to understand moral behavior, and his awareness allows him to reject his family's superficial values. However, the moral deficiencies of his own character allow him to behave immorally. Therefore, option B is incorrect. In their attitudes toward women, both characters represent the middle class of the time; therefore, choice C is incorrect.

43. C: All choices are titles of poems by the same author, Walt Whitman, and all are published in the volume *Leaves of Grass.* This particular excerpt is taken from "Song of Myself," Whitman's longest and perhaps most famous poem.

44. B: Whitman's masterpiece is his celebration ("singing") of a mystical experience revealing, among other themes, his unity with the universe and nature. This is reflected in the title, *Leaves of Grass,* that he gave his collection of poems including "Song of Myself." The meaning of the excerpt is not simply literal (A). It is also not a metaphor for social classes or roles (C), and it does not refer to mistreatment in a personal relationship (D).

45. B: *Leaves of Grass*, the book of poems containing "Song of Myself," was first published in 1855, and Whitman continued to make revisions over 36 years, releasing subsequent editions through 1891. Hence all editions were published in the 19th century.

46. B: These excerpts are from "The Love Song of J. Alfred Prufrock" by T. S. Eliot. The other choices are also by Eliot. "Prufrock" was one of his earliest poems (published in *Poetry* magazine in 1915 and in a collection, *Prufrock and Other Observations*, in 1917). "The Waste Land" (A), often considered his masterwork, was published in 1922. While these two share several similar themes, "The Waste Land" is far longer and is not written as a dramatic monologue. "Notes Toward the Definition of Culture" (C) is by Eliot, but it is an essay, not a poem. Eliot published his poem "The Hollow Men" (D) in 1925.

47. C: The persona in the poem is speaking about his mortality. His rhetorical questions about parting his hair and eating a peach do not indicate indecision (A) but rather allude to conditions of old age (balding and diarrhea), and the imagery of his dress and the beach allude to retirement—not a vacation (B). This excerpt does not mention drowning (D). (The third excerpt does, but is not literal.)

48. D: Options (A) and (C) both express meanings that can be interpreted from this verse. The speaker compares his existence to that of a crab to show his own sense of unimportance, which is consistent with other parts of the poem expressing his sense of low status (e.g., "No! I am not Prince Hamlet, nor was meant to be... Almost, at times, the Fool"). Moreover, the poet has chosen the image of a crab not only to fit with the poem's other sea imagery, but also because it is a scavenger. Eliot's essay "Tradition and the Individual Talent" suggests that art can rescue the bleakness of modern life by creating beauty from its refuse. The imagery ("ragged," "scuttling," "silent") reinforces this bleak view rather than expressing a simple, literal wish (B).

49. A: This line is an expression of the despair felt by the speaker, characterizing the poet's view of modern life as broken, fragmented, and both alienating and isolating to the individual. While the

speaker often mourns his aging throughout the poem ("I grow old... I grow old"), the statement about the mermaids is not literal as in options B and D. The mermaids represent the beautiful dream of the world of art; the speaker feels he cannot be included in or belong to it, even though he can perceive it. He is not saying the mermaids are not real (C) as in the previous line, he has said, "I have heard the mermaids singing." But they only sing to one another ("each to each"), not to him.

50. B: Hearing the mermaids singing to each other is part of Eliot's imagery, symbolizing the beauty found in art and in the beautiful dreams that both inspire it and are created by it. Prufrock's hearing them singing can also symbolize his glimpses of eternity, immortality, the ideal, and/or Paradise—things that art can portray or even achieve, but which he despairs of experiencing. His hearing them singing to each other but thinking they will not sing to him emphasizes his feelings of isolation and futility, which reflect Eliot's desolate view of the modern condition. The meaning is not primarily literal as in options A, C and D.

51. C: The fabliau is a humorous story including an incident that is nearly always indecent. In "The Miller's Tale," the cuckolded husband hangs his rear end out of the window and flatulates into the face of his wife's lover. "The Reeve's Tale," "The Shipman's Tale," "The Summoner's Tale," and others are additional instances of fabliau in *The Canterbury Tales.* "The Physician's Tale" (A) is an example of the literary form of the classical legend. "The Wife of Bath's Tale" (B), an Arthurian story, is an example of one version of the literary form of the romance. "The Pardoner's Tale" (D) is an example of the literary form of the *exemplum*, a type of instructional anecdote or story often used by preachers in sermons to illustrate moral points or principles.

52. D: *The Great Gatsby* by F. Scott Fitzgerald (1925) and *To the Lighthouse* by Virginia Woolf (1927) are both novels, but neither is a frame tale (a story or stories set within a story). Chaucer's *Canterbury Tales* is a 14th-century work that is rather famous for, among other things, being a frame tale containing multiple stories. Bocaccio's *Decameron* is likewise a 14th-century frame tale containing 100 tales. Each story-within-a-story is told by a different character in both *The Canterbury Tales* and *The Decameron* (A). Vyasa's Sanskrit epic the *Mahabharata* (circa 4th century) and Chaucer's 14th-century *The Parlement of Foules (Parliament of Fowls)* also use the frame tale structure—the former for historical, geographical, religious, and moral instruction and the latter framed in the form of a dream. The Gothic-Romantic novel *Frankenstein* (1818) by Mary W. Shelley and the Victorian novel *Wuthering Heights* by Emily Brontë (1847) also use the narrative structure of the frame tale (C).

53. C: Dante wrote his *Divine Comedy* between 1308 and 1321, consisting of three *canticas* (songs or chants): *Inferno* (Hell), *Purgatorio* (Purgatory) and *Paradiso* (Heaven). It was the first work ever published in vernacular Italian, the everyday language actually spoken by the people. Previously, all publications in Italy were issued in Latin, the language of the Roman Catholic Church. This was also true in other countries dominated by the Roman Empire; throughout the Middle Ages, as vernacular languages developed, books began to be published in the local languages. Cicero wrote *De re publica (On the Republic)* (A) between 54 and 51 BCE, an ancient Roman work published in Latin. Bocaccio finished writing *Il Decameron (The Decameron)* (B) around 1351-1353, after Dante's *Divine Comedy*. Umberto Eco's *Il nome della rosa (The Name of the Rose)* (D) is a novel published in modern Italian in 1980.

54. B: In this line, Yeats refers to the Trojan War, which has been indirectly attributed to the rape of Leda by the god Zeus in the form of a swan. This union produced the war-gods Castor and Polydeuces and also Helen of Troy and Clytemnestra. Helen's elopement with Paris triggered the Trojan War, a conflict powered by the war-gods. In the war, Agamemnon killed Clytemnestra's first husband and infant and took Clytemnestra as his wife. After his 10-year absence in the war,

Clytemnestra killed Agamemnon. As such, this part of Yeats's poem refers to both a murder *and* a war (D). The Trojan War occurred roughly around the 11th-12th century BCE. The Peloponnesian War (C) between Athens and Sparta occurred from 431-404 BCE, ending the Golden Age of Greece. The Punic Wars (A) between Rome and Carthage occurred from 264-246 BCE, establishing Roman dominance. Hence these both occurred far later than the Trojan War.

55. A: This poem is a sonnet. Specifically, it is the Petrarchan (Italian) sonnet form, composed of an octave (eight lines) and a sestet (six lines), with the transition from former to latter signaling a major change. (The Shakespearean or English sonnet is composed of three quatrains followed by a couplet.) The third line of the sestet is broken for emphasis. It is not a villanelle (B), which has 19 lines rather than the sonnet's 14 and uses a convention of repetition. This poem uses rhyme schemes of ABAB repeated in the octave and ABC repeated in the sestet, and is in iambic pentameter, hence it is not free verse (C). It is not a sestina (D), which dates back to 12th-century Provençal troubadours and has 39 lines rather than 14.

56. B: Yeats' question at the end of the poem best suggests the poignancy of the human condition, which is necessarily incomplete as we do not and cannot have the power or knowledge of the divine. Yeats asks whether, but does not state that, Leda "put on his knowledge with his power" (A). While certainly ancient Greece portrayed humans interacting differently with divinity than modern Western culture does (C), this is not Yeats's point. He uses this mythological event as a device for telescoping sex and history, showing how it generated ("engenders there") forces dominating the Western world, and musing about what Leda might have experienced in the moment. Line 13, "...his knowledge with his power" does not indicate she gained the latter but not the former (D). It asks if she "put on" the two together.

57. C: The Syntactic Cueing System is that set of cues available in the syntax. Syntax is the sentence structure and word order of language. The Phonological (A) Cueing System is that set of cues available in the phonological structure of language. Phonological structure is the language's speech sounds and the letters representing them. The Semantic (B) Cueing System is that set of cues available in the semantics. Semantics are the meaning (and meanings) of words and the morphemes (smallest units of meaning) that comprise words. The Three Cueing Systems model does not include a Pragmatic (C) system. However, it recognizes, as all linguists and reading instructors do, that pragmatic cues involve reader understanding of their reasons for reading and of how text structures operate. (In linguistics, pragmatics is the study of how language is used for social communication.)

58. D: Semantics refers to the meanings of words and language. The semantic system in the Three Cueing Systems model is the set of cues (including words, phrases, sentences, discourse, and complete text) that readers can use to recognize words based on meanings. Pragmatic cues (A) are based on reader purposes for reading and reader understanding of text structure. The phonological system (B) consists of cues related to the phonemic (or sound) structure of language. The syntactic system (C) consists of cues related to the sentence structure and word order of language.

59. C: Phonological cues are based on the speech sounds in words and their alphabetic representations in print. Readers can identify words by knowing sound-to-letter correspondences. Syntactic cues (A) are based on how words are arranged and ordered to create meaningful phrases, clauses and sentences. Semantic cues (B) are based on the meanings of morphemes and words and how they combine to create additional meanings. Pragmatic cues (D) are based on the readers' purposes for reading and their understanding of how textual structures function in the texts that they read.

60. B: Pragmatics is the study of how language is used socially for communication. In reading instruction, pragmatic cues relate to the reader's purposes for reading and the reader's understanding of the workings of textual structures. Although pragmatic cues are valid and important, the Three Cueing Systems model does not include a pragmatic "system." The three cueing systems named in this theory are the phonological system of sound cues (D), the Semantic system of meaning cues (C), and the Syntactic system of sentence-structure cues (A).

61. D: Reading instructors should teach students to activate their prior knowledge because it will improve their reading comprehension. Before reading (A), teachers should discuss and model connections with existing knowledge to prepare students by helping them consider what they already know about the subject of the text. While they read (B), students can make better sense of the text by considering how it fits with what they already know. After reading (C), teachers can lead discussions helping students focus on how the connections they made between the text and their previous knowledge informed their understanding of the text, and on how the text helped them build on their foundations of existing knowledge.

62. C: Certain cognitive strategies used by good readers have been identified through research. Teaching children these strategies and helping them apply these until they can do so independently are found to support mastery of reading comprehension. Good readers who use such successful strategies are not necessarily reading teachers, and it is not necessary for students to find different ways (A) to apply them. Such strategies are less likely to be used by beginning students, and always applying them with assistance (B) without ever graduating to independent application is less effective. These strategies are used by all proficient readers, not just published writers (D). Finally, creativity is important to many kinds of writing, but not necessary to understand what one reads.

63. A: The student making this observation is connecting reading of a mythological text (presumably Greek or Roman) s/he reads to the world—in this instance, to human nature—by noting that despite greater powers, the gods' emotional reactions and behaviors are like those of humans. The student statement in option B reflects a connection of text to text—fiction (a novel) to historical accounts of a period (for example, see Dickens's *A Tale of Two Cities)*. The student statement in option C reflects a connection of text to self: the student can relate to the feelings of a character in the text. Because each choice reflects a different one of the three kinds of student connections named, option D is incorrect.

64. C: Thinking about thinking, or understanding our own cognitive processes, is known as metacognition. Explicitly teaching effective reading comprehension strategies does more than deepen student understanding of reading: it also promotes the higher-order, abstract cognitive skill of metacognition. Schemata (A) (plural; singular is *schema*) is Piaget's term for mental constructs we form to understand the world. Piaget said we either assimilate new information into an existing schema or alter an existing schema to accommodate the new knowledge. Reading instruction experts may refer to experience or background knowledge as schemata because students undergo this cognitive process when they fit what they read to their existing knowledge/experience. Scaffolding (B), a term coined by Jerome Bruner, refers to the temporary support given to students as needed while they learn, which is gradually reduced as they become more independent. Reading instruction experts may also describe students' connections of text to prior experience as scaffolding. Metamorphosis (D) is a term meaning a transformation—literally in biology as with caterpillars into butterflies, or figuratively, as in Franz Kafka's *The Metamorphosis,* wherein protagonist Gregor Samsa becomes a cockroach.

65. B: Why the students participate in a reading/learning activity refers to the motivation for the activity. Option A refers to the timing of the reading/learning activity. Option C refers to the place

or physical setting of the learning activity. Option D refers to the way(s) in which the learning activity is defined and executed. All of these activity settings are factors that influence learning differently according to the different cultural, social, and economic factors involved in each specific situation.

66. A: The process of actively constructing meaning from reading is interactive, in that it involves the text itself, the person reading it, and the setting in which the reading is done: the reader interacts with the text, and the text interacts with the reader by affecting him/her; the context of reading interacts with the text and the reader by affecting them both; and the reader interacts with the reading context as well as with the text. Choice B is a better definition of the *strategic* aspect of the process. Options C and D are better definitions of the *adaptable* aspect of the process.

67. B: Researchers find that learners of both their native language (L1) and a second language (L2) go through all three developmental stages, which means that choices A and C are both incorrect. However, learners of a second language are often urged by teachers and others to skip the Silent Period, whereas young children acquiring their native languages are not similarly expected to speak immediately. L2 learners are not likely to undergo the third stage later (D) but sooner than or at a similar time as L1 learners, due either to having not yet learned all linguistic forms of the L2 or to being unable to access all of the L2's forms as they produce language.

68. C: L2s can be learned in a number of educational contexts, such as being segregated from the L1, formally taught via the medium of the L1, through submersion, or within the language classroom but not used to communicate outside it, among many others. They can also be taught/learned in several natural contexts: as the majority language to members of ethnic minority groups, as the official language of a country where learners are non-natives, or for international communication purposes separate from the L1 or official language. Therefore, it is not accurate that L2s are never learned in natural contexts (B and D). Unlike L2s, L1s are always first acquired in natural contexts, meaning choice A is inaccurate.

69. D: The process of fossilization occurs when some of the incorrect forms a learner of a second language has developed are not corrected over time, but become permanently fixed. (When a learner's L2 contains many such fossilized forms, it is termed an interlanguage.) Vygotsky's Zone of Proximal Development (A), in which a learner can accomplish tasks with assistance that s/he could not yet achieve independently, applies to the acquisition of both first and second languages. The hypothesis that there is a critical period for learning language (B) has also been applied to both L1 and L2 acquisition. In the same way, proponents of linguistic universals—both the typological universals proposed by Greenberg and the Universal Grammar described by Chomsky—find that in both first- and second-language learning, marked (language-specific) features do not transfer and are harder to learn, while unmarked (universal across most languages) features conform to general linguistic principles and are easier to learn. Fossilization is the only choice that occurs exclusively in second-language acquisition.

70. C: Omitting articles (for example, *a/an, the, these*) and plural endings (*–s*), which is common among Chinese ESL students, is not because they have not yet learned the English forms (A) or words for these. Nor are these omissions a way to avoid having to choose the correct form among various English irregularities (C). Nor are these errors due to the student's lack of understanding of the relationship between the Chinese and English versions of the forms (D). Rather, Chinese does not include articles or plural endings the way English does, so the student has no frame of reference or comparison. Therefore, the student's ESL pattern of absent articles and plurals reflects the nature and rules of the L1, which have transferred to the L2 but are incompatible with it.

71. B: As linguists have long pointed out, dialects are NOT non-standard versions of a language (A). In linguistics, dialects are *differing* varieties of any language, but these may be vernacular (nonstandard) OR standard versions of a language. They are often considered less socially acceptable, especially in educational, occupational and professional settings, than whichever standard version is most accepted. The linguistic features of dialects are not incorrect (C), but simply different. Their use does not indicate poor or incomplete language learning (D).

72. A: The formal version of Standard English is reflected in dictionaries and grammar books and applied in written language. In speech, Standard English is NOT universal (B): it differs in pronunciation between the regions of North America and between native English speakers in England, Ireland, Australia, India, and other English-speaking areas. Speech communities use a more flexible variety of *informal* Standard English rather than the Standard English of writing (C). The construct of Standard English actually includes a range of dialects (D) because formal Standard English is used in writing and not speech, which by nature dictates a less formal, more flexible version.

73. C: The Great Vowel shift was a huge shift in the phonemics of English pronunciation that occurred from the 15th to 18th centuries in all places where English was spoken and written.

74. B: During the Great Vowel shift, the location of the tongue in the mouth where the long vowels in English were produced eventually shifted to a higher position, altering the sounds of their pronunciation. For example, the letter "e," pronounced /e/ (the sound spelled as "-ay" by Modern English speakers) in Chaucer's day (as it is still pronounced in Romance languages), gradually changed to be pronounced /i/ (the sound spelled as "ee" in Modern English). The tongue's movement back (A), down (C), or front (D) in the mouth would produce respectively different phonemes.

75. A: Shakespeare lived from circa 1564-1616 and wrote most of his known plays and poems between 1589 and 1613, or in the late 16th and early 17th centuries. The Great Vowel Shift occurred from the 15th to 18th centuries. Thus, Shakespeare wrote his Elizabethan English during this major language change. Geoffrey Chaucer (B) lived from circa 1343-1400 and wrote his known works between roughly 1369 and 1399. Therefore, his Middle English was the form that existed *before* the Great Vowel Shift took place. Emily Dickinson (C) wrote her poetry during the 19th century, *after* the Great Vowel Shift. The Pearl Poet (D), author of the *Pearl* poem, *Sir Gawain and the Green Knight,* and other works was a contemporary of Chaucer, meaning his works were also written *before* the Great Vowel Shift.

76. B: Linguists generally analyze the Great Vowel Shift as having consisted of eight steps: Step 1 = /i/ and /u/ → /əI/ and /əU/; Step 2 = /e/ and /o/ → /i/ and /u/; Step 3 = /a/ → /æ/; Step 4 = /ɛ/ → /e/, /ɔ/ → /o/; Step 5 = /æ/ → /ɛ/; Step 6 = /e/ → /i/; Step 7 = /ɛ/ → /e/; and Step 8 = /əI/ and /əU/ → /aI/ and /aU/. Step 1 involved downward shifts, Step 3 a forward shift, and Step 8 downward shifts. However, the overall effect of the Great Vowel Shift across all of its steps was an upward shift in the placement of the tongue in the mouth in the pronunciation of all long English vowels.

77. D: The Great Vowel Shift ultimately changed the pronunciation of the long vowels in English completely. Consequently, it has affected orthographic conventions and rules (A), instruction in reading (B), and how easily the modern readers of English texts can comprehend literature written before the GVS (C), as in the works of Chaucer and others. The sources of difficulty (in addition to changes in vocabulary and usage) for modern readers include not only the earlier spellings, but also the pronunciations that affected those spellings, as well as rhymes.

78. C: The etymology, or origin, of the English word *debt* is the Latin word *debitum*. It came into English during the Middle English form of the language. Therefore, this word was not originally a Middle English word (A) but a Latin word. Because it came from Latin into Middle English, it did not exist as an Old English word with a voiced *b* (B) as Old English preceded Middle English. The origin of this word was not Greek (D) but Latin. NOTE: Early scribes and printers, described by some as "inkhorn scholars," introduced many silent letters to English spellings to indicate their Latin or Greek roots, as in this case.

79. B: In Old Italian, the word *disastro* meant unfavorable in one's stars. It was commonplace to attribute bad fortune to the influences of the stars in the Medieval and Renaissance eras. The Old Italian word came into English in the late 1500s as "disaster" and was used by Shakespeare (cf. *King Lear*). The word's Latin root is *astrum*, meaning "star," and the Latin prefix *dis-*, meaning "apart" and signifying negation. *Catastrophe* (A) and *misfortune* (C) are both Modern English meanings of the word "disaster," whereas the "ill-starred" meaning used in Elizabethan times has now become archaic or obsolete. The root means "star," not the aster flower (D).

80. A: The Latin word *sal* meant "salt." According to the famous ancient historian Pliny the Elder, "in Rome, a soldier was paid in salt," as it was a means of preserving food in the days before refrigeration and was thus a very valuable commodity. The Latin term *salarium*, from the root *sal*, originally meant the salt paid to soldiers but eventually became generalized to mean any kind of payment. (The expression "worth your salt" also derives from this origin.) "Salary" may sound similar to "celery" (B), but their roots and meanings are not the same. While salt eventually referred to any kind of payment including money or other kinds, it never originally meant *money* (C). "Earnings" (D) is a Modern English synonym for "salary" rather than the original meaning of its root word.

81. B: The word "brunch" is a blend of "breakfast" and "lunch". Blends of two or more words are known as portmanteau words. (*Portmanteau* is a French word meaning a suitcase.) "Fax" (A) is an example of clipping, or shortening a word, from its original "facsimile." "Babysitter" (C) is an example of compounding, or combining two or more words into one. "Saxophone" (D) is an example of proper noun transfer: A Belgian family that built musical instruments had the last name of Sax, and this wind instrument was named after them. These represent some of the ways that new words have entered—and still do enter—the English language.

82. C: Neologisms (from *neo-* meaning "new"), also known as "creative coinages," are new words sometimes invented by people which then become parts of our vocabulary. The word "quark" was first coined by the great Irish author James Joyce; he used it in his last novel, *Finnegans Wake*. The physicist Murray Gell-Mann then chose this word from Joyce's work to name the model of elementary particles he proposed (also proposed concurrently and independently by physicist George Zweig) in 1964. Blending (A) is another way new words come into our language; for example, "moped" is a blend of the respective first syllables of "motor" and "pedal." Conversion (B), also called functional shift, changes a word's part of speech. For example, the common nouns "network," "microwave," and "fax," along with the proper noun "Google" have all been converted to verbs in modern usage. Onomatopoeia (D) means words that imitate associated sounds, such as "meow" and "click."

83. D: This is an example of a compound-complex sentence. A simple (A) sentence contains a subject and a verb and expresses a complete thought. Its subject and/or verb may be compound (e.g., "John and Mary" as subject and "comes and goes" as verb). A complex (B) sentence contains an independent clause and one or more dependent clauses. The independent and dependent clauses are joined by a subordinating conjunction or a relative pronoun. A compound (C) sentence contains

- 135 -

two independent clauses—two simple sentences—connected by a coordinating conjunction. A compound-complex (also called complex-compound) sentence, as its name implies, combines both compound and complex sentences: it combines more than one independent clause with at least one dependent clause. In the example sentence given, the first two clauses, joined by "however," are independent, and the clause modifying "actual test questions," beginning with "which cover," is a relative, dependent clause.

84. C: A euphemism is an expression used instead of more literal words to make a harsh expression sound softer, to make an impolite description sound more polite, or to make a description less polite (such as saying "bit the dust" instead of "died" in a formal setting). Jargon (A) is the specialized terminology of a specific field or group. This example, however, is NOT medical jargon; a better example might be "expired" or "deceased." Ambiguity (B) means unclear and/or open to multiple interpretations. A better example of ambiguity in this scenario might be, "The surgery did not obtain all of the desired outcomes." This can mean a greater number of things than that the patient died. A connotation (D) is a suggested meaning associated with the literal meaning of a word. For example, "The surgery was abortive" does not state that the patient died, but if the surgery was meant to save the patient's life, the adjective "abortive," meaning unsuccessful or failing to obtain the desired result, could connote that the patient died.

85. B: Typically, after students write something, teachers may ask them to reflect on what they wrote, which would mean that this is NOT a prewriting activity. In writing exercises, teachers will typically ask students to plan (A) what they will write in order to clearly define their main topic and organize their work. Many teachers find it helps students to visualize (C) what they are reading and/or want to write about, and make drawings of what they visualize as preparation for writing. Brainstorming (D) is another common prewriting activity designed to generate multiple ideas from which students can select.

86. A: After prewriting (planning, visualizing, brainstorming), the correct sequence of steps in the writing process are drafting, in which the writer takes the material generated during prewriting work and makes it into sentences and paragraphs; revising, where the writer explores to improve the quality of the writing; editing, in which the writer examines his or her writing for factual and mechanical (grammar, spelling, punctuation) errors and correcting them; and publishing, when the writer finally shares what he or she has written with others who will read it and give feedback.

87. B: Researchers have found that the writing processes both form a hierarchy and are observably recursive in nature. Moreover, they find that when students continually revise their writing, they are able to consider new ideas and to incorporate these ideas into their work. Thus they do not merely correct mechanical errors when revising (A), they also add to the content and quality of their writing. Furthermore, research shows that writers, including students, not only revise their actual writing, during rewrites, they also reconsider their original writing goals rather than always retaining them (C), and they revisit their prewriting plans rather than leaving these unaffected (D).

88. C: Researchers have found that children know a great deal more about a given topic than what their writing usually reflects. Therefore, options A and D are incorrect. Furthermore, researchers have concluded that when children stop writing, they do not do so because they have run out of things to write about the topic (B), but rather because they have not yet developed the means to articulate their knowledge adequately. Educational experts find that these research findings inform writing instruction in that the process of continually rewriting helps children to access and articulate more of the knowledge they actually have.

89. D: This description is most typical of the process of peer review. Classmates read a peer's paper and then identify values in it, describe it, ask questions about it, and suggest points for revision. These are types of helpful feedback identified by experts on writing and collaborative writing. The other choices, however, are not typically collaborative. For a portfolio assessment (A), the teacher collects finished work products from a student over time, eventually assembling a portfolio of work. This affords a more authentic assessment using richer, more multidimensional, and more visual and tactile products for assessment instead of using only standardized test scores for assessment. Holistic scoring (B) is a method of scoring a piece of writing for overall quality (evaluating general elements such as focus, organization, support, and conventions) rather than being overly concerned with any individual aspect of writing. A scoring rubric (C) is a guide that gives examples of the levels of typical characteristics in a piece of writing that correspond to each available score (for example, scores from 1-5).

90. C: According to the Association of College and Research Libraries, Information Literacy is the set of skills that an individual must have for finding, retrieving, analyzing, and using information. It is required not just for reading and understanding information (A). Information Literacy does not mean learning and retaining a lot of information (B), or only sharing it with others (D), but rather knowing how to find information one does not already have and how to evaluate that information critically for its quality and apply it judiciously to meet one's purposes.

91. B: The early 21st century has been dubbed the Information Age primarily because, with widespread Internet use and other innovations in electronic communications and publishing, there are more sources of information and greater output of available information than ever before. While some agencies might require more information (A), this is only possible because such information is more readily available now. Professionals in higher education and research find that with this new explosion of information, college students cannot possibly gain enough information literacy by just reading texts and writing research papers, and cannot learn all they need to know in four years (C). This period is also not called the Information Age due to an increased student interest in acquiring information (D), but due to the increased access to information.

92. A: It is a standard of Information Literacy (IL) that students must use their own critical thinking skills to evaluate the quality of the information and its sources before they use it. Another standard is that the student should ascertain how much information s/he needs for his/her purposes first, deciding this after uncovering excessive information is inefficient (B). An additional IL standard is to access necessary information in an efficient and effective way. However, none of these standards include the idea that students will lose incidental learning or broadness of scope by doing so (C). IL standards include the principle that students *should* use the information they find in ways that are effective for attaining their specific purposes (D).

93. B: The MLA (Modern Language Association) system for documenting literary sources defines in-line citations in a paper as combining signal phrases, which usually include the author's name and introduce information from a source via a fact, summary, paraphrase, or quotation; parenthetical references following the material cited, frequently at the end of the sentence; and, except for web sources that are unpaginated, page number(s). MLA defines a list of works cited (A) as an alphabetized list found at the end of a research paper that gives the information sources referenced in the paper, including each source's publication information, quotations, summaries, and paraphrases. Guidelines for preparing the list of works cited are provided in the *MLA Handbook*. MLA information notes (C) are an optional addition to the MLA parenthetical documentation system. These notes can be used to add important material without interrupting the paper's flow, and/or to supply comments about sources or make references to multiple sources. They may be endnotes or footnotes. Because only one of the answers is correct, Option D is not possible.

94. C: On the Internet, the name of an author is usually provided but may not be visible at first glance. Web sources frequently include the author's name on another page of the same site, such as the website's home page, or in a tiny font at the very end of the web page, rather than in a more conspicuous location. In such cases, students doing online research may have to search more thoroughly than usual to find the author's name. Therefore, they should not immediately assume the author is not named (A). Also, many Web sources are sponsored by government agencies or private corporations and do not give individual author names. In these cases, the research paper *should* cite the agency or corporation name as author (B). Finally, it is much more common for online sources to omit an author's name than it is in print sources. In these cases, it is both permitted and advised by the MLA to cite the article or book title instead (D).

95. D: When online sources you are citing in your research paper are in PDFs and other file formats that have stable pagination, the MLA advises including the page number in the research paper's in-text citation because these numbers are valid and do not change. If a Web source has no pagination, as often happens, the MLA does NOT advise avoiding the citation (A), it advises simply making the citation without a page number because there is not one available. Unlike in PDFs (above), when citing a source from a printout, the MLA advises NOT including page numbers even if you see them because the same page numbers are not always found in all printouts (B). It is not true that in-text citations should never include page numbers (C).

96. D: The MLA guidelines for citing multiple authors of the same work in in-text citations (for both print and online sources) dictate using the first author's name plus "et al" for the other authors when there are four or more authors. If there are two (options A and B) or three (options B and C) authors, the guidelines say to name each author, either in a signal phrase [for example, "Smith and Jones note that… (45)" or "Smith, Jones, and Gray have noted… (45)"] or in a parenthetical reference ["(Smith, Jones, and Gray 45)."].

97. C: Persuasive writing has the purpose of expressing the writer's opinion and/or of convincing the reader of something. A movie review is one example of this writing purpose and type. Other examples include advertisements, editorials, book and music reviews, and literary essays. Narration (A) is a type of writing for telling stories. Description (B) is a type of writing for creating a picture using words that evoke imagery for the reader. Exposition (D) is a type of writing for informing and/or explaining.

98. B: Persuasive writing tries to convince readers to agree with the author's opinion or position regarding a topic. To convince others, writers must have sufficient knowledge about the topic, logical thinking skills, strong beliefs about the topic, and enough technical skill for making logical points, supporting one's opinions, and swaying the reader's emotions. Expository (A) writing aims to give information and/or explanations. It requires sufficient knowledge, practicality, and the technical skill for writing clarity, but it is not as hard as persuasion because it seeks not to convince the reader of anything, only to inform or explain. Descriptive (C) writing seeks to paint verbal pictures that make the described things real to readers through sensory details. This requires imagination and strong creative writing skills, but is not as difficult as persuading the reader to agree with the author's viewpoint. Narrative (D) writing tells a story and can be the easiest, as storytelling and enjoying stories are natural for most people.

99. A: *The Adventures of Huckleberry Finn* by Mark Twain is a fictional novel. *The Diary of a Young Girl* by Anne Frank is a non-fictional journal. "The Fall of the House of Usher" by Edgar Allan Poe is a fictional short story in the horror genre. Novels, personal narratives like diaries/journals, and short stories, as well as biographies and anecdotes are all types of narrative. Narration tells a story, often (but not always) advances chronologically, and has a beginning, middle, and end. Descriptive

writing (B) paints a word picture using sensory imagery to make an event, scene, thing, or person more real to the imagination of the reader. Other than character sketches, picture captions, and some kinds of advertising, most writing is not completely descriptive: narrative works typically include descriptive parts. Exposition (C) is found in news stories, encyclopedias, research papers, informational essays, and instruction manuals rather than fiction or journals. Persuasion (D) is more characteristic of editorials, reviews, ads, and literary essays than novels, short stories or diaries.

100. B: For any writing assignment, you should first target an audience, perform an audience analysis, and develop an audience profile to determine what you should include in and omit from your writing. Even though the assigning teacher may be the only one to read your writing, you should not assume s/he is your main audience (A) because the teacher may expect you to write for other readers. In addition to first knowing your purpose for writing before beginning, you should also consider what purpose your writing will meet for your readers (C) and how they are likely to use it. Considering your audience's attitude toward what you will write and their likely reactions are also important to shaping your writing and is NOT overthinking (D).

101. C: The kind of audience for your writing, as well as your purpose, will determine what style, tone, and wording you choose. Knowing your audience will enable you to select writing strategies, style and tone, and specific word choices that will be most understandable and appealing to your readers. Knowing the type of audience will also dictate how much time to spend on research (A). Some readers will expect more supporting evidence, while others will be bored or overwhelmed by it. Similarly, you will want to include more or less information depending on who will be reading what you write (B). And while the structure of your piece does inform how you organize your information, you should also vary your organization according to who will read it (D).

102. D: It is best to begin an essay or paper with a broader, more general introduction to the topic, and move to a more focused and specific point regarding the topic—not vice versa (C)—by the end of the introduction. This point is your thesis statement. Writing experts advise *against* the technique of beginning an essay with a dictionary definition (A) because it has been so overused that it has become ineffective and uninteresting. To engage the reader's interest in your topic, it is best to begin with some very attention-getting material rather than leaving it for later (B).

103. C: The first part of the introduction to an essay or paper should be some original, fresh material that will engage the attention of readers enough so they are interested in continuing to read. Following this should be the transitional portion of the introduction, which gives some pertinent background information about the piece's particular purpose (B). This informs the reader of your reason for focusing on your paper or essay's specific topic. The transitional portion moves the piece to the third part of the introduction: the thesis statement (A), which is a clear expression of the main point you are trying to make in your essay or paper. An optional part of the introduction is an explanation of how you will defend your thesis, giving readers a general idea of how your essay or paper's various points will be organized. This is sometimes described as a "road map" (D).

104. B: One recommended technique for beginning an essay is to cite a surprising statistic related to your essay's topic. This will get the readers' attention, while also giving some information about the topic to be discussed in the rest of the piece. Another effective technique is to begin with an interesting quotation that summarizes your position. This adds interest, support, and power; it is not true that you should use only your own words instead of quoting another's (A). It is also untrue that opening with a story or anecdote is contrary to the purposes of an essay or paper (C); when you have some personal interest in your topic, this technique is useful for emotionally engaging the readers in the subject matter. It is not true that asking rhetorical questions will only frustrate

readers (D): this is a technique that helps readers imagine being in different situations so they can consider your topic in new ways.

105. A: While students may sometimes regard the conclusion of their essay or paper as simply the last paragraph that includes all the pieces that they could not fit into earlier parts of the piece, this is an inadequate treatment of the conclusion. Because the conclusion is the last thing the audience reads, they are more likely to remember it. Also, the conclusion is an excellent opportunity to reinforce your main point, remind readers of the importance of your topic, and prod readers to consider the effects of the topic in their own lives and/or in the world at large. A good conclusion should restate your original thesis statement (B), pull together and/or summarize the main points you made (C), and make clear(er) your discussion's or argument's context (D).

106. B: Tone is the writer's overall way of expressing his or her attitude. Voice is who the reader hears speaking in the writing, the individual way the writer uses to express his or her tone—not vice versa (A). Style (options C and D) is the effect a writer creates through language, mechanics, and attitude or the sound (formal or informal) or impressions (seriousness, levity, grace, fluency) of the writing.

107. C: Diction refers to your overall choice of language for your writing, while vocabulary refers to the specific words in a discipline that you use when writing in or about that discipline—not vice versa (A). Jargon (B) is very specialized terminology used in a discipline that is not readily understood by readers outside of that discipline. It is hence less accessible than the vocabulary of the discipline, and only used in writing intended only for those who are already familiar with it. Style refers to the writer's effect through language and technique (D).

108. D: Knowing your purpose for writing means knowing what you want to achieve with the content of your writing, and thus what writing style to use. Your choice of words and how formal or informal your writing is—your diction—*does* affect your style (A). Diction and tone should be consistent in your writing style, and should reflect vocabulary and writing patterns that suit your writing purpose best. Style is not added later to give writing personality (B). It develops from your purpose for writing, or what you want to accomplish with your writing. Style *is* directly related to your control of the content (C) of your writing.

109. C: The verbs quoted all refer to interpreting information in your own words. This task targets the cognitive objective of comprehension. Tasks targeting knowledge recall (A) would ask you to name, label, list, define, repeat, memorize, order, or arrange the material. Tasks targeting application (B) would ask you to calculate, solve, practice, operate, sketch, use, prepare, illustrate, or apply the material. Tasks targeting evaluation (D) would ask you to judge, appraise, evaluate, conclude, predict, score, or compare the material.

110. B: The verbs quoted all refer to taking pieces or parts of information or knowledge and bringing them together to create a whole, and to building relationships among the parts to fit new or different circumstances. Analysis (A) is the opposite of synthesis—breaking information down into its component parts and demonstrating the relationships among those parts. An assignment for analysis would ask you to compare, distinguish, test, categorize, examine, contrast, or analyze information. Evaluation (C) is making judgments based on given criteria, confirming or supporting certain preferences, and persuading the reader. An assignment targeting evaluation would use words like evaluate, predict, appraise, conclude, score, judge, or compare. Application (D) is using knowledge in new contexts. The assignment would ask you to apply, prepare, practice, use, operate, sketch, calculate, solve, or illustrate.

111. A: Evaluation is the most complex of the thinking/writing strategies listed in these choices because it commonly incorporates the other thinking strategies. Knowledge recall (D) requires showing mastery of information learned. Comprehension (C) requires showing understanding of the information learned. Application (B) requires taking the information learned and using it in new or different circumstances. These processes are not as complex as evaluating (or making critical judgments about) the information learned. Analysis and synthesis are also more complex than knowledge recall, comprehension, and application, though less so than evaluation.

112. D: Comparing and contrasting, explaining cause and effect relationships, and analyzing are the most commonly used forms of analysis in college-level writing. Supporting an opinion (C) you have stated in your writing is one of the most commonly used forms of *synthesis*, not analysis, in college-level writing.

113. C: Proposing a solution to some problem or situation is one of the most commonly used forms of synthesis strategies in college-level writing. The other most commonly used synthesis writing strategy is stating an opinion and supporting it with evidence. Explaining cause and effect (A) and comparing and contrasting (B) are two of the most commonly used *analysis* (not synthesis) writing strategies. Using persuasion (D) to convince the reader is typically combined with the other strategies named to add credibility and acceptance to the position stated by the writer.

114. B: A white paper, opinion survey, annotated bibliography, and problem solution are all examples of the exploratory discourse aim. So are definitions, diagnoses, marketing analyses, feasibility studies, and literature (*not* literary) reviews. The expressive (A) discourse aim is reflected in vision statements, mission statements, proposals, constitutions, legislative bills, etc. Examples of writing reflecting the informative (C) discourse aim include news and magazine articles, reports, and encyclopedia articles. Examples of writing reflecting the persuasive (D) discourse aim include political speeches; editorials; ad campaigns; and works of artistic, social, or political criticism.

115. A: This sentence is an analogy, which compares similarities between two concepts to establish a relationship. Analogy can enhance comprehension of a new concept via comparison to an older/more familiar concept. Allegory (B) uses symbolism to represent a more abstract concept with a more concrete concept. Allusion (C) is a passing reference to a specific work/place/person/event. For example, saying "Susan loves to help and care for other people so much that her friends call her Mother Teresa" is an allusion to a famous person for effectiveness. Antithesis (D) juxtaposes words/phrases/sentences with opposite meanings, balancing these to add insight. A good example is Neil Armstrong's statement during the moon landing: "That's one small step for man, one giant leap for mankind."

116. D: All these choices use the literary device of an extended metaphor, as does the quoted Shakespeare passage wherein Romeo describes Juliet as the sun. In option A, Eliot describes the fog as a cat ("...rubs its back... rubs its muzzle... licked its tongue... Let fall upon its back the soot... curled once about the house, and fell asleep.") Similarly, Carl Sandburg's (1916) poem "Fog" (C) describes the fog that "comes on little cat feet." In option B, Frost uses the extended metaphor of two roads that "diverged in a wood" to describe the journey of life.

117. C: This sentence appeals to the reader's emotions by stating simply that it is dangerous and "really stupid" to use a cell phone while driving; it does not provide any evidence or logic to support the statement. Choice A offers a logical, common-sense argument in that steering one-handed makes driving more dangerous. Choice B refers to statistics of greater accident risk to support the statement that cell phone use while driving is dangerous. Such supporting evidence is an appeal to

logic. Choice D cites the fact that many state laws ban cell phone use while driving to support the idea that it is dangerous, and also refers to data on more accidents from doing so. These pieces of supporting evidence also appeal to logic rather than emotion.

118. A: A fallacy of inconsistency exists in a statement that contradicts itself or defeats itself. Saying there are exceptions to all general statements is itself a general statement; therefore, according to the content, this statement must also have an exception, implying there are NOT exceptions to all general statements. Option B is an example of a fallacy of irrelevance: passing or failing is determined by course performance, so asking to pass because parents will be upset if one fails is an irrelevant reason for appealing to a teacher for a passing grade. Option C is an example of a fallacy of insufficiency: a statement is made with insufficient supporting evidence. A lack of evidence of innocence is not enough to prove one is guilty because there could also be an equal lack of evidence of guilt. Option D is an example of a fallacy of inappropriate presumption: asking someone if s/he has stopped cheating presumes that s/he has cheated in the past. The person being asked this question cannot answer either "yes" or "no" without confirming that s/he has indeed been cheating. If the person being asked has not been cheating, then the person asking the question is making a false assumption.

119. B: A clustering illusion is a cognitive bias of attributing cause and effect and patterns to unrelated or random events. The character described considers the phone's ringing an effect caused by flushing the toilet, when in reality the two are unrelated. It was mere coincidence that the first ring occurred after he flushed; subsequent rings always occur at preset time intervals, and his repeated flushes simply coincided with these. The above-average effect (A) is the cognitive bias of overestimating our own abilities. The confirmation bias (C) is our tendency to focus on information confirming our pre-existing beliefs while overlooking conflicting information. In comparing ourselves with other people, we notice others' errors more and our own errors less. The framing bias (D) is being influenced by how information is framed rather than the facts. For example, whether a doctor presents the success or failure rate of an operation can influence the patient's decision to undergo it, even if both rates reflect identical data.

120. A: The statement reflects a stereotype. A stereotype is an assumption or generalization made about everybody in an identified group. Assumptions (C) can be made about many things, not just about the members of a certain group. Generalizations (D) also apply to a great many subjects, not just to the characteristics of a specific group of people. An inference (B) is a conclusion based on available evidence rather than on an overt statement of fact. For example, if Archie said, "That man is Asian, so he must be a terrible driver," he would be making an inference based on his stereotype of Asian people. Therefore, stereotype is the most precise definition of the statement.

How to Overcome Test Anxiety

Just the thought of taking a test is enough to make most people a little nervous. A test is an important event that can have a long-term impact on your future, so it's important to take it seriously and it's natural to feel anxious about performing well. But just because anxiety is normal, that doesn't mean that it's helpful in test taking, or that you should simply accept it as part of your life. Anxiety can have a variety of effects. These effects can be mild, like making you feel slightly nervous, or severe, like blocking your ability to focus or remember even a simple detail.

If you experience test anxiety—whether severe or mild—it's important to know how to beat it. To discover this, first you need to understand what causes test anxiety.

Causes of Test Anxiety

While we often think of anxiety as an uncontrollable emotional state, it can actually be caused by simple, practical things. One of the most common causes of test anxiety is that a person does not feel adequately prepared for their test. This feeling can be the result of many different issues such as poor study habits or lack of organization, but the most common culprit is time management. Starting to study too late, failing to organize your study time to cover all of the material, or being distracted while you study will mean that you're not well prepared for the test. This may lead to cramming the night before, which will cause you to be physically and mentally exhausted for the test. Poor time management also contributes to feelings of stress, fear, and hopelessness as you realize you are not well prepared but don't know what to do about it.

Other times, test anxiety is not related to your preparation for the test but comes from unresolved fear. This may be a past failure on a test, or poor performance on tests in general. It may come from comparing yourself to others who seem to be performing better or from the stress of living up to expectations. Anxiety may be driven by fears of the future—how failure on this test would affect your educational and career goals. These fears are often completely irrational, but they can still negatively impact your test performance.

> **Review Video: 3 Reasons You Have Test Anxiety**
> Visit mometrix.com/academy and enter code: 428468

Elements of Test Anxiety

As mentioned earlier, test anxiety is considered to be an emotional state, but it has physical and mental components as well. Sometimes you may not even realize that you are suffering from test anxiety until you notice the physical symptoms. These can include trembling hands, rapid heartbeat, sweating, nausea, and tense muscles. Extreme anxiety may lead to fainting or vomiting. Obviously, any of these symptoms can have a negative impact on testing. It is important to recognize them as soon as they begin to occur so that you can address the problem before it damages your performance.

> **Review Video: 3 Ways to Tell You Have Test Anxiety**
> Visit mometrix.com/academy and enter code: 927847

The mental components of test anxiety include trouble focusing and inability to remember learned information. During a test, your mind is on high alert, which can help you recall information and stay focused for an extended period of time. However, anxiety interferes with your mind's natural processes, causing you to blank out, even on the questions you know well. The strain of testing during anxiety makes it difficult to stay focused, especially on a test that may take several hours. Extreme anxiety can take a huge mental toll, making it difficult not only to recall test information but even to understand the test questions or pull your thoughts together.

> **Review Video: How Test Anxiety Affects Memory**
> Visit mometrix.com/academy and enter code: 609003

Effects of Test Anxiety

Test anxiety is like a disease—if left untreated, it will get progressively worse. Anxiety leads to poor performance, and this reinforces the feelings of fear and failure, which in turn lead to poor performances on subsequent tests. It can grow from a mild nervousness to a crippling condition. If allowed to progress, test anxiety can have a big impact on your schooling, and consequently on your future.

Test anxiety can spread to other parts of your life. Anxiety on tests can become anxiety in any stressful situation, and blanking on a test can turn into panicking in a job situation. But fortunately, you don't have to let anxiety rule your testing and determine your grades. There are a number of relatively simple steps you can take to move past anxiety and function normally on a test and in the rest of life.

> **Review Video: How Test Anxiety Impacts Your Grades**
> Visit mometrix.com/academy and enter code: 939819

Physical Steps for Beating Test Anxiety

While test anxiety is a serious problem, the good news is that it can be overcome. It doesn't have to control your ability to think and remember information. While it may take time, you can begin taking steps today to beat anxiety.

Just as your first hint that you may be struggling with anxiety comes from the physical symptoms, the first step to treating it is also physical. Rest is crucial for having a clear, strong mind. If you are tired, it is much easier to give in to anxiety. But if you establish good sleep habits, your body and mind will be ready to perform optimally, without the strain of exhaustion. Additionally, sleeping well helps you to retain information better, so you're more likely to recall the answers when you see the test questions.

Getting good sleep means more than going to bed on time. It's important to allow your brain time to relax. Take study breaks from time to time so it doesn't get overworked, and don't study right before bed. Take time to rest your mind before trying to rest your body, or you may find it difficult to fall asleep.

> **Review Video: The Importance of Sleep for Your Brain**
> Visit mometrix.com/academy and enter code: 319338

Along with sleep, other aspects of physical health are important in preparing for a test. Good nutrition is vital for good brain function. Sugary foods and drinks may give a burst of energy but this burst is followed by a crash, both physically and emotionally. Instead, fuel your body with protein and vitamin-rich foods.

Also, drink plenty of water. Dehydration can lead to headaches and exhaustion, especially if your brain is already under stress from the rigors of the test. Particularly if your test is a long one, drink water during the breaks. And if possible, take an energy-boosting snack to eat between sections.

> **Review Video: How Diet Can Affect your Mood**
> Visit mometrix.com/academy and enter code: 624317

Along with sleep and diet, a third important part of physical health is exercise. Maintaining a steady workout schedule is helpful, but even taking 5-minute study breaks to walk can help get your blood pumping faster and clear your head. Exercise also releases endorphins, which contribute to a positive feeling and can help combat test anxiety.

When you nurture your physical health, you are also contributing to your mental health. If your body is healthy, your mind is much more likely to be healthy as well. So take time to rest, nourish your body with healthy food and water, and get moving as much as possible. Taking these physical steps will make you stronger and more able to take the mental steps necessary to overcome test anxiety.

> **Review Video: How to Stay Healthy and Prevent Test Anxiety**
> Visit mometrix.com/academy and enter code: 877894

Mental Steps for Beating Test Anxiety

Working on the mental side of test anxiety can be more challenging, but as with the physical side, there are clear steps you can take to overcome it. As mentioned earlier, test anxiety often stems from lack of preparation, so the obvious solution is to prepare for the test. Effective studying may be the most important weapon you have for beating test anxiety, but you can and should employ several other mental tools to combat fear.

First, boost your confidence by reminding yourself of past success—tests or projects that you aced. If you're putting as much effort into preparing for this test as you did for those, there's no reason you should expect to fail here. Work hard to prepare; then trust your preparation.

Second, surround yourself with encouraging people. It can be helpful to find a study group, but be sure that the people you're around will encourage a positive attitude. If you spend time with others who are anxious or cynical, this will only contribute to your own anxiety. Look for others who are motivated to study hard from a desire to succeed, not from a fear of failure.

Third, reward yourself. A test is physically and mentally tiring, even without anxiety, and it can be helpful to have something to look forward to. Plan an activity following the test, regardless of the outcome, such as going to a movie or getting ice cream.

When you are taking the test, if you find yourself beginning to feel anxious, remind yourself that you know the material. Visualize successfully completing the test. Then take a few deep, relaxing breaths and return to it. Work through the questions carefully but with confidence, knowing that you are capable of succeeding.

Developing a healthy mental approach to test taking will also aid in other areas of life. Test anxiety affects more than just the actual test—it can be damaging to your mental health and even contribute to depression. It's important to beat test anxiety before it becomes a problem for more than testing.

Review Video: Test Anxiety and Depression
Visit mometrix.com/academy and enter code: 904704

Study Strategy

Being prepared for the test is necessary to combat anxiety, but what does being prepared look like? You may study for hours on end and still not feel prepared. What you need is a strategy for test prep. The next few pages outline our recommended steps to help you plan out and conquer the challenge of preparation.

Step 1: Scope Out the Test

Learn everything you can about the format (multiple choice, essay, etc.) and what will be on the test. Gather any study materials, course outlines, or sample exams that may be available. Not only will this help you to prepare, but knowing what to expect can help to alleviate test anxiety.

Step 2: Map Out the Material

Look through the textbook or study guide and make note of how many chapters or sections it has. Then divide these over the time you have. For example, if a book has 15 chapters and you have five days to study, you need to cover three chapters each day. Even better, if you have the time, leave an extra day at the end for overall review after you have gone through the material in depth.

If time is limited, you may need to prioritize the material. Look through it and make note of which sections you think you already have a good grasp on, and which need review. While you are studying, skim quickly through the familiar sections and take more time on the challenging parts. Write out your plan so you don't get lost as you go. Having a written plan also helps you feel more in control of the study, so anxiety is less likely to arise from feeling overwhelmed at the amount to cover. A sample plan may look like this:

- Day 1: Skim chapters 1–4, study chapter 5 (especially pages 31–33)
- Day 2: Study chapters 6–7, skim chapters 8–9
- Day 3: Skim chapter 10, study chapters 11–12 (especially pages 87–90)
- Day 4: Study chapters 13–15
- Day 5: Overall review (focus most on chapters 5, 6, and 12), take practice test

Step 3: Gather Your Tools

Decide what study method works best for you. Do you prefer to highlight in the book as you study and then go back over the highlighted portions? Or do you type out notes of the important information? Or is it helpful to make flashcards that you can carry with you? Assemble the pens, index cards, highlighters, post-it notes, and any other materials you may need so you won't be distracted by getting up to find things while you study.

If you're having a hard time retaining the information or organizing your notes, experiment with different methods. For example, try color-coding by subject with colored pens, highlighters, or post-it notes. If you learn better by hearing, try recording yourself reading your notes so you can listen while in the car, working out, or simply sitting at your desk. Ask a friend to quiz you from your flashcards, or try teaching someone the material to solidify it in your mind.

Step 4: Create Your Environment

It's important to avoid distractions while you study. This includes both the obvious distractions like visitors and the subtle distractions like an uncomfortable chair (or a too-comfortable couch that makes you want to fall asleep). Set up the best study environment possible: good lighting and a comfortable work area. If background music helps you focus, you may want to turn it on, but otherwise keep the room quiet. If you are using a computer to take notes, be sure you don't have any other windows open, especially applications like social media, games, or anything else that could distract you. Silence your phone and turn off notifications. Be sure to keep water close by so you stay hydrated while you study (but avoid unhealthy drinks and snacks).

Also, take into account the best time of day to study. Are you freshest first thing in the morning? Try to set aside some time then to work through the material. Is your mind clearer in the afternoon or evening? Schedule your study session then. Another method is to study at the same time of day that you will take the test, so that your brain gets used to working on the material at that time and will be ready to focus at test time.

Step 5: Study!

Once you have done all the study preparation, it's time to settle into the actual studying. Sit down, take a few moments to settle your mind so you can focus, and begin to follow your study plan. Don't give in to distractions or let yourself procrastinate. This is your time to prepare so you'll be ready to fearlessly approach the test. Make the most of the time and stay focused.

Of course, you don't want to burn out. If you study too long you may find that you're not retaining the information very well. Take regular study breaks. For example, taking five minutes out of every hour to walk briskly, breathing deeply and swinging your arms, can help your mind stay fresh.

As you get to the end of each chapter or section, it's a good idea to do a quick review. Remind yourself of what you learned and work on any difficult parts. When you feel that you've mastered the material, move on to the next part. At the end of your study session, briefly skim through your notes again.

But while review is helpful, cramming last minute is NOT. If at all possible, work ahead so that you won't need to fit all your study into the last day. Cramming overloads your brain with more information than it can process and retain, and your tired mind may struggle to recall even previously learned information when it is overwhelmed with last-minute study. Also, the urgent nature of cramming and the stress placed on your brain contribute to anxiety. You'll be more likely to go to the test feeling unprepared and having trouble thinking clearly.

So don't cram, and don't stay up late before the test, even just to review your notes at a leisurely pace. Your brain needs rest more than it needs to go over the information again. In fact, plan to finish your studies by noon or early afternoon the day before the test. Give your brain the rest of the day to relax or focus on other things, and get a good night's sleep. Then you will be fresh for the test and better able to recall what you've studied.

Step 6: Take a practice test

Many courses offer sample tests, either online or in the study materials. This is an excellent resource to check whether you have mastered the material, as well as to prepare for the test format and environment.

Check the test format ahead of time: the number of questions, the type (multiple choice, free response, etc.), and the time limit. Then create a plan for working through them. For example, if you have 30 minutes to take a 60-question test, your limit is 30 seconds per question. Spend less time on the questions you know well so that you can take more time on the difficult ones.

If you have time to take several practice tests, take the first one open book, with no time limit. Work through the questions at your own pace and make sure you fully understand them. Gradually work up to taking a test under test conditions: sit at a desk with all study materials put away and set a timer. Pace yourself to make sure you finish the test with time to spare and go back to check your answers if you have time.

After each test, check your answers. On the questions you missed, be sure you understand why you missed them. Did you misread the question (tests can use tricky wording)? Did you forget the information? Or was it something you hadn't learned? Go back and study any shaky areas that the practice tests reveal.

Taking these tests not only helps with your grade, but also aids in combating test anxiety. If you're already used to the test conditions, you're less likely to worry about it, and working through tests until you're scoring well gives you a confidence boost. Go through the practice tests until you feel comfortable, and then you can go into the test knowing that you're ready for it.

Test Tips

On test day, you should be confident, knowing that you've prepared well and are ready to answer the questions. But aside from preparation, there are several test day strategies you can employ to maximize your performance.

First, as stated before, get a good night's sleep the night before the test (and for several nights before that, if possible). Go into the test with a fresh, alert mind rather than staying up late to study.

Try not to change too much about your normal routine on the day of the test. It's important to eat a nutritious breakfast, but if you normally don't eat breakfast at all, consider eating just a protein bar. If you're a coffee drinker, go ahead and have your normal coffee. Just make sure you time it so that the caffeine doesn't wear off right in the middle of your test. Avoid sugary beverages, and drink enough water to stay hydrated but not so much that you need a restroom break 10 minutes into the test. If your test isn't first thing in the morning, consider going for a walk or doing a light workout before the test to get your blood flowing.

Allow yourself enough time to get ready, and leave for the test with plenty of time to spare so you won't have the anxiety of scrambling to arrive in time. Another reason to be early is to select a good seat. It's helpful to sit away from doors and windows, which can be distracting. Find a good seat, get out your supplies, and settle your mind before the test begins.

When the test begins, start by going over the instructions carefully, even if you already know what to expect. Make sure you avoid any careless mistakes by following the directions.

Then begin working through the questions, pacing yourself as you've practiced. If you're not sure on an answer, don't spend too much time on it, and don't let it shake your confidence. Either skip it and come back later, or eliminate as many wrong answers as possible and guess among the remaining ones. Don't dwell on these questions as you continue—put them out of your mind and focus on what lies ahead.

Be sure to read all of the answer choices, even if you're sure the first one is the right answer. Sometimes you'll find a better one if you keep reading. But don't second-guess yourself if you do immediately know the answer. Your gut instinct is usually right. Don't let test anxiety rob you of the information you know.

If you have time at the end of the test (and if the test format allows), go back and review your answers. Be cautious about changing any, since your first instinct tends to be correct, but make sure you didn't misread any of the questions or accidentally mark the wrong answer choice. Look over any you skipped and make an educated guess.

At the end, leave the test feeling confident. You've done your best, so don't waste time worrying about your performance or wishing you could change anything. Instead, celebrate the successful completion of this test. And finally, use this test to learn how to deal with anxiety even better next time.

> **Review Video:** **5 Tips to Beat Test Anxiety**
> Visit mometrix.com/academy and enter code: 570656

Important Qualification

Not all anxiety is created equal. If your test anxiety is causing major issues in your life beyond the classroom or testing center, or if you are experiencing troubling physical symptoms related to your anxiety, it may be a sign of a serious physiological or psychological condition. If this sounds like your situation, we strongly encourage you to seek professional help.

Thank You

We at Mometrix would like to extend our heartfelt thanks to you, our friend and patron, for allowing us to play a part in your journey. It is a privilege to serve people from all walks of life who are unified in their commitment to building the best future they can for themselves.

The preparation you devote to these important testing milestones may be the most valuable educational opportunity you have for making a real difference in your life. We encourage you to put your heart into it—that feeling of succeeding, overcoming, and yes, conquering will be well worth the hours you've invested.

We want to hear your story, your struggles and your successes, and if you see any opportunities for us to improve our materials so we can help others even more effectively in the future, please share that with us as well. **The team at Mometrix would be absolutely thrilled to hear from you!** So please, send us an email (support@mometrix.com) and let's stay in touch.

If you'd like some additional help, check out these other resources we offer for your exam:

http://MometrixFlashcards.com/GACE

Additional Bonus Material

Due to our efforts to try to keep this book to a manageable length, we've created a link that will give you access to all of your additional bonus material.

Please visit http://www.mometrix.com/bonus948/gaceenglish to access the information.